Quilting
for
People Who
Still Don't
Have Time
to
Quilt

by Marti Michell

Bobbie Matela, Managing Editor

Carol Wilson Mansfield, Art Director

Linda Causee, Editor

Meredith Montross, Associate Editor

Kathryn Smith, Assistant Editor

Christina Wilson, Assistant Editor

Ann Davis Nunemacher, Illustrations

Graphic Solutions inc-chgo, Book Design

Photography by Norton Photography,
Starkman Photography and Bread and Butter Studios

Shown on covers: Scrappy Basket Weave, Radiant Squares,
Basket Weave in Vivid Colors, Victorian Posy and Where's Elvis?

Acknowledgments:

Writing assistance at Quilter's Ink, Inc. was provided by Jenny Lynn Price.

Hand-dyed fabrics: Stacy Michell, Shades Hand-Dyed Textiles,
585 Cobb Parkway, South, The Nunn Complex, Studio O, Marietta, GA 30062

The Sophie Scissorhands doll, page 132, was adapted from Yobo the Clown,
designed by elinor peace bailey. For pattern ordering information write to her at
1779 East Avenue, Hayward, CA 94541.

Special thanks for sharing their quilts in this book go to: Guðfinna Helgadóttir,
Lisa Wesmiller Benson and Diane Hicks

All other quilts were designed by Marti Michell and made by her or Marti Michell
Studio Associates: Patti Bachelder, Ann Cookston, Martha Dudley, Sheri Gravel,
Jennifer Kay and Camellia Pesto.

For a full-color catalog including books
on quilting, write to:

American School of Needlework®
Consumer Division
1455 Linda Vista Drive
San Marcos, CA 92069

Published by American School of Needlework®, Inc.
ASN Publishing
1455 Linda Vista Drive, San Marcos, CA 92069

ISBN:0-88195-863-8   All rights reserved.   Printed in USA.

About the Author

Marti Michell, a pioneer in the current quiltmaking revival, was also a leader in the introduction of the rotary cutter and strip techniques. The rotary cutter was invented in Japan in 1979. By 1981, Yours Truly, Inc., the company then owned by Marti and her husband, Dick Michell, had developed acrylic rulers and was offering week-long seminars on strip techniques. Hundreds of teachers and shop owners learned the benefits of rotary cutting and were introduced to strip technique patchwork.

Marti's first book, *Quilting for People Who Don't Have Time to Quilt,* was published by American School of Needlework in 1988. Marti is constantly delighted by the number of people who thank her for that book, many saying, "That was my first quilting book!" This revised version, *Quilting for People Who* Still *Don't Have Time to Quilt,* should be enjoyed equally by Marti's loyal readers and patchwork newcomers.

In 1995, their appreciation of quick cutting methods and tools led Marti and Dick to launch the From Marti Michell Perfect Patchwork Templates: acrylic templates for rotary cutting.

Born and raised in Iowa, Marti started sewing in 4-H and was graduated from Iowa State University in Home Economics Journalism with a minor in Textiles and Clothing. In 1991, Marti was the first recipient of the quilt industry's prestigious Michael Kile Award, commonly called the Lifetime Achievement Award. The Michells have lived in the Atlanta suburbs since 1969. They have two children who are grown and gone, and two cats who refuse to leave home.

Table of Contents

Introduction

For Best Results with This Book

Naturally, as the author, I believe that "Best Results" means learning everything you can about strip techniques. If you agree, please read this book from beginning to end, just like a novel, and make as many quilts as you can along the way. While *Quilting for People Who Still Don't Have Time to Quilt* doesn't pretend to have the suspense of a Whodunit?, I like to think it will help you solve the mystery of strip techniques. I trust you will see how the plot thickens as techniques learned in one quilt are expanded upon in another. I like to think that any reader who loves quilts will find some real characters between these covers!

The step-by-step projects are presented in a natural progression starting with the first basic quilt, the *Fence Rail Basic Quilt*, and building with new skills in each project. The instructions for the first basic quilt are especially important (and long!) because they detail so many procedures you will use on nearly every strip technique quilt in the future. Written instructions for strip techniques are usually much longer than for traditional techniques.

It doesn't sound very flashy, but I also like to emphasize good work habits. The greatest colors and designs in the world are spoiled by lumpy, bumpy, crooked quilts. The *Quilting for People Who Still Don't Have Time to Quilt* techniques are designed to make sure the quality of your work justifies your investment of money and time.

The most effective way to master these techniques is to make quilts. The first quilt in the book is a full-size bed quilt. If you are new to quiltmaking, I especially encourage you to start with it. Then, you are a quiltmaker! Too often, people start with a pillow and when the project is completed, they are just a pillow maker.

To Make Just One Quilt

If your preference is to make a specific quilt shown, you don't need to read cover to cover. It may, however, be necessary to read several sections in addition to the specific quilt's instructions.

1. If you are new to strip techniques, please read Before You Begin, page 12, for an overview. If you are new to quiltmaking, look for basic information in Tips on Fabric Selection, Tools and More, page 172.

2. Every quilt in the book is either a basic quilt, or a variation of one. It is a good idea to read the instructions for the appropriate basic quilt before starting any other quilt. The instructions for all of the basic quilts in the book may seem long, because each set contains detailed construction information. Simple variations don't take much space as they can refer to the basic quilt for directions. Detailed instructions for techniques used in the basic quilt projects are not repeated in subsequent instructions. This saves space, and more importantly, helps to reinforce the entire concept of strip techniques.

3. Read all of the instructions for the quilt top you plan to make before you select or cut fabric. It should prevent surprises or incorrect assumptions.

4. For finishing instructions, read Finishing Your Quilt, page 179.

How To Use the Snapshots

As you become more familiar with the techniques this book teaches, long instructions can be replaced by the snapshots. For example, this simple statement would become all the information you would need to make the *Fence Rail Basic Quilt*: "Interior of quilt is 10 unit blocks by 13 unit blocks. The strips are cut 1³/4 inches wide and the borders are cut 3 inches, 4 inches and 5 inches wide." Hence, the instructions for each quilt in the book are preceded by this special "Snapshot" feature. In fact, if you already understand strip techniques, the "Snapshot" version of each quilt is the perfect formula for making any of the quilts shown. However, please try to read or at least skim the rest of the book for tips and techniques to add to your repertoire.

Most Importantly, Please Enjoy!

No matter how you choose to use the book, my wish is that the techniques, quilts and ideas will open new doors of creativity, productivity and fun!

Marti Michell

Yes, You Do!
Yes, You Can!

Quilts are a universal symbol of love and warmth. For centuries, men and women alike have been

protected by quilts,
intrigued with their history,
inspired by their beauty,
and fascinated with the process of making quilts.

The antique quilts we enjoy today are indeed slices of history. We examine them carefully. We look at quilts for clues about the maker's life. We see a quilt and remember a grandmother or our own childhood events fondly. Most of us try to preserve and protect these heirlooms. Sometimes we forget that quilts were originally made to be used. For every quilt existing today perhaps dozens more were made and used. Think how much love and comfort those quiltmakers provided.

With electric blankets and central heat available, no one quilts to keep warm. So why do people quilt today? There is no single reason, but here are a few of the answers:

"To satisfy my creative urges."
"For relaxation."
"I love working with fabrics."
"To leave something of myself."
"For gifts."
"To use up fabric."
"It's infectious, I can't quit."
"As a showcase for my needlework."
"To make a scrapbook or memory quilt."
"To express my love and provide comfort for my family and friends."
"I've just always wanted to make a quilt."

Perhaps you've thought that last comment, but just as quickly thought, "I just don't have time to make a quilt," or "I can't make a quilt." Stop right there. Yes, you do! Yes, you can! Wipe your mental slate clean, and get ready for fun.

Think Positively

If there is one paramount myth about quiltmaking, it's the "I could never do that" syndrome. Many people look at quilts like they are all monumental, never-ending projects. Perhaps it is because we all know at least one person who has been working on the same quilt for 30 years. The truth is, that person hasn't really worked on the quilt for 30 years; they just haven't finished the quilt for 30 years.

It is important to start with an open mind and a positive attitude. If you've ever thought of quiltmaking as cutting out hundreds of little pieces, one little piece at a time, and then sewing them back together, one little piece at a time, forget it! As you go through this book, you are going to learn that many traditional quilt designs can be translated into accurate, time-saving strip-sewing methods. You will learn how to recognize designs which can be adapted.

The Emphasis Is on Quilts to Use

The *Quilting for People Who Still Don't Have Time to Quilt* techniques presented in this book will show you how to enjoy making quilts for people to enjoy using! You will be making quilts that can be finished in hours,

not months or years. The techniques include multiple cutting, rotary cutting, machine piecing and machine quilting.

I avoid using the words "easy" or "fast" or "quick" because too many people turn up their noses and say "Humph! That means big pieces, sloppy workmanship, low standards." No-No-No! Every technique introduced here is easier, faster and more accurate than what could be called traditional techniques.

As your quiltmaking productivity becomes public knowledge, I recommend you learn to talk about loving the clever methods and the accuracy and meticulousness of the techniques. Later, when people exclaim over your quilts, please say, "Thank you," but never, never say, "Oh, these? They were so easy!"

One of the fabulous by-products of making quilts with these techniques is the mental freedom. Because you aren't investing weeks or months in a quilt, it is easy to have a relaxed attitude. You can make quilts just to satisfy yourself. You aren't making quilts to please me or your mother-in-law or a quilt show judge or a snooty sister. Instead, you can make quilts that you like, that express your own creative urges, make a statement or tell a joke. You can use the quilt or give it to someone—no strings attached.

Imagine another scenario. You've worked on the "heirloom" quilt for five years when your son, your first born, announces he's getting married. Then the big decision. You'll give them the quilt for a wedding present.

What do you think happens on your first visit? The thing you want to see first is the quilt. You are discreetly looking and suddenly you see it. "Oh no! Is that cat on my quilt?!?" They can't please you. You'll be mad if they don't use it and mad if they do!

What about masterpiece quilts? You may want to make quilts that are "too good to use," the kind that only sit on a shelf in an acid-free box to be brought down on momentous occasions. Or you may decide competition quilting is your goal. That's fine. These techniques will allow you to make those quilts more quickly and accurately, too.

You know what heirloom quilts are, don't you? Quilts that are too good for your family to use, but not too good for an heir to use or for some complete stranger to take to the beach in a hundred years, are heirloom quilts! When you sit down to make an "heirloom," every decision becomes crucial. I prefer the relaxed attitude I call "automatic heirloom quiltmaking." My recommendation is to flood your family with quilts you have enjoyed making. Make so many they can't use them all up. Then there will be plenty for future generations.

Make Quality Quilts Quickly

You can make quality quilts quickly. You do have to follow a couple of simple rules.

Rule #1: You must be selective.

It is important to understand that not every quilt you've ever seen can be made using strip techniques. You'll notice there are no curved seams or complicated pointed designs in this book. There are, however, more quilts that can be made using these techniques than anyone will live long enough to accomplish.

There are so many popular quilts that are made with just strips and squares that all of the quilts in this book are made with those two basic shapes, or, we could say, are made from strips. That doesn't mean that everything in the finished quilt is a strip. It just means that the first cut on every piece is a strip.

Rule #2: You must be selective.

You always pick out the pattern and fabrics for every quilt. You never agree or offer to make a quilt for any person who wants to pick the design and fabrics. This may sound rude, but if they want to do the picking, they do the piecing. If you get to pick, you'll piece. (You'll understand this better if you ever weaken and agree to make a quilt someone else selected.)

Warning: Once you even say you're thinking about making a quilt, someone you care about a lot will say, "Oh, will you make one for me?" Remember, if you say "Yes," to add "as long as I get to make all the decisions."

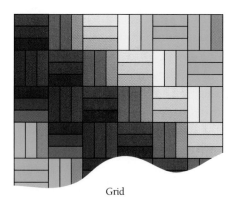
Grid

No grid

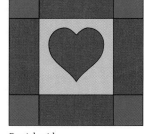
Partial grid

No grid

Learn to See and Think in Patchwork Grids

Patchwork is the procedure of sewing together small pieces of different fabrics, usually cut into geometric shapes, into pleasing patterns. Appliqué is the process of applying cut fabric shapes (usually not geometric) directly onto another layer of fabric. We will be making patchwork quilt tops. There are hundreds of different patchwork designs. To make quilts using the techniques in this book, you must learn to identify the shapes used to make the quilt top. Then make sure you work with shapes that benefit from strip techniques.

The most frequently used shapes in patchwork are strips, squares and right angle triangles. Squares, of course, are just strips cut so their length is the same as their width. Right angle triangles can be cut from squares. All of them can be drawn on a grid such as graph paper. The quilt blocks in this book deal exclusively with strips and squares. In this book, triangles are used only as a device for completing rows in diagonal set quilts.

8

Repetition in the order of the fabrics is the second crucial ingredient for efficient strip techniques. When the size and shape of a piece repeats consistently and frequently, strip techniques can be used most effectively.

Grid - Repetition
see Double Irish Chain

Grid - Repetition

Grid - No repetition

There are No Pattern Pieces in this Book!

You do not need pattern pieces or templates if the quilt design can be drawn on a grid. Instead, you will learn to use the grid to represent measurements and eliminate pattern pieces. Perhaps the most empowering feature of quilts drawn on grids is that you decide what size pieces to work with. You are not confined to fixed pattern piece sizes and only one fin-

ished size block. The size of the first strip you cut determines the scale and finished size of the project. For example, in **Diagram A**, there is a grid four squares wide by five squares high. If each square represented 1 inch, the shape would be 4 inches by 5 inches; if each square represented 2 inches, the shape would be 8 inches by 10 inches; if each represented 10 inches, the shape would be 40 inches by 50 inches; and if each square represented 3 cm, the finished shape would be 12 cm by 15 cm, etc.

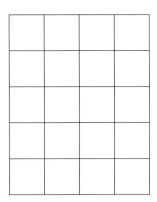

Diagram A

Strip techniques in cutting mean that, for every square in a repeating grid pattern, you will cut a strip. The strip will be as wide as the finished size of the square plus 1/2 inch (two 1/4-inch seam allowances). The strip will be as long as you want or is convenient. My routine length is 27 inches cut on the lengthwise grain, but I will occasionally use 45 inches cut on the crosswise grain.

It may sound strange, but everything you can Sew-Before-You-Cut is more accurate, faster and easier. Sew-Before-You-Cut is one way of describing strip piecing techniques. Strip techniques are the backbone of this book. You will quickly learn to appreciate these techniques by actually doing them yourself in the quiltmaking section of this book. It is hard to do them justice in words. In this case, a few minutes of action is worth a thousand words. We say "Sew-Before-

You-Cut," but really you cut strips first, then sew them together before you cut "pieces." That brings us to the rotary cutter.

Tools for Accurate Cutting

IN A NUTSHELL
Learn to use rotary cutting tools and techniques.

Some of my quiltmaking friends love the quilting most, some prefer the piecing process, but I don't know anyone who says, "I can't wait to get home and cut!" Yet accurate cutting is the first crucial step in accurate patchwork.

One of the reasons the techniques in this book are so effective is the use of the rotary cutter, a relatively new tool introduced in 1979. It is used with a protective mat and an acrylic ruler to speed you through the cutting process and get you to the fun part. Let's face it: cutting can be pretty tedious, especially if you are looking at a quilt and seeing nearly 1,000 squares to cut. Doesn't it sound better to say 100 strips? Or, by cutting multiple layers, 25 cuts? Even more important than speed is accuracy. The rotary cutting system is quicker and more precise than cutting with scissors, and has revolutionized the task of cutting most shapes, especially strips!

The reason I stress this so much is that I ignored the rotary cutter for a year or so after I first saw it. After all, I reasoned, I had good scissors and I could use them well. Surely this advanced pizza cutter was just a gadget—right? Wrong! Today it is much more likely that you will have been introduced to the rotary cutter than when my first books appeared, but just in case you haven't, now is the time.

There are several rotary cutters on the market. They came in two sizes for years, but recently a very large cutter has been introduced. Some people feel more comfortable starting with the smallest cutter. If you want to keep your initial investment down, it is also less expensive. Because I am almost always doing multiple layer cutting, I prefer either of the larger cutters.

People say to me, "How can you use that to cut fabric and not cut your table?" You can't!! That's where the protective mat comes in. You must use the cutter on the mat if you don't want your table to look like the bottom of a used pizza pan!

Don't try a homemade substitute for a protective mat. Leftover linoleum doesn't work. Old stacks of newspaper won't work. The mat designed for the job is self-healing and does not dull the blade like other surfaces might. There are many sizes and as you might suspect, the larger the mat, the more expensive. For cutting strips, a long thin mat can be selected. It is a little less expensive but also considerably less convenient.

I have a small mat that I keep near the ironing board. It is perfect for the second cut right after pressing. The 18-inch by 24-inch mat fits perfectly on the kitchen counter when I am working at home, and the 24-inch by 36-inch mat is on my table in the studio.

Back to the actual cutting process. To be effective in cutting strips with a rotary cutter, you need a strong straight edge. There are many different acrylic rulers on the market, 5 inches or 6 inches wide and 24 inches long. The grid on the ruler surface is extremely helpful in assuring accuracy. Most of the rulers also have angles and other special features printed on them.

1. *The blades are very sharp. All of the brands currently available have guards. Make sure they are in place when the cutter is not in use. This protects both you and the blade. If you drop the cutter or accidentally cut across a pin, the blade often becomes nicked. Then instead of cutting the fabric where the blade is nicked, it perforates the fabric. The blades are replaceable, but the need can be minimized if you will just keep the guard in place.*

2. *A fresh blade will cut six to 12 layers of fabric easily with very little pressure. Bearing down too hard is not necessary and can do irreparable damage to the protective mat. It's harder to accurately fold and stack 12 layers of fabric than to cut them. For that reason, I generally cut four to eight layers even though the cutter could cut more.*

3. *When cutting, the blade side, not the guard side, goes immediately next to the acrylic ruler.*

4. *Cut away from, not toward, your body.*

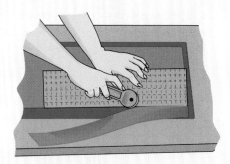

5. *To get straight strips, it is imperative that the ruler be perpendicular to the fold on folded fabrics and/or parallel to the selvage. The preliminary cut is usually to trim off the selvage (cutting strips on the lengthwise grain) or to straighten a store cut edge (cutting strips on the crosswise grain), either of which creates one side of the first strip. Cutting the second side of the strip requires changing hands, going to the other side of the mat, or turning the mat. My favorite method is to cut the first strip left-handed—not as hard as it sounds if you have a good ruler—and the rest right-handed, which is my favored hand; then I don't have to change table sides or turn the fabric or mat.*

6. *Take advantage of the grids on the mat and on the ruler to maximize your accuracy.*

7. *No matter what the final shape is to be, it is most common first to cut a strip that is the same width as one dimension of the desired piece, then cut across the strip to get the shape needed.*

8. *Specific guidelines for using the rotary cutting system to cut sewn strip sets are included in The Second Cut, page 16.*

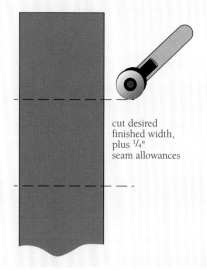

cut desired
finished width,
plus $1/4$"
seam allowances

What About Metric?

This book includes finished size measurements, in both U.S. and metric terms, for all quilts shown and for the unit blocks in each quilt. The strip measurements are cut sizes and are given only in inches. The reason is that, for quiltmakers who work in inches, the 1/4-inch seam allowance is well-accepted. However, my metric-measuring friends tell me there is not yet unanimity on the standard metric seam allowance. They say that even though 1/4 inch is closest to 6 mm, many quilters use either 5 mm or 7.5 mm for a seam allowance. Therefore, they say cut measurements don't really convert to metric very well.

One of the wonderful things about strip techniques is that the actual width of either the strip or the seam allowance is not as important as consistency. So the easy way for you to convert is to compare the U.S. measurement with the metric measurement and round up or down to the most convenient metric size.

If you are really concerned about making a project the same size as one shown, take our cut measurement, subtract 1/2 inch, and multiply by 2.54 to find the finished size in centimeters. One inch equals 2.54 centimeters, **Diagram B**. Based on your seam allowance preference, decide on the easiest cut width for your strips. As long as you are consistent, the design will come out right. As long as you come out close to the desired size, or size shown, you can make final adjustments with borders.

Write the metric measurement, including your choice of seam allowance, in the book.

> **TIP** ♦ ♦ ♦ ♦ ♦ ♦ ♦ ♦
> *Use these numbers for actual mathematical conversions:*
>
> 1 meter = 39.37 inches
>
> 1 inch = 2.54 centimeters
>
> yards x .9144 = meters
>
> inches x 2.54 = centimeters

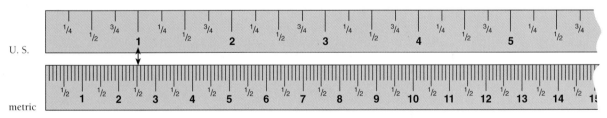

Diagram B

Before You Begin

Even though I hope you are really eager to start making quilts, there are a few general things I feel must be said before you begin. To make this as painless as possible, most of the following sections include boxed "In a Nutshell" summaries. If you don't want to read the backup information, just skip to the next "In a Nutshell."

The Sew-Before-You-Cut Techniques

IN A NUTSHELL
How you actually sew the pieces together unlocks the secrets of the Quilting for People Who Still Don't Have Time to Quilt *techniques. Erase completely from your mind the idea of making a quilt piece by little piece. Remember, everything that you can Sew-Before-You-Cut is more accurate, faster and easier.*

Analysis

Sew-Before-You-Cut is almost revolutionary. It's different from anything you were taught in sewing class. It will be stressed in this book over and over. The old patchwork ways of cutting and sewing one piece at a time incorporated very little thought. You do need to think ahead and organize a little for the Sew-Before-You-Cut methods to be most effective. The first thing is to analyze the pattern and develop a plan for what pieces you can Sew-Before-You-Cut.

Analysis and thinking ahead will be emphasized even when cutting. For example, often the first two strips that are going to be sewn together are also the same dimension. If you place the

fabrics face to face when you cut, you have eliminated a step, and as a bonus, the strips are more accurately positioned for sewing the seam.

Find the Unit Block

Look for the unit block in **Diagram H** of *Fence Rail Basic Quilt* on page 23. It doesn't always work, but start in the upper left corner. Look to the right until you see the same piece appear. Go back to the corner and look down until the same piece appears. This smallest repetitive unit is the unit block. The purpose of finding it is to streamline the construction. When you need to make many units of the same thing, every step can be more efficient. Sometimes the quilt block is the same as the unit block, but not always.

Most unit blocks can be broken into sub-units for easier assembly. Frequently the same block can be divided different ways into different sub-units. See *No-Name Four Patch Duo*, page 63, *and Nine Patch Delight*, page 122.

The sub-units for a quilt's unit block may even be common quilt blocks (see *Burgoyne Surrounded Basic Quilt*, page 155). Sometimes when you look at a single quilt block, one method of assembly appears obvious; however, if you look at the same block repeating across the quilt interior, another assembly method appears which would be easier, or would create fewer distracting seams.

Learning About Grainline

IN A NUTSHELL
Crosswise grain, lengthwise grain and bias have very different characteristics.

LENGTHWISE
The best way to study grainline properties of woven fabric is by feel. With a piece of fabric about 18 inches square, preferably with one selvage intact, you can learn to identify grainline properties. Grasp the fabric with both hands on the selvage edge. Pull in opposite directions to make fabric

---

A Quilt Block is the recognizable visual design that often occurs in a square. It is the design you would see in a book of quilt blocks. It may be helpful to think of the quilt block as the part of a quilt that could be used alone to make a pillow top.

A Unit Block is the most efficient construction unit for a particular quilt. It should be the smallest repetitive unit, but it is not usually the same as the recognizable quilt block. Sometimes there are two unit blocks (see Sticks and Stones, *page 36, or* Double Irish Chain Basic Quilt, *page 137).*

When there are many recognizable unit blocks, I find it easier to talk about a Master Unit and sub-units, as in Burgoyne Surrounded Basic Quilt, page 155.

A Sub-unit is a portion of the Unit Block or Master Unit. Breaking a larger unit into smaller sub-units sometimes makes construction easier.

taut. That's the lengthwise grain; see **a** in **Diagram A**. The fabric has very little stretch in that direction, but it does have some stretch.

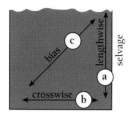

Diagram A

CROSSWISE

Now hold the fabric with one hand on the selvage and the other hand on the opposite end of the fabric. Pull again. Isn't that a surprise? That's the crosswise grain, **Diagram A**; see **b**. With the same pressure, it will stretch two and one-half to three times farther than the lengthwise grain. Most commercial dress patterns suggest placement on lengthwise or crosswise grain. The inference is that they are the same. The fact is that they are not the same; the lengthwise grain is much firmer.

BIAS

Bias isn't a four letter word. Well it is, but it's one you need in your sewing vocabulary, and you need to know how to use it! Go back to the 18-inch square of fabric and put your hands on opposite corners. Pull. Now that's stretch! Bias runs diagonally across the lengthwise and crosswise grains of the fabric, and is the most stretchy direction of a piece of fabric, **Diagram A**; see **c**. There are times when that property will drive you crazy and times when it may save your project. The important thing is to understand it exists; it is a property of the fabric that does not change. Understand how to work with it.

Using Grainline Characteristics

For starters, you need to know that you do not want bias on the longest dimension of a piece. You do not want it on the long outside edge of a block or a quilt where you will probably be adding borders or sashing. But if you need flexibility and stretch, like on a narrow rolled binding along a scalloped edge, you'll bless bias.

STRIP PIECING AND GRAINLINE

When I started doing strip piecing, I cut across the fabric from selvage to selvage. It was the easy thing to do. Then I began to think about my training in garment construction and design. The lengthwise grain of the fabric was usually placed on the height of the body for good reason. Now, I stress using the lengthwise grain on the longest dimension of the cut piece whenever possible. Placing the long dimension of a border on the lengthwise grain adds stability, especially if the item is intended as a wallhanging and has an obvious top. When patchwork is being made into garments, whenever possible and when not contrary to the design statement, the lengthwise grain should run from head to toe.

In solid-colored fabrics, there is often a visible difference between pieces cut on the lengthwise grain and those cut on the crosswise grain. This is especially visible in larger pieces, such as plain squares that alternate with patchwork blocks.

Another important reason for cutting strips on the lengthwise grain revolves around the fabric problem called "bowing," **Diagram B**. That is the word used to describe the problem of threads being pulled out of position during the printing and finishing process. Crosswise threads, instead of being perfectly perpendicular to the selvage, are arched. If you then cut crosswise strips, you are cutting (breaking) every crosswise thread you hit. Everywhere threads are cut, they will ravel. (Theoretically, if you were cutting crosswise strips, you would be cutting between two perfectly parallel crosswise threads and only cutting lengthwise threads.)

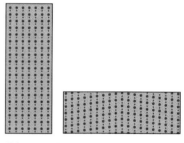

Diagram B

In addition, when fabric is bowed, any directional design in the fabric is pulled out of position, too. Cutting crosswise strips makes that distortion more obvious. Bowing barely affects lengthwise grain. Cutting strips on the lengthwise grain keeps printed patterns more accurate and greatly reduces raveling. Strips cut on the lengthwise grain will have smoother seams and be easier to keep straight while pressing.

SO WHAT'S THE CATCH?

The catch is that if you are accustomed to buying only a quarter yard of fabric, the longest strip you can get is 9 inches. You can hardly call that a strip. That is why 27 inches (3/4 yard) has become my standard speculative purchase length. I have found that I much prefer the 27-inch strip to the 45-inch strip. (If by chance you have already calculated the number of 45-inch strips needed for certain quilt designs, just double the number for 27-inch strips. Yes, 27 doubled is 54, not 45, but sometimes cutting from 27-inch strips is not as efficient as cutting from 45-inch strips, so you may need the extra length to get the same number of pieces.

You need not become obsessed with the issue of lengthwise grain. Just try to think ahead. Before long, it becomes natural. There are times when the "trade-offs" required to cut strips on the lengthwise grain aren't worth it, such as:

1. Overriding design reasons. If the fabric has an obvious directional design that is an integral part of the design and contradicts the lengthwise grain choice—design is more important. **Example:** a printed stripe runs lengthwise. You want the stripe to go crosswise on the border for its dramatic effect. The longest dimension ends up cut on the crosswise grain—go for it!

2. Simple economics. You aren't willing to buy 3 to 3 1/2 yards of fabric 45 inches wide to cut four full-size borders on lengthwise grain that will only use 12 inches of width. That's legitimate. You are the only one who can make that decision. However, since you will have to piece to cut your borders crosswise, why not buy the fabric needed and still cut strips lengthwise and piece? You may end up with more seams on the long side, but I believe it's worth the trade-off. (Refer to Borders and Grainline, page 179.)

3. It's already sewn when you remember. You are the only one who can decide how big a problem something has to be before you rip.

Cutting the Fabric in Steps

Don't cut everything at once. When using strip techniques, the finished size of one sub-unit often determines the size to cut the next component. If the seam allowance you are using is slightly larger or smaller than 1/4 inch, the finished size of your sub-unit will be slightly smaller or larger than the mathematically correct measurement (MCM) for that sub-unit. You will learn that in most cases, your one and only (O&O) personal measurement replaces the MCM in subsequent steps, but I'm getting ahead of myself. See page 15 for a discussion of MCM and O&O.

Although I stress planning for cutting the borders by saving a long piece of fabric along the selvage, it is important to not actually cut the border strips until the quilt interior is completed. One reason is that your choice of border widths, colors and fabrics may change after the unit blocks are assembled. Another reason is that the quilt interior may be a slightly different size from what you expected! (Refer to Before Cutting Borders, page 179.) The same holds true for binding.

Strip Piecing

The first step in Sew-Before-You-Cut is usually strip piecing. When you study a quilt design and see the same two squares of fabric side by side repeatedly, you realize that you can either cut lots of each square and sew them together, or you can cut a few

strips of fabric as wide as the squares, sew the strips together and then cut the sewn strips into pieces as long as the squares, **Diagram C**. Likewise, you will quickly learn to recognize three, four or more fabrics repeating in a way that would make sewing strips of those fabrics together advantageous, **Diagram D**. That is what analysis is all about.

With a little practice you will see how to put the simple concept of strip piecing to work to make you look like a miracle quilter. Your friends will not believe how fast you can do patchwork. You are not required to share these secrets. If, however, you decide to be generous and tell your friends about your newly-learned skills, never, never say it's easy. Say it's clever, say it's smart, say it's a brilliant new technique you've learned, but never say it's easy. It is, of course; we just don't say so.

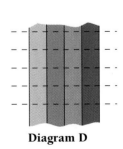

TIP ◆ ◆ ◆ ◆ ◆ ◆ ◆ ◆ ◆ ◆
Regardless of the speed and efficiency of strip techniques, cut just enough strips to make some sample blocks first. Even the most experienced quilter can be surprised by the way selected fabrics look when they are pieced. If you decide to make a change, you haven't wasted time cutting strips and your fabric is still in big pieces. If you like the results when a few blocks are together, strip techniques allow you to proceed full steam ahead.

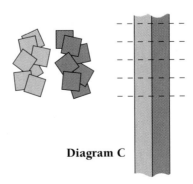

Diagram C

Diagram D

The Actual Sewing

Seam Allowance

If you are new to quilting and patchwork, you may not have entered the world of the 1/4-inch seam allowance yet. After using 5/8-inch seam allowances in dressmaking, the first 1/4-inch seam allowance will look impossibly thin. Try to remember that many of the 5/8-inch seam allowances survive being trimmed to narrower than 1/4 inch, turned inside out and poked. Not only is the 1/4-inch seam allowance adequate for patchwork, but should it be necessary to make a narrower seam allowance, don't worry until you get below 1/8 inch. Some people who enjoy doing miniature patchwork (finished pieces smaller than 1/2 inch) regularly use a 1/8-inch seam allowance.

On a few sewing machines, the outside edge of the presser foot is exactly 1/4 inch from the center of the needle hole. An easy way to check is to put a tape measure under your presser foot. Put any inch mark at the needle. Put the presser foot down, **Diagram E**. If it's 1/4 inch, you're lucky. If it isn't, there are several other ways to create the 1/4-inch seam allowance. For now, when you are just sewing strips, a guide on the throat plate or a piece of tape can be lined up to show where to run the edge of the fabric. Check with your sewing machine dealer to see if there is a 1/4-inch presser foot attachment available for your machine. Many newer machines have a variable

needle position that may create a perfect 1/4-inch seam allowance.

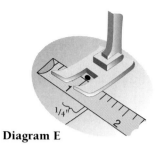

Diagram E

THERE'S MORE TO PERFECT PATCHWORK THAN A 1/4-INCH SEAM ALLOWANCE

In the final analysis, it's the size of what you see that is really important, not the size of the seam allowance. The seam allowance is there to keep the sewing threads from ripping out and to allow you to make adjustments if necessary. The object is to have a perfect 1-inch square in the finished patchwork, for example, not to have a perfect 1/4-inch seam allowance. Too often people get all hung up on sewing exactly 1/4 inch from the cut edge. This is fine when it works, and when you have both a perfect finished piece and a perfect seam allowance you can feel very smug, but the most important thing is the perfect size finished patchwork.

Usually, It's Consistency that Counts

It is also true that, in all of the quilts in this book or in any quilt that uses strip techniques, it is consistency that counts. Cutting, sewing and pressing perfectly result in "mathematically correct measurements." What happens if the edge of your presser foot makes a seam just a little larger or smaller than 1/4 inch? The size of your finished unit is just a little smaller or larger, and is called your "one-and-only" unique measurement. As long as all of the seams are the same, don't worry. When a unit block or quilt interior is just a little larger or smaller than intended, adjustments to the finished quilt size can be made easily by slightly changing the size of borders or sashing strips.

Cut measurements are given for strips. With strip techniques, I emphasize the cut size and cutting accuracy. Then with consistent sewing, the finished sizes are accurate shapes. This simplicity is why people who love being productive love making quilts using Sew-Before-You-Cut techniques.

This is not true if there are angles or curves in any of the shapes in your

---

What Do MCM and O&O Mean?

Throughout this book, you will find many measurements that are designated as MCM, or "mathematically correct measurements." The MCM is the size a piece would be at that point in the construction if you had cut perfectly, stitched a perfect 1/4-inch seam allowance and pressed perfectly. MCMs are given for sub-units, unit blocks, quilt interiors, cut sizes for batting and backing, border and binding strips and finished quilts.

In reality, seldom are all pieces cut perfectly, sewn with a perfect 1/4-inch seam allowance and pressed perfectly. The result is that your unit ends up a slightly different size. When you are making quilts using strip techniques, that's okay, as long as you are consistent! The size of your unit is your "one-and-only" unique measurement, or O&O. It is good if the MCM and O&O are close to matching, but don't panic if they aren't identical. Consistency is more important than perfection.

quilt. Then you must know exactly what size seam allowance is on the pattern and double-check while sewing to be sure you are really stitching on the correct line.

My recommendation is that you go ahead and learn to make 1/4-inch seam allowances now.

Math vs. Patchwork

Math is an exact science; sewing is not. Patchwork is a cross between them. Paper patterns and measurements that are mathematically correct may not end up exact when interpreted in fabrics. Learning how to spot strategic warning signals as you proceed, and how to make necessary adjustments, comes with practice. Examples are discussed in the project section.

Pressing

In A Nutshell
Pressing is not an option!

It is smart to make your iron one of your best friends as you embark on patchwork. My preference is a steam iron. When pressing seams in patchwork, both seam allowances go in the same direction, not open as in dressmaking. When in doubt, press them toward the darker fabric.

When I am pressing a set of strips, I usually put the strips across the ironing board instead of end to end. With the seam allowances right side up, I hold onto the fabric with my left hand and put the iron down on the other edge of the strips. With the weight of the iron holding the right hand side of the fabric, I put just a little tension on the left side. That causes the seam allowances to stand up, and with the steam iron, I can press them down flat. Keep the strips straight; don't press curves into your strips. It is easiest when all seams go in the same direction, but many times the instruc-

tions say to press toward the darker fabric. That often means that seams need to go in opposite directions on the same strip. Sometimes you can press from each side in toward the center. Sometimes you have to hold the strip at the end and work your way down the middle. You do what you have to do to get it right! Time spent pressing carefully is time well spent.

Honoring the philosophy that once is not enough, I then turn the strips over and press from the right side of the fabric. The object is to eliminate any tiny folds I might have pressed into the seam. Tiny 1/32-inch folds don't seem like much until you multiply that times two for each seam, and times four or five seams for a block, and times ten or 12 for the number of blocks. I admit to being a fanatic about perfect pressing!

DIRECTIONAL PRESSING

In the step-by-step section, you will see how directional pressing becomes a crucial part of ease and accuracy in sewing. You will learn how to plan pressing to your advantage. This may not seem very flashy, but it simplifies your stitching life and gives you lots more time for the fun stuff. Along this line, a side effect of directional pressing is what I call "automatic pinning." It is first mentioned in the *Fence Rail Basic Quilt* on page 24, but probably best described in Introducing the Basic Four Patch, page 62.

Typically, you will press between each step. Some people like to set up a pressing area right beside the sewing machine and stay seated while pressing. I don't mind getting up to press. I usually have sewn so many strips or sets together while at the machine that getting up to press gives me a chance to stretch.

SHORTCUT PRESSING

Sometimes finger pressing can postpone pressing for one step; but be very careful about trying to go longer than that without pressing. Using the combination of your fingers and the presser foot tension to hold the seam allowance in place, you can usually stitch across the most recent seam adequately. You have to decide which is more important to you: perfect, flat seams or saving a few minutes on every quilt you make for the rest of your life. Everything is a trade-off.

The Second Cut

This is really your first opportunity to put the Sew-Before-You-Cut theories to work. Now that your first strips are cut, pieced and pressed, you make the "second cut" that forms the second dimension of the patchwork piece (see **Diagram C**, page 14).

The width of the strips formed the first dimension. Again, go to the rotary cutter and mat, and perhaps switch to a shorter acrylic ruler. Accurately cut a new common line across the sewn pieces. This ensures more accurate dimensions on the pieced unit. It allows you to work with larger pieces, and it is easier to be accurate with larger pieces. Stated another way, an error of 1/16 inch is a much greater problem on a 2-inch piece than an 8-inch piece.

There are times that the second cut is an exact measurement. In *Radiant Squares,* page 146, for example, if the first strip is cut 1 1/2 inches wide, then the second cut must also be 1 1/2 inches. At other times, as in the *Fence Rail Basic Quilt,* page 20, you measure across the finished strip sets to determine the segment length for the second cut.

When making the "second cut" across sewn strip sets, line up the ruler with any horizontal seams. It is more important that the second cut be perpendicular to the seams than be parallel to the end of the strip set.

Chain Piecing

Strip piecing is the process of sewing two strips together (see **Diagram C**, page 14). Chain piecing means continuously feeding the pieces to be joined under the presser foot without cutting the thread, **Diagram F**. Even though the strips are actually chain pieced, chain piecing more commonly refers to the piecing done after the "second cut," **Diagram G**. As you place the same combination of pieces in position one after the other, it is easy to see any obvious visual differences. These are visual warnings. Likewise, it is easy to make a consistent slight change to correct a problem from the previous step. This is something that you will have to look at and analyze as you sew; each quilt is different and I could write words forever, but experience is the real teacher.

Diagram F

Diagram G

Correcting Any Differences

Measure several units to determine if they match the MCM or are your O&O. If you have several different O&Os for the same unit, adjustments are necessary! After measuring several units, you will know whether a slight adjustment or a huge one is required.

If the sub-units or unit blocks are of slightly varying sizes, there are several possible solutions. Double-check your pressing: you may have pressed folds into the seams, which can be corrected with re-pressing. Look at the seam allowances: are they consistent? Check the strips themselves: were they cut evenly? It may be necessary to take out a few seams to make adjustments. The wide acrylic rulers with grids printed on them can be very useful for checking the accuracy of sizes, confirming that seams are perpendicular and using with the rotary cutter to accurately trim edges.

If the variance is large, you will need to carefully measure each unit and sort by size. If you made extras, they come in handy now; you can set aside the most out-of-whack units to be used later for accessories. If you didn't make extras and there are only one or two very large or small units, you may prefer to make replacements rather than compromise all the others.

TO RIP OR NOT TO RIP

Because my stitch length preference is relatively small, and I really don't like ripping, my own guideline is rather harsh. If the mistake, once seen, is the first thing I see when I look at the quilt top, I rip. It's not worth being aggravated forever for a few minutes of ripping. If I were planning to enter the quilt in a competition, I'd rip, but competitions aren't really my thing. If I were giving the finished piece

away and I thought it wouldn't be noticed, I might not rip. After all, if they found the mistake, they would probably be proud of finding something I had missed, or they would think it was my "humility block." (In some societies, it is believed that, as only God can make something perfect, a quiltmaker must make an obvious mistake; hence, humility blocks.) There are only two ways to avoid ripping: by never making a mistake, or by not caring when you do. Each of us has to set our own standard of perfection.

SOME TIPS ON RIPPING

If you must rip, the gentlest way is the best. On one side of the seam, cut about every sixth stitch. A little experimentation will let you know if you can get by with clipping every seventh or eighth stitch. Then turn the fabric over and pull the thread on the other side. When you cut at the right intervals, the thread just pops out as you pull. Go back to the first side and brush away the clipped threads. I can do about 10 inches per minute or 1/100th of a mile per hour!

Another ripping technique is to pull one thread, gathering the fabric on the seam, until it breaks. Then go to the other side of the fabric and pull the opposite thread until it breaks. Proceed back and forth until the seam is removed. This is faster and neater, but it is harder on the fabric and more likely to cause distortion.

Sometimes straightening a seam is necessary because there is an equal error in both pieces of fabric. As long as the new seam allowance can be wider than the old one, straightening simply requires a new seam, no ripping. The old stitching can stay in the seam allowance.

What Else?

Some Terms to Know as You Read This Book

Patchwork is easier when you are acquainted with these quilting terms.

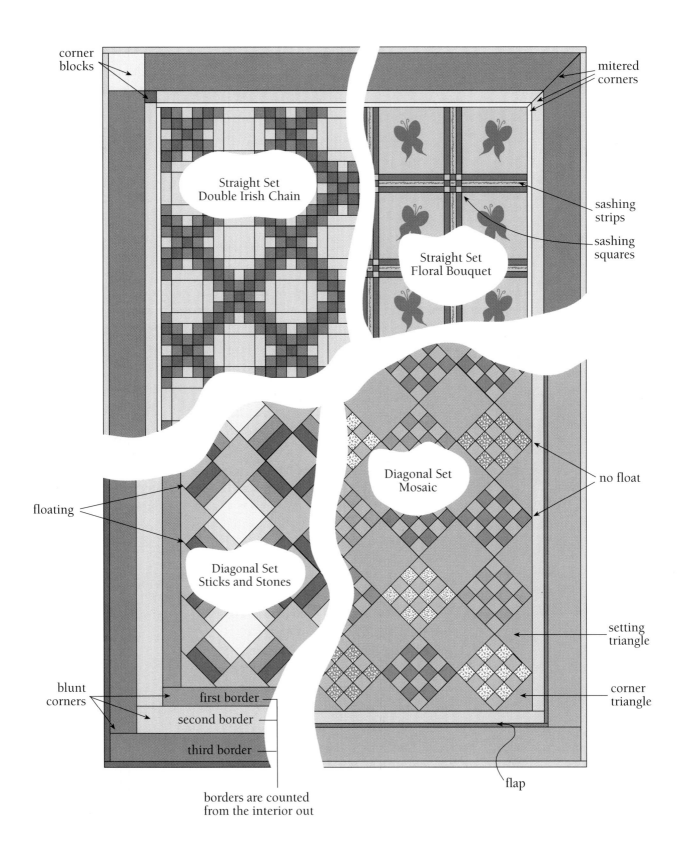

corner blocks

mitered corners

Straight Set Double Irish Chain

sashing strips

sashing squares

Straight Set Floral Bouquet

Diagonal Set Mosaic

no float

floating

Diagonal Set Sticks and Stones

setting triangle

corner triangle

blunt corners

first border

second border

third border

borders are counted from the interior out

flap

Now Hear This!!

Unless Otherwise Stated:

- All seam allowances are ¼ inch.

- All pieces are sewn right sides together.

- All measurements for strips are cut sizes—assuming the strips have ¼-inch seam allowances, the finished size should be ½ inch smaller than the cut size.

- Mathematically Correct Measurements (affectionately referred to as MCMs) are given for pieces in progress. When an MCM is given for a newly-sewn strip set or pieced sub-unit, presumably pieces were cut accurately, sewn with exact ¼-inch seam allowances, and pressed perfectly. Because the MCM includes two seam allowances, the finished size should be ½ inch smaller.

- Your One and Only unique measurement (O&O) will, in most cases, replace the MCM. If the pieces are not cut, sewn and pressed perfectly, the resulting unit will be a slightly different (O&O) size. That's okay, because it is consistency that counts. See pages 15 and 17 for more discussion of MCM, O&O and the implications when using strip techniques.

- All quilt sizes given are MCM for the quilt shown, including borders and binding as indicated. Remember that quilting will take up 2 to 4 inches of this MCM size in each direction, depending upon how heavily you choose to quilt.

- All block sizes given are finished measurements.

- All MCMs for borders are for blunt corners unless stated otherwise, page 182. For mitered corners, multiply the cut width by two, and add that to every border length. Borders are numbered from the patchwork interior toward the outer edge.

- All bindings are made using the French-fold technique on page 188. Binding measurements referred to are for finished width.

Snapshots:

- At the beginning of each quilt, the snapshot box includes all the basic information needed to make the quilt. See page 5 for a more detailed description of snapshots.

Remember!

MCM = Mathematically Correct Measurement

O&O = One and Only unique measurement

&

Your One and Only unique measurement (O&O) will, in most cases, replace the MCM.

Fence Rail Basic Quilt

Snapshot

- Unit Blocks: 130
- Interior Arrangement: set 10 across by 13 down, **Diagram H**, page 23
- Strip Width: 1³/4" cut
- Borders: 3", 4" and 5" cut
- French-fold binding: ¹/2" finished

Unit Block

Queen/Double Quilt Size:

84¹/2" by 103¹/4"
214.6 cm by 262.3 cm

Block Size:

6¹/4" square
15.9 cm square

Materials Required:

³/4 yard each of twenty different fabrics for quilt blocks and pieced backing (four light fabrics, four dark fabrics and twelve medium fabrics)

³/4 yard of ecru fabric for first border

1 yard of rose fabric for second border

1⁷/8 yards of dark green fabric for third border

³/4 yard of fabric for French-fold binding

packaged quilt batting, larger than 85" x 104"

If tying your quilt:
60 yards of smooth, sport-weight yarn
large-eyed, sharp-pointed needle

Before beginning to work on your quilt, read Now Hear This!! on page 19.

Selecting the Fabric

In fabric selection, especially for multi-colored quilts, light, medium and dark tonal ranges are often more important than the actual colors. For this quilt, four light fabrics (they were all ecru or pink and ecru) and four dark fabrics (burgundy, navy, green and brown) were chosen first. The remaining 12 fabrics were chosen to develop a compatible range of mediums in the rose, blue and green color families. Notice the variety in the size and type of designs.

For most quilts, I recommend selecting border fabrics after the blocks are pieced, allowing the finished look of the quilt interior to help determine the borders. If, however, you are making a multi-colored quilt such as the *Fence Rail Basic Quilt*, and it has to coordinate with the color scheme of a particular room, it is best to select border fabrics first to fulfill those color needs. This quilt's borders make it look very pink and green, with blue accents. If ecru, slate blue and navy blue borders had been selected, the quilt would appear very blue, with pink and green accents.

Finding the Unit Block

When you are making a quilt using strip techniques, the first step is to find the unit block. The unit block is the smallest repetitive unit. Although this won't always work, start by looking in the upper left corner. Look to the right until you see the same shape repeating. Then look down from the corner to find the same shape repeating. In the *Fence Rail Basic Quilt*, the unit block is a square made with five strips, light to dark going right to left or top to bottom, **Diagram A**. In this quilt, there are 130 unit blocks, each finishing to 6¹/4 inches square. The unit block and the quilt block are one and the same for this quilt. That is not always true, of course.

Unit Block
Diagram A

Cutting the Fabric

Using the piece-by-piece approach to patchwork, you would have to cut 650 rectangular pieces 1³/4 inches by 6³/4 inches, and piece them together into the unit blocks for the *Fence Rail Basic Quilt*. This book is all about

Fence Rail Basic Quilt *makes a great first quilt to introduce strip techniques, because the unit block is made entirely from strips and the finished design is complemented by tying.*

making strip sets using Sew-Before-You-Cut techniques. It is a much more efficient use of your time!

MAKING STRIP SETS

The development of appropriate strip sets is key to your success with Sew-Before-You-Cut techniques. Typically, a strip set is made for a portion of the block (row, etc.). Because the Fence Rail unit block is composed of strips only, the strip set, cut into the appropriate length, makes the block. A separate strip must be cut for each strip position in the block, even if the fabrics are repeated within the block. The number and length of the strip sets is determined by the size of the quilt.

Although 27 inches is my standard strip length (page 174), 27 inches is not always practical. Here I am, on the first and easiest quilt, already making exceptions to my rules! The MCM for the second cut is $6^{3}/4$ inches, so 27 inches would allow cutting exactly four unit blocks per strip. Such exactness is too tight for my comfort. If you are purchasing fabric, you can't buy 28-inch lengths; but if you are cutting from scraps, you can make the strips a little longer.

On the lengthwise grain, cut ten strips, $1^{3}/4$ inches wide by 28 inches long, from each of the 20 fabrics selected. If your fabric strips are a perfect 27-inch length, cut 11 or 12 strips from each fabric. Cut a 22-inch fabric square for the pieced back at the same time you cut the strips, **Diagram B**. (If you are using scraps, the minimum, no-mistakes number of $1^{3}/4$-inch by 28-inch strips needed is 165.) Cutting extra strips (one or two extra of each of 20 fabrics) gives you the opportunity to reject combinations you don't like, and leaves extra for accessories.

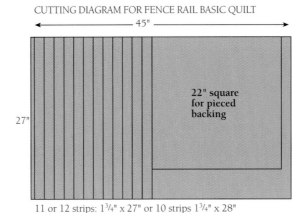

CUTTING DIAGRAM FOR FENCE RAIL BASIC QUILT

45"

27"

22" square for pieced backing

11 or 12 strips: $1^{3}/4$" x 27" or 10 strips $1^{3}/4$" x 28"

Diagram B

Making the Unit Block

Remember that everything you can Sew-Before-You-Cut is easier, faster, and more accurate; the first step in Sew-Before-You-Cut is strip piecing.

STRIP PIECING

Strip piecing is the process of sewing two or more strips together into a set. Chain piecing means continually feeding the same pieces in the same order under the presser foot without cutting the thread. Although not always the case, for this quilt, you will be chain piecing as you are strip piecing.

1. Sew five strips together before you cut them to length (strip piecing). You need 40 sets (or 33 using the minimum, no-mistakes number of strips). Begin with 40 strips of the darkest fabrics, and sew a medium strip to each one. No pinning is necessary. When you finish the first pair, don't stop and cut the threads; instead, just feed the next pair right under the presser foot (chain piecing), **Diagram C**. It doesn't need to be speed sewing, just a nice steady pace with a consistent seam allowance. You may prefer pressing as you go, but it's really more efficient to wait until you have completed sewing all five strips into a set.

2. When you have sewn the 40 pairs of strips together, start again, adding

another medium strip to the second strip, **Diagram D**. Make sure that the darkest strip is always on the left, and the third strip (and each successive strip) is progressively lighter than the previous strip. The quilt will be more interesting if you vary the arrangement of specific fabrics within the sets of strips, while keeping them all dark to light.

3. Add the fourth strip, **Diagram E**. It should be lighter than the third strip, and darker than the fifth.

4. Add the fifth strip, **Diagram F**, which should be from the fabrics you have selected as the lightest.

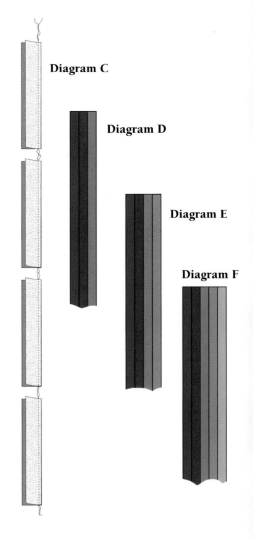

Diagram C

Diagram D

Diagram E

Diagram F

5. Press all seam allowances in the same direction, toward the darkest strip.

MAKING THE SECOND CUT

1. Measure across several of the sewn and pressed strip sets. The MCM ("mathematically correct measurement") for five 1³/4-inch-wide strips sewn together with accurate ¹/4-inch seam allowances and pressed flat is 6³/4 inches wide. If that's what you have, great. If not, the next best thing is to have a consistent finished width, affectionately called your O&O ("one-and-only") unique width. If your strip sets are all slightly smaller or slightly larger than 6³/4 inches, all that happens is that your quilt interior is slightly smaller or larger than mine. You can still get the same finished size by adjusting the border widths. For significant differences, you can add or subtract a row of unit blocks, if desired. (Refer to pages 15, 17 and 19 for more information about MCM and O&O.)

> ◆ **TIP** ◆ ◆ ◆ ◆ ◆ ◆ ◆ ◆
> *Most rulers are only 6 inches wide. Use an auxiliary ruler, such as a 1-inch by 6-inch, beside the original ruler to take the measurement more easily.*

If the strip sets are varying widths instead of consistent, it means a lot of adjustments later, or a bumpy finished quilt resulting from uneven seams. Double-check your pressing: you may have pressed folds into the seams that have made the strip sets uneven; that can be corrected with a simple re-pressing. Look at the seam allowances: are they consistent? Check the strips themselves: were they cut evenly? It may be necessary to take out a few seams and adjust. Or if you made extra sets, lay aside the most uneven sets and work with the best.

2. The unit block is created by making the second cut across the sewn strip sets. Whether the average width is the MCM, 6³/4 inches, or your O&O, that width determines the size of the unit block square, and thus determines the position of the second cut.

To make the unit block squares, work with one strip set at a time. With your ruler perpendicular to the long edges and the seams, straighten one end of the strip set. Using the width of the strip sets as the increment measurement, measure from the newly cut edge, mark and cut or just cut, if you are using the rotary cutting system, **Diagram G**. You should get four squares from a 28-inch strip set. (In this particular quilt, if your seam allowances are a little narrow, your strip sets will be wider than 6³/4 inches, so you will only be able to get three squares from a strip set.) Cut at least 130 squares. Save any remaining strip sets to sew together for pillow ruffles, etc.

Assembling the Quilt Interior

Do the next step on the floor or a large design wall so the entire quilt interior can be seen simultaneously.

This MCM or your O&O=increment measurement

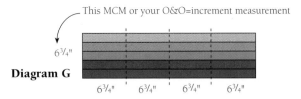

6³/4"

Diagram G

6³/4"   6³/4"   6³/4"   6³/4"

cut 3"

cut 4"

cut 5"

Diagram H

23

ARRANGING THE BLOCKS

Following the full quilt layout, **Diagram H**, arrange the blocks into 13 horizontal rows of ten blocks each. To develop the fence rail pattern, arrange the horizontal blocks with the dark strip at the bottom, and the vertical blocks with the dark strip on the left. Study the block assembly, and rearrange if necessary to avoid a concentration of one color or a particular fabric in one area. Strive for a comfortably random yet balanced look, but don't go crazy rearranging blocks.

PUTTING PAIRS TOGETHER

You may think that you will sew all ten blocks in the first row together, then in the second row, etc., and finish by sewing the long rows together. Although you can do this, I prefer sewing pairs of blocks together, then pairs of pairs, then two pairs of pairs, etc., **Diagram I**. The reasoning behind this is that if all ten blocks in each row were sewn together, nine seam intersections would have to match when sewing the rows together. If you are off anywhere, it means you have to adjust continually along the seam. When sewing by the pairs method, many seams will only have one seam intersection to match, so that any discrepancies can fall into the seam allowances.

1. Take each block in the second vertical row and turn it face down on its partner in the first row, as if they were already hinged together. This puts them in the proper position for sewing.

2. Starting at the top of the quilt, pick up the pairs, maintaining the correct position by stacking them so that Pair #1 is on top of Pair #2, which is on top of Pair #3, etc. It's smart to pin a paper with each row number on the top pair as a reference as you handle the blocks, especially if you won't complete this step in one session, **Diagram J**.

3. Hold the blocks in front of you, making sure you don't change hands or the position of the blocks! The "hinged" side must stay on the right, and Pair #1 on top! Go to the machine and start sewing the first pair.

As you finish the first pair, feed the second pair right under the presser foot, and then the third, etc. Do not cut the pairs apart; the chain piecing will automatically keep them in the correct order.

4. When you have finished with vertical Rows 1 and 2, repeat with Rows 3 and 4, 5 and 6, etc.

PAIRS OF PAIRS, ETC.

1. As you press the pieced pairs, you can create automatic pinning. On each pair, press both seam allowances toward the vertical strips, so they alternate left and right down the row. You can feel the little ridge that

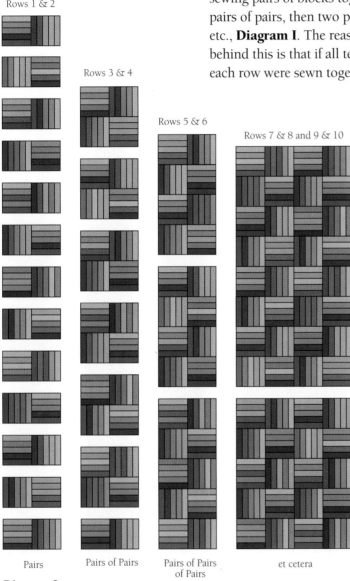

Rows 1 & 2

Rows 3 & 4

Rows 5 & 6

Rows 7 & 8 and 9 & 10

Pairs

Pairs of Pairs

Pairs of Pairs of Pairs

et cetera

Diagram I

Diagram J

24

develops as you press the seam allowance. Those ridges will act like little grippers as you put the pairs right sides together for the next seam. With a little practice, as you position the pairs, the ridges just meet, no space between, no overlapping, and no pinning necessary. The seam lines in the next seam will match perfectly.

2. Now sew the pairs of pairs. Four unit blocks are being sewn together, but there is still only one seam to match. Don't cut the thread keeping the vertical rows in line yet. It is more important to keep the positioning accurate than to take advantage of chain piecing, even though it means you need to handle each seam individually. Because there are 13 horizontal rows, there will be one block left at the end.

3. Time to press again. Think ahead. If you press all of the seam allowances

in Rows 1 and 2 up, 3 and 4 down, 5 and 6 up, etc., you will create automatic pinning for the vertical seams. All of this leads to a neat, flat quilt interior.

4. Now sew pairs of pairs of pairs together. There will be eight unit blocks and still only one seam intersection to match. Sew the extra pair to the last group of eight on each row.

5. Continue sewing larger units together until the interior is completely assembled. The last seam will probably be the horizontal seam between Rows 8 and 9. It may seem complicated now, but this planning becomes natural, and it is worthwhile for the orderliness that it develops and the problems that it prevents.

The MCM for the assembled quilt interior is 63 inches by 81¾ inches. Press the quilt interior.

PIECING THE QUILT BACK

If you cut 22-inch squares from the 20 fabrics you purchased or from your scraps, you're ready to piece the quilt back. Arrange the blocks in a pleasing layout of five horizontal rows of four blocks each. Sew the squares together in each row; then sew the rows together.

FINISHING THE QUILT

Modified Quilt-As-You-Sew borders are a nice way to finish a tied top. See page 181 of Finishing Your Quilt for details. The borders were cut 3 inches, 4 inches and 5 inches wide; the binding strips were cut 2⅝ inches wide. Layer the quilt with batting and backing. The photographed quilt features pieced backing, and was hand-tied with yarn at the quilt block corners.

On the Flip Side

These days, I find more and more of my quilt backs incorporating some degree of patchwork. I make eye-catching quilt backs and use up left-over fabrics at the same time, so I can buy new fabrics for tops! The *Fence Rail Basic Quilt* is the first quilt in this book that features a pieced back. Throughout the book, you will see the flip side of several more quilts and find ideas and tips for making them. If you plan to hand quilt, pieced backs introduce more seams that can interrupt the rhythm of your stitch. For machine quilting, the biggest problem with pieced backs revolves around what color thread to use in the bobbin.

Basket Weave

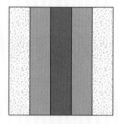

Basket Weave is a perfect example of a simple, but effective, monochromatic color scheme. The light, medium and dark slate blue prints provide the needed contrast. It is the light, medium and dark values and symmetrical arrangement of fabrics that make the basket weave so obvious.

Crib Quilt Size:

40³/4" by 53¹/4"
103.5 cm by 135.3 cm

Block Size:

6¹/4" square
15.9 cm square

Materials Required:

³/4 yard of ecru and blue print fabric
1¹/4 yards of medium blue fabric, including French-fold binding
³/4 yard of dark blue fabric
1⁵/8 yards of fabric for backing
1⁵/8 yards of batting, or packaged crib-size batting
⁷/8 yard of dark blue fabric for border (cut crosswise and pieced)

As the Basket Weave *is simply a different fabrication, a set variation and a smaller size than the* Fence Rail Basic Quilt, *these instructions are condensed. Please refer to the* Fence Rail Basic Quilt, *page 20, for further guidance.*

Basket Weave is the name for a quilt set in which the unit blocks are made of parallel strips (or fence rail blocks) that alternate vertically and horizontally to create a woven effect.

Selecting the Fabric

One of the things I really enjoy about quiltmaking is that you can change the colors of a block, or change the set, and most people don't even recognize it as the same quilt. Without even changing the strip size, the *Fence Rail Basic Quilt* becomes the *Basket Weave*.

Cutting the Fabric

On the lengthwise grain, cut 18 light strips, 18 medium strips and nine dark strips, 1³/4 inches wide by 27 inches long. For a real savings of time, layer the light and medium fabrics right sides together when cutting the strips with a rotary cutter. The fabrics will be automatically positioned with the raw edges together for all of the first seams.

Making the Unit Block

Although the unit block for the *Basket Weave* is made with five strips, the same as the *Fence Rail Basic Quilt*, **Diagram A**, the traditional arrangement of the light, medium and dark fabrics is different. In this quilt, the darkest strip is in the middle, flanked by medium and then light fabrics, **Diagram B**.

1. Using **Diagram B** as a guide, sew the strips together to make nine strip sets for the unit block.

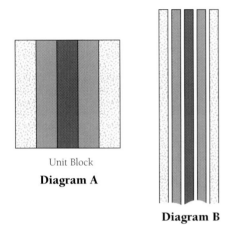

Unit Block
Diagram A

Diagram B

2. Press seam allowances toward the dark fabric. The MCM for the finished strip sets is 6³/4 inches wide.

3. The unit block is created by the second cut, **Diagram C**. (If your strip sets are not 6³/4 inches, use your O&O for the second cut.) Cut four unit blocks from each strip set, making a total of 35 blocks.

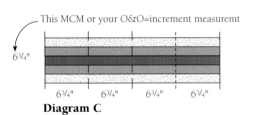

This MCM or your O&O=increment measuremt

6³/4"

6³/4"   6³/4"   6³/4"   6³/4"
Diagram C

Assembling the Quilt Interior

Lay out the blocks into seven horizontal rows of five blocks each, **Diagram D**. To develop the basket weave set, alternate block strips vertically and horizontally. It is fun to arrange unit blocks and see the pattern develop. However, because all of the blocks are identical, you can skip the full arrangement now. Make 14 pairs with the horizontal strips on the bottom and the vertical on top. Press all seam allowances toward the vertical block. To make six pairs of pairs, turn one pair around and take advantage of automatic pinning while sewing the units of four into the correct position. At this point, you may want to arrange all of the blocks and incorporate the remaining blocks to assure the proper layout.

The MCM for the quilt interior is 31³/4 inches by 44¹/4 inches. Press the quilt interior.

Finishing the Quilt

The border strips were cut 4¹/2 inches wide; the binding strips were cut 3⁵/8 inches wide for a ³/4-inch-wide French-fold binding. See Finishing Your Quilt, page 179, for more finishing ideas.

Diagram D

Basket Weave Discovery

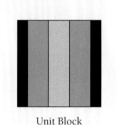
Wallhanging Size:
41" by 41"
104.1 cm by 104.1 cm

Block Size:
4" square
10.2 cm square

Materials Required:
eight fat-eighths of assorted red hand-dyed fabrics

eight fat-eighths of assorted blue hand-dyed fabrics

1 yard of black fabric, including second border

1 3/8 yards of 60"-wide fabric for backing

1 3/8 yards of batting

3/4 yard of dark blue hand-dyed fabric for first and third borders

5/8 yard of floral print fabric for French-fold binding

Basket Weave Discovery *features two strip widths in the unit block. Instructions for this variation of the* Fence Rail Basic Quilt *are condensed. Please refer to the Basic Quilt, page 20, for further guidance.*

A New Idea for a Basket Weave Quilt

While I've always thought the *Basket Weave* is very pleasant, I have had a gnawing question. Since dark colors recede and light colors advance, shouldn't I put dark strips on the outside edges of the unit block, and a light one in the middle to get a greater effect of woven dimension? Several times I tried it, but the dark areas always looked like big, gaping holes in a basket too loosely woven.

It took me 20 years to realize that just because the Fence Rail and Basket Weave strips are traditionally all the same width, it doesn't mean they have to be! I'm a grown woman, some even say a woman of the 90s and I can cut my strips any width I want! So I decided to put dark strips on the outside, but I would not cut them as wide as the other strips, **Diagram A**. I couldn't wait to try it. This is the first quilt made implementing this idea. I think the results are just great!

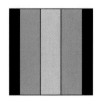

Unit Block

Diagram A

Selecting the Fabric

The photographed quilt features 16 fat-eighths of hand-dyed fabrics, eight blue and eight red. Although these fabrics are not really value gradations, the progressive arrangement of fabrics in the blocks, and blocks in the quilt, creates that effect. Refer to the photograph of the quilt, page 29.

Cutting the Fabric

Arrange the red fabrics from lightest to darkest, then sort them into pairs. Start with the lightest red and second lightest red and continue so that each pair is progressively darker. Arrange and pair the blue fabrics likewise.

From each pair of fabrics, cut two strips from the lighter of the two fabrics and four strips from the darker, 1 1/2 inches wide by 18 inches long. Cut black fabric into 32 strips, 1 inch wide by 18 inches long. Cut all strips on the lengthwise grain.

*The distinctive design
of Basket Weave Discovery is created by
varying the strip width to refine and enhance the woven effect.*

Making the Unit Block

A single strip of the lightest value fabric is flanked by strips of the next lightest value, and bordered by strips of black, **Diagram A**.

1. Using **Diagram B** as a guide, sew the strips together into sets for the unit block. Begin with the pair of the two lightest blue strips, combined with two narrow strips of black fabric, to make the first strip set. Continue sewing progressively darker values of strips into sets. Make four blue strip sets and four red strip sets.

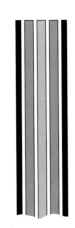

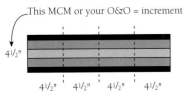

This MCM or your O&O = increment

4¹/₂"

4¹/₂"   4¹/₂"   4¹/₂"   4¹/₂"

Diagram B

2. Press seam allowances toward the dark fabric. The MCM for the sewn strip sets is 4¹/₂ inches wide.

3. The unit block is created by the second cut, **Diagram B**. (If your strip sets are not 4¹/₂ inches, use your O&O for the second cut.) Cut eight unit blocks from each combination, making a total of 32 red and 32 blue blocks.

Assembling the Quilt Interior

Following the quilt layout, **Diagram C**, assemble the blocks into eight rows of eight blocks each. The blue blocks are arranged horizontally from lightest to darkest, from top to bottom. The red blocks are positioned vertically lightest to darkest, left to right. Each combination is used in two rows.

The quilt interior is assembled by sewing pairs of blocks together, then pairs of pairs, then two pairs of pairs, etc. See page 24. The MCM for the assembled quilt interior is 32¹/₂ inches by 32¹/₂ inches. Press the quilt interior.

Finishing the Quilt

The borders for the photographed quilt were cut 1 inch, 1¹/₂ inches and 3 inches wide. They were added traditionally. The quilt was layered with batting and backing, and machine quilted in the ditch between the quilt blocks, using invisible thread. A ¹/₂-inch French-fold binding (strips cut 2⁵/₈ inches wide) completes the quilt. See Finishing Your Quilt, page 179, for details on finishing.

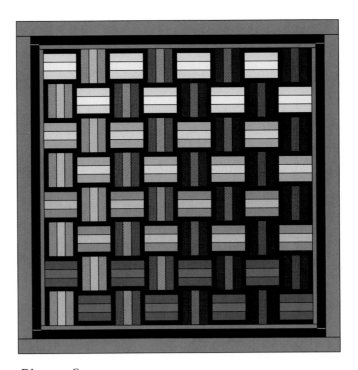

Diagram C

Basket Weave in Vivid Colors

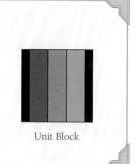

Snapshot

- Unit Blocks: 144
- Interior Arrangement: set 12 across by 12 down, **Diagram H,** page 32
- Strip Widths: 1¹⁄₈" and ³⁄₄" cut
- Borders: 1", 1" and 2¹⁄₂" cut
- French-fold binding: ³⁄₈" finished

Unit Block

Wallhanging Size:

35¹⁄₄" by 35¹⁄₄"
89.5 cm by 89.5 cm
as shown in color picture, page 33, and illustration in **Diagram I,** *page 34.*

Block Size:

2³⁄₈" square
6 cm square

Materials Required:

24 fat-sixteenths in rainbow spectrum of hand-dyed fabrics, **or**

12 fat-eighths, includes second border, pieced from blue fabrics

1 yard of black fabric for strips, first and third borders and French-fold binding

1¹⁄₄ yards of fabric for backing

1¹⁄₄ yards of batting or crib-size packaged batting

Like Basket Weave Discovery, Basket Weave in Vivid Colors *utilizes narrow dark strips along the outside edges of the unit blocks to create the woven illusion. As this quilt is a variation of the* Fence Rail Basic Quilt *and* Basket Weave Discovery, *instructions are condensed. Please refer to the instructions for those quilts if necessary.*

Selecting the Fabric

If the effect you want is a true Basket Weave, I recommend using an odd number of strips with symmetrically-positioned matching fabric, **Diagram A.** The desired result in this quilt, however, was to create an abstract, woven-looking piece without giving up the strip techniques. I love playing with color wheel fabrics, so that was a natural for this project. It looks complicated in writing, but in reality, the strips follow a natural rotation. The strips are positioned as part of that color rotation, **Diagram B.** The black strips are very narrow, and do a great job of creating the woven illusion, along with the alternating vertical and horizontal blocks.

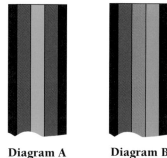

Diagram A   **Diagram B**

The photographed wallhanging was made using a packaged set of 24 hand-dyed fabrics in the full rainbow spectrum. The fat-sixteenths package was perfect. Each piece is 9 inches by 11 inches. These 24 fabrics are divided into two sets, for making vertical and horizontal weave blocks. Each unit block is composed of three rainbow fabric strips, bordered by narrow strips of black fabric, **Diagram C.**

Unit Block

Diagram C

> *Option: A set of 12 rainbow colors could also be used by making the vertical and horizontal blocks from identical sets of fabric. See Twelve-Color Option, page 35.*

Cutting the Fabric

Because the dramatic pattern of this wallhanging is created by the arrangement of color, it is important first to understand how the fabrics are sorted before beginning to cut. The basic color wheel has six colors: red, orange, yellow, green, blue and violet. It is easy to expand that by adding all the in-between blends: red-orange, yellow-orange, yellow-green, blue-green, blue-violet and red-violet, **Diagram D.** The hand-dyed fabrics used for this quilt contained 12 addi-

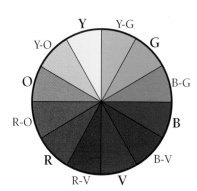

Diagram D

tional gradations of color, one between each of these colors, **Diagram E**. Working clockwise around the color wheel, sort and number the fabrics from one to 24; then separate the odd- and even-numbered fabrics. The first fabric in the photographed quilt is from the blue family.

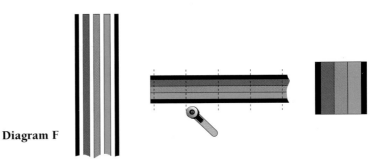

Diagram F

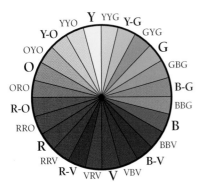

Diagram E

From each of the 24 rainbow fabrics, cut three strips, 1¹/₈ inches wide by 18 inches long (or six strips 1¹/₈ inches by 9 inches if using packaged fabric). Cut the black fabric into 48 strips, ³/₄ inch wide by 18 inches long. Cut all strips on the length-wise grain.

Making the Unit Block

Each strip set is composed of three rainbow fabric strips, bordered by narrow strips of black fabric, **Diagram F**. Each fabric is repeated in three consecutive strip sets, rotating to the next position in each new set, **Diagram G**. Make your own keys to show your color rotation, as in **Diagram G**, and block rotation, as in **Diagram H**.

1. Using **Diagrams F** and **G** as guides, sew the strips together into strip sets for the unit blocks, keeping even- and odd-numbered strips separate. Begin with fabrics numbered 24, 2 and 4, combined with two narrow strips of black fabric, to make Strip Set **a**. Continue sewing strips into sets.

Color rotation of 24 colors in the 24 strip sets and blocks

Position vertically

Block name	Fabric Numbers		
a	24	2	4
b	2	4	6
c	4	6	8
d	6	8	10
e	8	10	12
f	10	12	14
g	12	14	16
h	14	16	18
i	16	18	20
j	18	20	22
k	20	22	24
l	22	24	2

Position horizontally

Block name	Fabric Numbers		
m	23	1	3
n	1	3	5
o	3	5	7
p	5	7	9
q	7	9	11
r	9	11	13
s	11	13	15
t	13	15	17
u	15	17	19
v	17	19	21
w	19	21	23
x	21	23	1

Diagram G

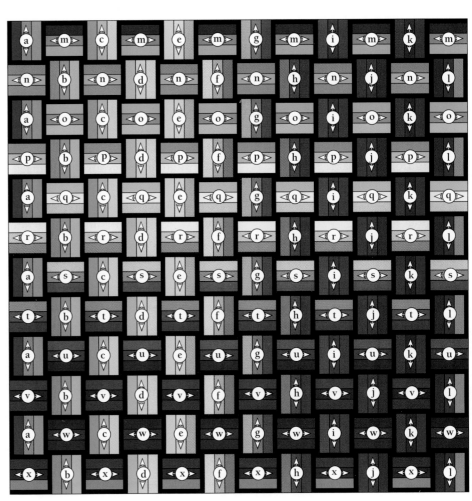

Diagram H

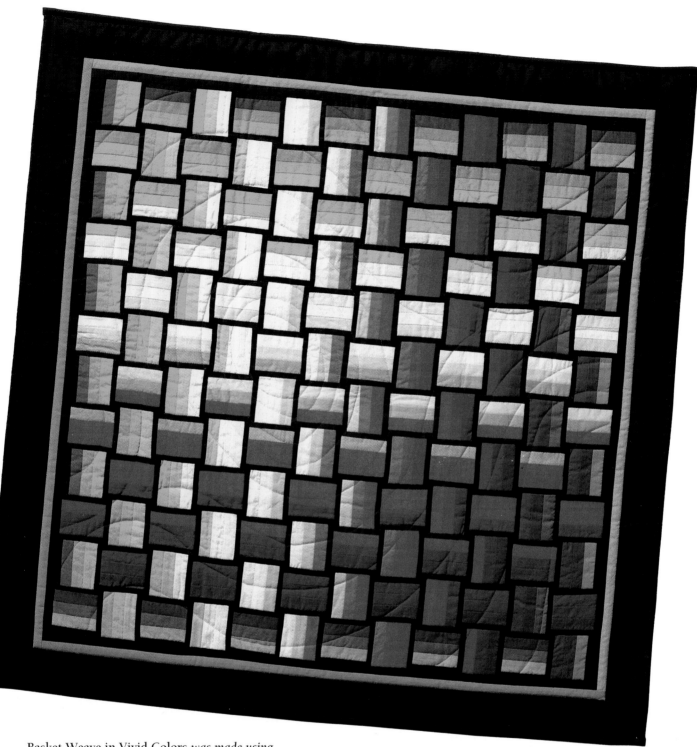

Basket Weave in Vivid Colors *was made using*
a packaged set of 24 hand-dyed fabrics in the full rainbow spectrum.
Narrow dark strips along the outside edges of the unit blocks create the woven
illusion. Notice the effect of the free-form quilting design.

Make 24 strip sets, **a** through **x**. As you complete each set, it is a good idea to label it **a**, **b**, **c**, etc., according to its fabric rotation, for making Block **a**, **b**, **c**, etc. Refer to **Diagram G**.

2. Press seam allowances toward the dark fabric. The MCM for the finished strip sets is 2⁷/8 inches wide.

The unit block is created by the second cut, **Diagram F**. (If your strip sets are not 2⁷/8 inches, use your O&O for the second cut.) Be careful to keep strip sets for horizontal and vertical blocks separated as you cut. Cut six unit blocks from each strip set, making 144 blocks.

Assembling the Quilt Interior

Following the quilt layout, **Diagram H**, assemble the blocks into 12 rows of 12 blocks each. The progression of colors in each block, and blocks in the quilt, develops the full rainbow spectrum. To create the basket weave set, Blocks **a** through **l**, made from even-numbered strips, are positioned vertically; Blocks **m** through **x**, made from odd-numbered strips, are positioned horizontally. Horizontal and vertical blocks alternate. To develop the pattern as shown, place the six matching blocks in the same row.

The quilt interior is assembled by sewing pairs of blocks together, then pairs of pairs, then two pairs of pairs, etc. See page 24. The MCM for the assembled quilt interior is 29 inches by 29 inches. Press the quilt interior.

Diagram I

34

Finishing the Quilt

The borders on the photographed quilt were cut 1 inch, 1 inch and 2 1/2 inches wide. They were added traditionally. The quilt was layered with batting and backing, and machine quilted using invisible thread, **Diagram I**. Beginning around the lightest block, quilt in concentric flowing ovals. Use the quilt blocks shown in the diagram to help position your quilting lines. Because this is a free-form design, the idea is more important than the actual position of the quilting lines. A 3/8-inch-wide (strips cut 2 1/8 inches wide) French-fold binding completes the quilt. See Finishing Your Quilt, page 179, for details.

Bonus:
Scraps of Vivid Color

Read Tips for Making Mini and Miniature Quilts, page 177.

Scraps of Vivid Color is a three-strip variation of the *Fence Rail Basic Quilt*, page 20.

I always say there are three kinds of scraps. A few scraps actually get thrown away; others are folded and put away for another day. Then there are creative scraps. They are so appealing they demand to be used. That was the case with these scraps. The border print is a perfect example of why you should buy things you like when you see them, even if you have no definite plans for their use. I knew I would "need" such a great print one day! Don't despair if you don't own this particular fabric; many other prints would work as well. I have a small col-lection of primary-colored letters, teddy bears, bal-loons, etc. on black—any of which would be great. Or, if you have lots of scraps, use them to make a border.

To make the quilt as shown, scraps of all 24 hand-dyed rainbow fabrics from the *Basket Weave in Vivid Colors* were required. Each unit block is composed of three different rainbow fabric strips. If you used only 12 fabrics in the *Basket Weave in Vivid Colors*, you will need to repeat the rotation twice to make this quilt. The strips in the photographed quilt were cut 1 1/8 inches wide. The border size was determined by the print.

Scraps of Vivid Color is a three-strip variation of the Fence Rail Basic Quilt.

Sticks and Stones

Wallhanging Size:
41³/₄" by 41³/₄"
106 cm by 106 cm

Block Size:
6" square
15.2 cm square

Materials Required:

1¹/₄ yards of light ecru and pink fabric, including third border and French-fold binding

1¹/₈ yards of medium pink plaid fabric, including second border

³/₄ yard of dark blue floral fabric

1¹/₄ yards of 60"-wide fabric for backing

1¹/₄ yards of batting, or crib-size packaged batting

¹/₄ yard of medium pink print fabric for first border, cut crosswise

It will take only a few moments to recognize that this quilt, called *Sticks and Stones,* employs many of the construction techniques of the *Fence Rail Basic Quilt.* Let's compare the two. In this quilt, the Fence Rail unit blocks are created with three strips instead of five. Half of the squares have no piecing. The set of the blocks is different: it is neither the diagonal fence rail nor the basket weave already shown. In actual construction, *Sticks and Stones* has fewer pieces and is really easier than the *Fence Rail Basic Quilt.* However, it has a few "tricky" concepts that may make it seem more complex.

Selecting the Fabric

This is a quilt where the selection of fabrics based on value is especially important. "Value" refers to the lightness or darkness of a color. In this case, the light, medium and dark fabrics are good examples of relative value. That is, the slate blue print that serves as the darkest fabric in the quilt is not really very dark compared to *all* colors, but it is dark in relationship to the other fabrics in the quilt. The soft colors selected make a very pretty quilt. The design is also quite striking when made with strong, high-contrast solid colors.

Do not select a fabric with a one-way directional design unless you are willing to forego most of the advantages of strip techniques. A two-way directional design will require some special attention, but could be very effective.

Finding the Unit Block

When beginning in the upper left corner of **Diagram B** and looking right, you will see that the first piece is a square, followed by a square made of three strips. The first piece to repeat is the unpieced square. It, too, is followed by a square with three strips, but the value placement of fabrics is different. It is necessary to include four small squares to find a complete repeat. The same situation occurs going down the quilt from the upper left corner. It would be easy to call this the unit block.

Remember that the unit block is defined as the smallest repetitive unit. The purpose of finding it is to streamline construction. If you need to make many units of the same thing, every step can be more efficient. If you look within this set of 16 squares in the upper left corner of the quilt, **Diagram B,** you can see two repeats. The easiest description is that this quilt has two unit blocks, **Diagram A.** The design is created by alternating the unit blocks in both directions. Looking closely, you will see that in addition to 13 Unit Blocks A and 12 Unit Blocks B, there is a row of half blocks or sub-units on one side and the bottom of the quilt, **Diagram B.**

Unit Block A   Unit Block B

Diagram A

Sticks and Stones employs many of the construction techniques of the Fence Rail Basic Quilt *except that the unit blocks are created with three strips instead of five and half of the squares are not pieced.*

The reason for this is something I call "The Rule of Matching Corners." Quilt designs with alternating unit blocks are nearly always more appealing if all of the quilt's corners have the same design element, in this case a dark square. The extra rows of half blocks complete the design and keep it in balance. When the unit blocks are all alike, as in the *Fence Rail Basic Quilt* or *Basket Weave*, matching corners are not as important. The quilts in this book have already been designed with this theory, but as you develop your own designs, you may realize that adding design elements to create matching corners is the solution you need.

> **TIP** ◆ ◆ ◆ ◆ ◆ ◆ ◆
> *The Rule of Matching Corners states that geometric quilt designs are almost always more appealing if the corners match.*

Making the Unit Blocks

After the unit block is defined, break it down into smaller parts, or sub-units—always looking to be efficient in construction techniques—to think smarter.

CUTTING AND SEWING THE NARROW STRIPS

Don't cut all the fabrics now. Cut the smallest sub-unit components first (in this quilt, strips for the "sticks"). After the strip sets are assembled, measure your strip sets to determine if you will be using the MCM or your O&O when cutting the next components (strips for the "stones").

1. The sticks in the unit blocks are made from strips. From each of the light, medium and dark fabrics, cut nine strips on the lengthwise grain, 1¹/₂ inches wide by 27 inches long. If you are using a different strip length, the minimum total length needed from each fabric is 215 inches, or

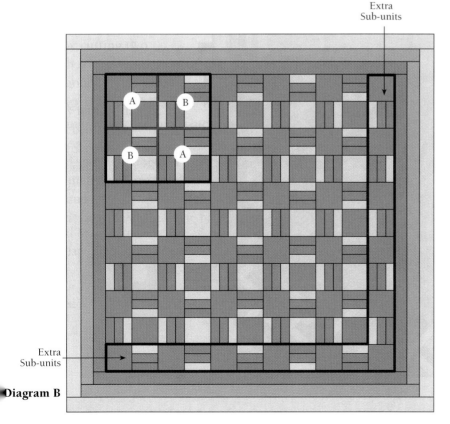

Extra Sub-units

Extra Sub-units

Diagram B

enough to cut 60 segments 3½ inches long after piecing.

All of the strip sets for the sticks in both unit blocks are assembled in the same sequence. To save time when making the strip sets, remember to put two adjoining fabrics face to face before cutting.

2. Using **Diagram C** as a guide, sew the strips together into sets. Press seam allowances toward the dark fabric. The MCM for the strip sets is 3½ inches wide.

Diagram C

ADDING THE "STONES"

(If your strip sets are not 3½ inches, substitute your O&O measurement for 3½ inches in every step of this section.)

1. Before making any second cuts across the strip sets, look at **Diagram D**. Strips for the two "sticks and stones" combinations with vertical strips can be sewn together before being cut. Anything you can Sew-Before-You-Cut is quicker, easier and more accurate.

For the stones, cut two strips of light fabric on the lengthwise grain, 3½ inches wide (or your O&O) by 27 inches long. From dark fabric, cut seven strips the same size.

2. For the first sub-unit of the Unit Blocks A, sew a wide dark strip to the light side of two strip sets. Cut across these strip sets in 3½-inch increments, making 13 pairs of sticks and stones, **Diagram D**.

For the first sub-unit of the Unit Blocks B, sew a wide light strip to the dark side of two strip sets. Cut 12 pairs of sticks and stones, **Diagram D**.

3. For the remaining sub-unit of each unit block, the strip sets must be cut before they can be joined to the wide strips or stones. Cut thirty-six 3½-inch squares from the strip sets. Turn the squares so that the strips are horizontal, and sew them to the five remaining wide dark strips. Study **Diagram E** carefully: keeping the wide dark strip on the bottom, sew 18 squares of sticks with the dark strip at the top, and 17 with the light strip at the top. Press the seam allowances toward the wide dark strip.

Cut across these strip sets in 3½-inch increments. Cut 18 pairs of sticks and stones with the dark strip on top; 13 for the Unit Blocks A, and five for the extra row of sub-units along the bot-tom and right side of the quilt. Cut 18 pairs of sticks and stones with the dark strip on the bottom; 12 for the Unit Blocks B, and six for the extra row of sub-units. The final "stone" will be used to complete the lower right corner of the quilt.

4. Now sew pairs of pairs together, completing 13 Unit Blocks A and 12 Unit Blocks B, **Diagram A**. Pay special attention to the position of light and dark when assembling the blocks. The MCM for the unit blocks is 6½ inches square.

Assembling the Quilt Interior

Following the quilt layout, **Diagram B**, page 37, assemble the unit blocks into five rows of five blocks each, as well as the extra row of sub-units along the bottom and right side of the quilt (the remaining pairs from Adding the Stones, step 3). This quilt

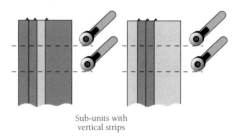

Sub-units with
vertical strips

Diagram D

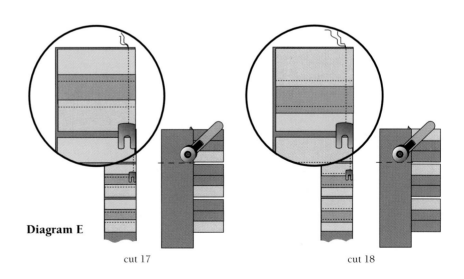

Diagram E

cut 17

cut 18

interior is assembled by sewing pairs of blocks together, then pairs of pairs, then two pairs of pairs, etc. Refer to page 24. The MCM for the assembled quilt interior is 33½ inches by 33½ inches. Press the quilt interior.

Finishing the Quilt

The borders were cut 1¾ inches, 1¾ inches and 1⅞ inches wide; binding strips were cut 2⅝ inches wide. See Finishing Your Quilt, page 179, for finishing information. This quilt was machine quilted with invisible thread. The borders were added using the Modified Quilt-As-You-Sew method.

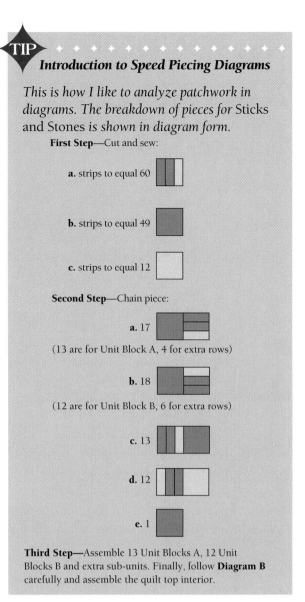

TIP

Introduction to Speed Piecing Diagrams

This is how I like to analyze patchwork in diagrams. The breakdown of pieces for Sticks and Stones is shown in diagram form.

First Step—Cut and sew:

a. strips to equal 60

b. strips to equal 49

c. strips to equal 12

Second Step—Chain piece:

a. 17

(13 are for Unit Block A, 4 for extra rows)

b. 18

(12 are for Unit Block B, 6 for extra rows)

c. 13

d. 12

e. 1

Third Step—Assemble 13 Unit Blocks A, 12 Unit Blocks B and extra sub-units. Finally, follow **Diagram B** carefully and assemble the quilt top interior.

Bonus:
Pinwheel Sticks and Stones

In this quilt, the pinwheel is made from two strips pieced and cut into squares. Rotate and join the squares to make the quilt block; alternate with matching-size empty blocks and finish as desired.

If the first strip is 1½ inches wide, the quilt will be approximately 31 inches by 39 inches with borders. Use larger strips and/or more blocks for a larger quilt.

Unit Block

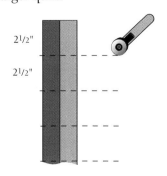

2½"

2½"

Introducing Diagonal Set Quilts

If you are serious about learning the secrets of *Quilting for People Who* Still *Don't Have Time to Quilt*, this is a good opportunity to start making diagonal set quilts. Up to this point, all of the quilts have been straight set. That means the quilt block or unit block is resting flat on one side. When the unit blocks are tipped or set on point instead of resting flat, it is called a diagonal set.

Busy quilters must learn to maximize the results they get for the time spent. One of the easiest ways to do that is to work with designs that feature strong diagonal lines. Many quilt blocks feature a diagonal design line and when the blocks are set together in a straight set, the resulting quilt still has a strong diagonal look. (See *Victorian Posy*, page 104, *Double Irish Chain*, page 137, and *Burgoyne Surrounded*, page 155, as examples.) Other times it is necessary to position the unit blocks on point to create a diagonal design line.

It is said in design that there are only three basic shapes: the square, the circle and the triangle. Reduced to its simplest interpretation, squares are rigid, circles are restful, and triangles are dynamic. Diagonal lines equate with triangles; that is why they almost always result in a more interesting quilt. When you are working with diagonal set quilts, you may have to tilt your head or turn the book or quilt so you can see the unit blocks in flat rows. When you set blocks on point, you will see that there are triangles at the end of each diagonal row. They are called setting triangles.

Making the next quilt, *Sticks and Stones on Point Basic Quilt*, is an easy way to learn about diagonal set quilts and The Secret of the Setting Triangles. Corner triangles are also needed for the quilt. While the triangles look alike, they aren't; that is part of the secret.

If you happen to be a serious fabric collector, but a novice at diagonal set quilts, you may prefer the *Scrappy Basket Weave*, page 49, as your first diagonal set quilt.

Sticks and Stones on Point Basic Quilt

Snapshot
- Unit Block A: 16
- Unit Block B: 9
- Interior Arrangement:
  7 diagonal rows with setting and corner triangles,
  Diagram E, page 42
- First Strip Width: 1³/₄" cut
- Border: 3¹/₄" cut
- French-fold binding:
  ³/₈" finished

Unit Block A   Unit Block B

**4 light
4 bright
1 dark**

Wallhanging Size:
27¹/₄" by 27¹/₄"
69.2 cm by 69.2 cm

Block Size:
3³/₄" square
9.5 cm square

Materials Required:
¹/₄ yard of black (dark) fabric, including setting and corner triangles
¹/₈ yard of black checked (medium dark) fabric, including corner blocks
¹/₂ yard of red (medium/bright) fabric, including setting triangles
¹/₈ yard of light gray (medium light) fabric
¹/₈ yard of white (light) fabric

¹/₂ yard of "theme" fabric for border, cut crosswise
⁷/₈ yard of fabric for backing
⁷/₈ yard of batting or one packaged crib-size batting
¹/₄ yard of fabric for French-fold binding, cut crosswise

If available, fat quarters are sufficient for every fabric requirement except setting triangles, border, backing and binding.

This simple diagonal set version of *Sticks and Stones* has a completely different appearance than the *Sticks and Stones Basic Quilt*, page 36. The difference is mainly the diagonal set and, secondly, the change in value place-

The diagonal set and contrasting placement of fabric values give Sticks and Stones on Point a completely different appearance than the Sticks and Stones Basic Quilt.

way to describe the border print. In a quilt this small, the border is a good place to position a theme fabric, whether it is wild animals, teddy bears or tropical fish.

Finding the Unit Block

> **TIP** ♦ ♦ ♦ ♦ ♦ ♦ ♦ ♦ ♦ ♦
> *One quilt's sub-unit is another's unit block.*

This quilt is so small that it is not practical to use the larger unit blocks; instead, just work with sub-units. In other words, the sub-units of the original quilt are the unit blocks in this quilt. The two unit blocks, **Diagram A**, are three narrow strips ("sticks") sewn into matching strip sets and cut into squares and matching unpieced squares ("stones"). It is easier to assemble the units into diagonal rows and then sew the rows together, **Diagram H**, than to make the larger unit blocks used in the Basic Quilt.

Unit Block A

4 light
4 bright
1 dark
Unit Block B

Diagram A

ment of the fabrics. By positioning the dominant fabric as the middle strip instead of the outside strip, it connects with the alternate square in an entirely different way. You will see that the construction method is also different.

Before beginning to work on your quilt, read Now Hear This!! on page 19.

> **TIP** ♦ ♦ ♦ ♦ ♦ ♦ ♦ ♦ ♦
> *If you like the looks and design of a quilt, but don't want to duplicate the colors, substitute words that describe the relative values, from darkest to lightest, for the colors of the fabrics in the quilt. Then select fabrics in another color scheme that fit the new description.*

Selecting the Fabric

As in the straight set version, the value of the fabrics selected is especially important. "Value" expresses the lightness or darkness of a color. In this quilt, it is very easy to establish the position of the dark, medium dark, medium/bright, medium light and light fabrics. In addition, there are some other descriptive words to consider. The brightness of the red fabric in the medium position is also crucial to the design of the quilt.

The border fabric, however, is the fabric that holds this quilt together. The Oriental characters in the fabric set the mood and the full white, red and black color scheme is established. "Theme fabric" seems like a good

Making the Unit Blocks

The unit blocks for this diagonal set version of Sticks and Stones are assembled the same as the sub-units for the straight set version, page 36.

CUTTING AND SEWING THE "STICKS"—UNIT BLOCK A

1. Cut the narrow strips for the sticks. From the black, red and gray (dark, medium/bright, medium light) fabrics, cut four strips 1³/4 inches wide by 18 inches long, or eight strips 1³/4 inches wide by 9 inches long. Remember to put two adjoining fabrics face to face before cutting to save time when sewing.

2. Using **Diagram B** as a guide, sew the strips together into sets. Press seam allowances toward the dark fabric. The MCM for the finished strip sets is 4¼ inches wide.

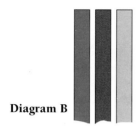

Diagram B

ADDING THE "STONES"— UNIT BLOCK B

Remember, anything you can Sew-Before-You-Cut is quicker, easier and more accurate. Before making any second cuts across the strip sets, look at **Diagram C**. Strips for the white "sticks and stone" combination are made entirely of vertical strips. These stone strips can be joined to the sticks strip sets before cutting.

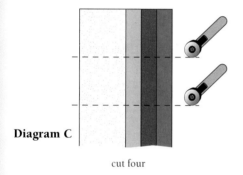

Diagram C

cut four

(If your strip sets are not 4¼ inches, substitute your O&O measurement in every step of this section.)

1. From both red and white (medium/bright, light) fabrics, cut one strip 4¼ inches wide by 18 inches long, or two strips 4¼ inches by 9 inches. From black (dark) fabric, cut one 4¼-inch square. The black square will be an unpaired Unit Block B.

2. For the white (light) sticks and stone combinations, sew a white strip to the light side of one strip set. Press seam allowances toward the sticks. Cut across these strip set combina-

tions in 4¼-inch increments, making four pairs of sticks and stones, **Diagram C**.

3. For the red (medium/bright) combinations, the strip sets must be cut before they can be joined to the wide strips. Cut four 4¼-inch squares from the strip sets. Turn the squares so the strips are horizontal, and sew them to the red strip. Study **Diagram D** carefully: keeping the wide red stones strip on the bottom, sew two squares with the horizontal dark strip at the top and two with the horizontal light strip at the top. Press the seam allowances toward the red strip. Cut across the pressed strip sets in 4¼-inch increments.

4. Cut eight 4¼-inch squares from the remaining strip sets. These are used as unpaired Unit Blocks B.

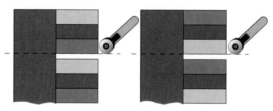

Diagram D

Assembling the Quilt Interior

Because this quilt features a diagonal set, setting and corner triangles must be used to fill in the outer edges of the quilt interior.

1. To make the setting triangles, cut two 7-inch squares from red fabric and one 7-inch square from black fabric. Cut each square on both diagonals to yield eight red and four black setting triangles.

2. For the four corner triangles, cut two 3¾-inch squares from black fabric, and cut each square once diagonally.

ASSEMBLING THE DIAGONAL ROWS

1. Lay the sticks and stone combinations and unpaired unit blocks out on a flat surface, or use a design wall, page 178. Fill in edges with setting triangles and corners with corner triangles as shown, **Diagram E**.

continued on page 44

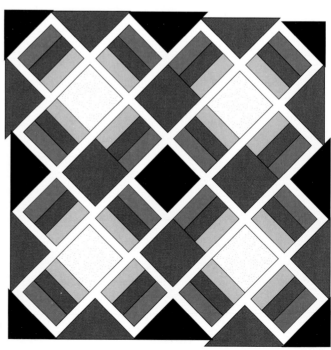

Diagram E

42

THE SECRET OF THE SETTING TRIANGLES

In a quilt with a diagonal set, such as the Sticks and Stones on Point Basic Quilt, the units are set on point, rather than parallel to the sides of the quilt. These diagonal rows create the need for half squares or setting triangles at each end.

Cutting these triangles can be tricky, unless you know the secret. It's no secret that two right angle triangles can be made by cutting a square in half diagonally. However, when the squares are fabric and they have been cut on grain, the hypotenuse of the new triangles would be a perfect bias and very stretchy. When the triangles are added to the end of the row, that stretchy edge is on the outside of the quilt, an arrangement that is difficult at best, disastrous at worst.

*It is obvious that setting triangles with the hypotenuse, or longest side, on the straight grain are preferred. How to do that is the Secret of the Setting Triangles. Just cut a larger square on both diagonals to yield four setting triangles (**A**). To determine the size of the larger square, measure the diagonal of the finished size unit block, and add 1¼ inches (**B**). This is the size square to quarter for perfect-fit, no-mistakes-allowed setting triangles. I prefer to add 1½ inches to 2½ inches to the diagonal measurement of the block. That size square will yield slightly larger setting triangles which allow the design blocks to float inside the borders (**C**).*

*The more you add, the more the quilt blocks float. Floating is good insurance against nipping off the corners of the quilt blocks when adding the borders, which will happen if the setting triangles don't fit perfectly (**D**). A narrow float actually makes your piecing look more crisp because you can see the corner points of the quilt blocks. A wide float can serve as a narrow first border. Excess can be trimmed away later if you decide you don't want a floating set.*

*When cutting the right angle triangles for the corners, the desired grainline is just the opposite. The hypotenuse should be on the bias and the legs on the straight grain. Four corner triangles can be cut from two squares that are the same finished size as the unit block. Cut each square in half diagonally to yield triangles with the legs on the straight grain (**E**). These triangles will be oversized enough to match floating setting triangles. Don't panic if they don't match perfectly. Excess fabric can be trimmed away later.*

Always analyze your right angle triangles carefully. If you want the hypotenuse to be on the straight grain, quarter a square diagonally. If you want the legs or short sides to be on the straight grain, halve a square diagonally.

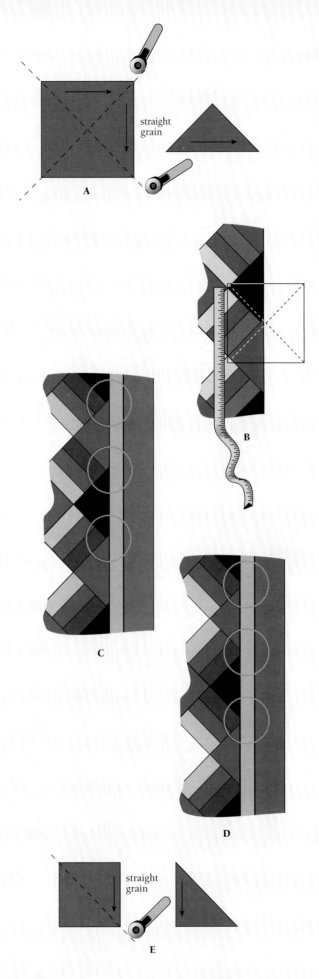

43

2. The easiest way to piece the diagonal rows is to join the unit blocks within each row first. Press the seam allowances toward the stones.

3. Sew the setting triangles in place to complete the rows. Line up the right angle of the triangle with a corner of the adjacent unit so the hypotenuse will become the outside edge of the quilt interior. The tips of the triangles will extend beyond the unit block, **Diagram F**. Be careful not to stretch the bias edges of the triangles when sewing. Press the seam allowances toward the triangles.

4. Beginning in the upper left corner of the quilt interior, join the completed rows to each other. With right sides together and seams matching, sew Row 1 to Row 2, **Diagram G**. Row 3 is then joined to Row 2, and so on, **Diagram H**. Continue until all the diagonal rows have been sewn together.

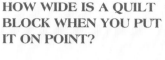

TIP *When joining the rows, the extending tips of the triangles will be sewn one over the other, thus creating the effect of a floating set. Because this particular quilt features setting triangles in alternating colors, the floating effect was minimized. Extra fabric will be trimmed later. For other quilts with a floating set, be sure to sew the rows together so that the same tip (upper or lower) of all triangles will be sewn over consistently.*

5. The corner triangles are last to be added, and will finish the quilt interior. With right sides together, sew the triangles in place at each corner, taking care not to stretch the bias edge when sewing, **Diagram I**.

HOW WIDE IS A QUILT BLOCK WHEN YOU PUT IT ON POINT?

Looking at a straight set design, it is easy to say, "If one square in the grid equals one inch, the quilt is as many inches wide as the design is squares wide." When you start playing with blocks on point, it is not so easy; the significant measurements change. It is the diagonal measurement of a quilt block that determines the width and length of the quilt. The formula for finding the hypotenuse of a right triangle when you know the length of one leg is the geometry lesson that solves the puzzle.

You may not recognize it yet, but chances are you are going to fall in love with diagonal set quilts. This formula turned into a tip is how you will know the size a design is going to be when completed before it is done. If you are working on graph paper when designing, don't forget to properly allow for the size each square represents to calculate the size of the block, then multiply by 1.41.

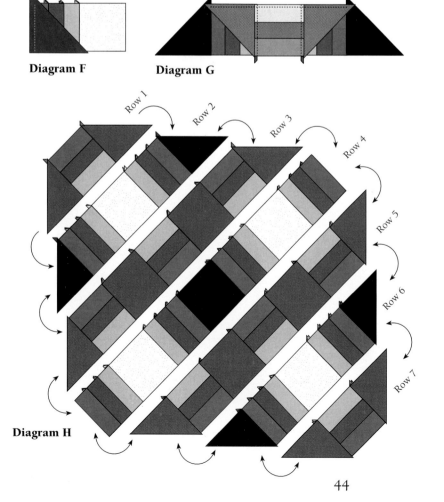

Diagram F   **Diagram G**

Diagram H

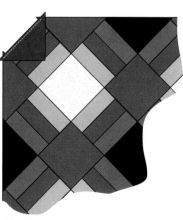

Diagram I

6. Trim the excess fabric from the setting and corner triangles in order to square up the quilt interior, page 179. The MCM for the assembled quilt interior is 21½ inches by 21½ inches from block to block. Due to the alternating color setting triangles, the photographed quilt has no additional float.

Finishing the Quilt

The 3¼-inch border for the photographed quilt was added traditionally, with corner blocks. The cut width of this border was determined by the fabric design. The quilt was layered with batting and backing, and machine quilted in the ditch between the quilt blocks, using invisible thread. A ³⁄₈-inch-wide (strips cut 2⅛ inches wide) French-fold binding completes the quilt. See Finishing Your Quilt, page 179, for details.

TIP

What you see is not necessarily what you sew.

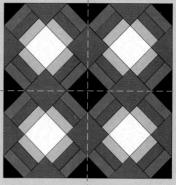

Look at the quilt as a whole in the photograph on page 41, before deciding on the pieces and sewing method. The quilt block, right, would appear to be made of eight triangles, four pieced squares and one plain square. Do you see how many more pieces and seams it would take to make four blocks like that than the whole quilt just completed?

Sticks and Stones on Point—Act II

Snapshot

- Unit Block A: 9
- Unit Block B: 4
- Interior Arrangement: 5 diagonal rows with extra sub-units and setting and corner triangles, **Diagram E**, page 47
- First Strip Width: 1½" cut
- Borders: 1¼", 1³⁄₈" and 1⁵⁄₈" cut
- French-fold binding: ³⁄₈" finished

Unit Block A   Unit Block B

Wallhanging Size:
37" by 37"
94 cm by 94 cm
as shown in color picture, page 46

Block Size:
6" square
15.2 cm square

Materials Required:
1⅛ yards of dark green print fabric, including third border and French-fold binding
⅛ yard of alternate dark green print fabric
⅛ yard of medium green print fabric
¾ yard of medium plum print fabric, including second border
¾ yard of ecru print fabric, including first border
³⁄₈ yard of plum fabric for setting and corner triangles
1¼ yards of fabric for backing
1¼ yards of batting

This quilt is a cross between the Sticks and Stones on Point Basic Quilt, *page 40, and the original* Sticks and Stones, *page 36. If necessary, read the instructions for those basic quilts before beginning this quilt.*

This diagonal set version of Sticks and Stones bears little resemblance to the *Sticks and Stones On Point Basic Quilt* on page 40. Act II has many more pieces so it makes sense to use the larger unit blocks as in the straight set *Sticks and Stones*, page 36. It also uses the same fabric value arrangement as the original Sticks and Stones. Larger unit blocks mean larger spaces along the sides when the blocks are set on point. Those spaces may be filled with more sub-units or with larger setting triangles. For our example, larger setting triangles were selected. This variation creates an attractive peaked border effect and reduces the amount of piecing.

This quilt is a cross between the Sticks and Stones on Point Basic Quilt *and the original* Sticks and Stones. Sticks and Stones On Point-Act II *has many more pieces and uses the same fabric value arrangement as the original* Sticks and Stones *while being set on point.*

composed of two pieced sub-units of three narrow strips ("sticks"), and two small unpieced squares ("stones"), **Diagram A**. They are assembled the same as for the straight set version, page 36.

Unit Block A   Unit Block B

Diagram A

1. From the ecru, plum and dark green fabrics, cut six strips each on the lengthwise grain, 1^{1}/2 inches wide by 27 inches long.

2. Sew the strips into sets, **Diagram B**. Press seam allowances toward the dark fabric. The MCM for the finished strip sets is 3^{1}/2 inches wide. If your measurements differ, substitute your O&O unique measurement in the following steps.

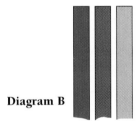

Diagram B

Remember how extra sub-units were used along two sides of the *Sticks and Stones*, page 36, to create matching patchwork corners? On point, the extra sub-units are used along the length of the center row and at one end of each row.

Selecting the Fabric

The two dark green and plum prints came from the same fabric group. Although either of the dark green fabrics could have been used for both unpieced squares in Unit Block A, by using two similar prints a pleasant secondary pattern was created. If you prefer to use just one, you may.

Making the Unit Blocks

The unit blocks for this diagonal set version of Sticks and Stones are each

3. For the stones, cut the following 3^{1}/2-inch wide strips on the lengthwise grain when possible: four strips of dark green fabric, 27 inches long; two strips of alternate green fabric, 18 inches long; one strip of medium green fabric, 15 inches long. Also cut one dark green 3^{1}/2-inch square for the individual sub-unit in the center row.

4. Strips for the two "sticks and stone" combinations with vertical strips can be sewn together before cutting. For the first sub-unit of the Unit Blocks A, sew an alternate green strip to the light side of two strip sets. Cut in 3^{1}/2-inch increments to make nine sub-units, **Diagram C**.

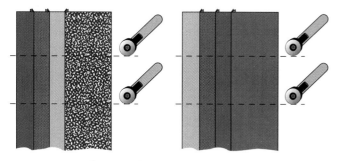

Sub-units with vertical strips

Diagram C

Cut 16 for Unit
Block A and
Sub-unit A

Cut 7 for Unit
Block B and
Sub-unit B

Diagram D

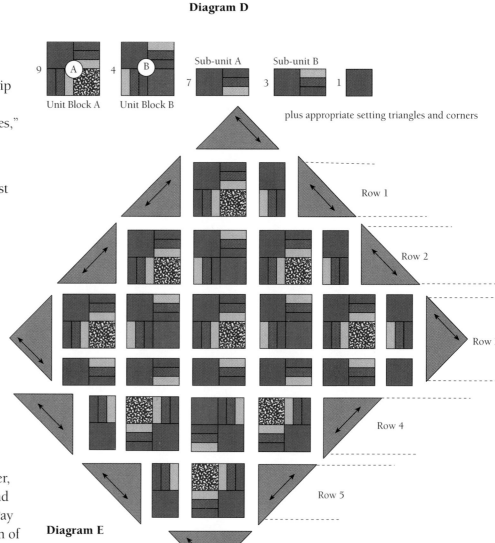

9 (A) 4 (B) Sub-unit A Sub-unit B

Unit Block A Unit Block B 7 3 1

plus appropriate setting triangles and corners

Row 1

Row 2

Row 3

Row 4

Row 5

Diagram E

For the first sub-unit of the Unit Blocks B, sew a medium green strip to the dark side of one strip set. Cut four pairs of "sticks and stones," **Diagram C**.

5. For the remaining sub-unit of each unit block, the strip sets must be cut before they can be joined to the wide strips or stones. Cut twenty-three 3½-inch squares from the strip sets. Turn the squares so the strips are horizontal, and place them on top of the remaining dark green strips. Sew 16 squares with the horizontal dark strip on top, and seven with the horizontal light strip on top, **Diagram D**. Press the seam allowances toward the wide dark strip. Cut across these strip sets in 3½-inch increments.

6. Now sew pairs of pairs together, completing nine Unit Blocks A and four Unit Blocks B, **Diagram A**. Pay special attention to the orientation of light and dark strips. The MCM for the 13 blocks is 6½ inches square.

Assembling the Quilt Interior

Remember that the setting triangles for this quilt are cut large enough to fit the complete unit block, rather than single sub-units; the corner triangles are cut large enough to fit the unit block with the additional row of sub-units.

CUTTING THE SETTING AND CORNER TRIANGLES

1. To make setting triangles, cut two 10½-inch squares from plum fabric. Cut each square on both diagonals to yield eight setting triangles.

2. To make corner triangles to fit the center row, cut two 9-inch squares from plum fabric. Cut each square once diagonally to yield four corner triangles.

ASSEMBLING THE DIAGONAL ROWS

Lay the unit blocks out on a large flat surface or design wall. Fill in the edges with extra sub-units and setting triangles as shown, **Diagram E**. This diagram shows the blocks sitting flat and the quilt on point. Sew extra sub-units and setting triangles into place and complete the rows, **Diagram F**. Join the rows and add corner triangles to complete the quilt interior.

The MCM for the completed quilt interior is 30$^{1}/_{4}$ inches by 30$^{1}/_{4}$ inches from edge to edge. The photographed quilt has an additional $^{1}/_{2}$ inch of float on each side; allow for a floating set on your quilt as desired. Trim the excess fabric from the setting and corner triangles in order to square up the quilt, page 179.

FINISHING THE QUILT

Borders could be added traditionally, but this quilt interior was centered on batting and backing the size of the finished quilt. It was machine quilted in the ditch and in the setting triangles, using invisible thread, before the borders were added. See Finishing Your Quilt, page 179, for details. The Modified Quilt-As-You-Sew borders were cut 1$^{1}/_{4}$ inches, 1$^{3}/_{8}$ inches and 1$^{5}/_{8}$ inches wide; binding strips were cut 2$^{1}/_{8}$ inches wide for a $^{3}/_{8}$-inch-wide French-fold binding.

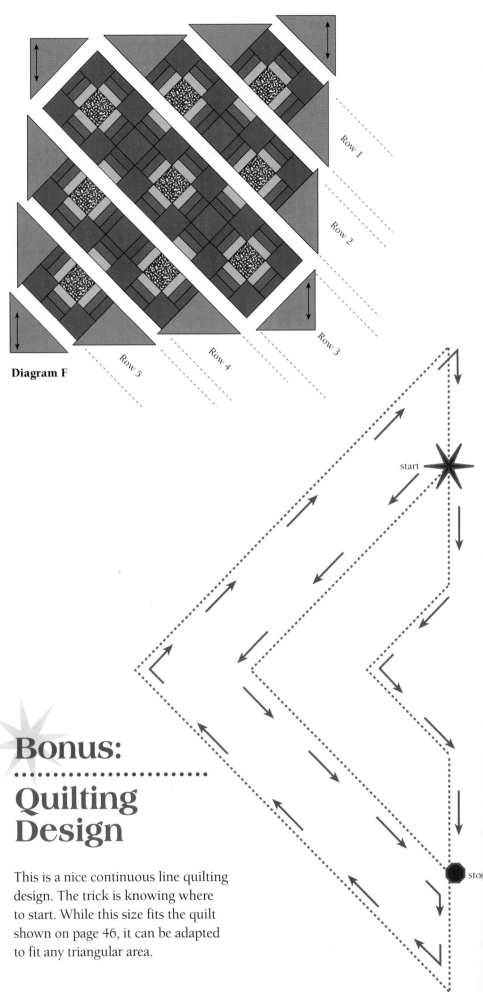

Diagram F

Row 1

Row 2

Row 3

Row 4

Row 5

Bonus:
Quilting Design

This is a nice continuous line quilting design. The trick is knowing where to start. While this size fits the quilt shown on page 46, it can be adapted to fit any triangular area.

start

stop

Scrappy Basket Weave

Snapshot

- Unit Blocks: 145
- Interior Arrangement:
  17 diagonal rows with
  setting and corner triangles,
  Diagram C, page 51
- Strip Width: 1¹/₂" cut
- Borders: 1³/₄", 1³/₄"
  and 3¹/₂" cut
- French-fold binding:
  ³/₈" finished

Unit Block

Wallhanging Size:

51¹/₂" by 51¹/₂"
130.8 cm by 130.8 cm
as shown in color picture, page 50.

Block Size:

3" square
7.6 cm square

Materials Required:

1³/₄ to 2¹/₂ yards total of approximately 70 assorted light, medium and dark scrap fabrics

³/₄ yard of teal and purple print fabric for setting and corner triangles and first border

1/2 yard of plaid fabric for second border

⁷/₈ yard of teal print fabric for third border

3 yards of fabric for separate backing*

3 yards of batting

⁵/₈ yard of fabric for French-fold binding

* If piecing the quilt backing from scraps, refer to On the Flip Side, page 52.

The Scrappy Basket Weave *quilt is a three-strip variation of the Basket Weave quilts on pages 26, 28 and 31. The diagonal set and scrappy shading combine to create a new look. Refer to the* Sticks and Stones on Point Basic Quilt, *page 40, for more information about diagonal sets, if necessary.*

The *Scrappy Basket Weave* unit blocks, **Diagram A**, are diagonally set in a weaving pattern. By taking advantage of the wide variety of fabrics, the definite dark and light fabrics in the unit blocks both become lighter toward the center of the quilt, and the colors and prints blend more softly.

Unit Block
Diagram A

TIP

Although this quilt is shown as a square wallhanging, it could also be used as a medallion quilt center, or the concept could be developed as a rectangle into a full-size quilt.

Selecting the Fabric

Approximately 70 fabrics were used in the photographed scrap quilt. The teal and purple print for the setting and corner triangles and first border was selected first; you might call it the theme fabric. In this case, it set the color scheme, but sends no other message. All the remaining fabrics had to "work with" that one. Remember, I said "work with," not "match"; too much matching will ruin a scrap quilt. Some of the fabrics would even clash on close inspection, but in whole they look great.

Cutting the Fabric

The *Scrappy Basket Weave* unit block is composed entirely of three-piece strip sets. Each set has a matching pair of strips on the outside edges and a lighter strip on the inside. Some people prefer to select the pair of fabrics and then cut strips; others would rather cut a lot of strips, then join them into sets. Whichever way you choose, cut 1¹/₂-inch wide strips on the lengthwise grain. Cut the strips a minimum of 3¹/₂ inches long, and in increments of 3¹/₂ inches. The equivalent of 25 inches total length from each of 70 fabrics is the mathematical minimum required. But, it is not quite so simple since each unit block requires twice as much of one fabric as the other. Typically, two or three 18-inch strips were cut from each fabric used in the photographed quilt. Although this provided more scraps than were required, it allowed for greater freedom in pairing the fabrics to make the strip sets.

The Scrappy Basket Weave *quilt is a three-strip variation of the Basket Weave quilts. The unit blocks are diagonally set in a weaving pattern and use a wide variety of fabrics. The definite dark and light fabrics in the unit blocks become lighter toward the center of the quilt.*

Making the Unit Block

1. Pair the fabrics for the strip sets in any combination desired. In this quilt, the darker fabric is always used for the two outer strips of the strip set. The inner strip, while always lighter, was sometimes selected to show high contrast and other times very low, or anywhere in between. When making strip sets for the photographed quilt, the same fabric was used in several sets, sometimes paired with a lighter fabric, and sometimes with a darker fabric. Variety is important. This is an excellent opportunity to experiment with value as the most important feature of a fabric.

In addition to studying the picture and layout diagram of this quilt, please jump ahead and look at the *Mini Scrappy Basket Weave* that follows. Look for features that you like less or better. Did you notice that some of the strip sets have the lighter fabric in the outside position?

2. Using **Diagram B** as a guide, sew the strips together to make three-strip sets. The more strip set combinations you make, the scrappier you will be able to make the quilt without repetition. A minimum of 75 strip sets is required if you plan to cut two blocks from each set, and use lots of repetition in your quilt. Because I love scrap quilts, I feel the more, the merrier! Nearly 100 strip sets, 8 to 12 inches long, were made for the photographed quilt.

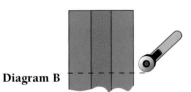

Diagram B

3. Press seam allowances toward the dark fabric. The strip set MCM is 3¹/2 inches wide.

4. The unit block is created with the second cut. (If your strip sets are not 3¹/2 inches, use your O&O for the second cut.) Cut 3¹/2-inch squares from the strip sets, **Diagram B**. Although a minimum of 145 blocks is required, do not expect to make the minimum if you want to achieve real scrappiness! It is always smart to make extra blocks, especially when making a scrap quilt. See On the Flip Side, page 52, and you won't worry about extra blocks.

Assembling the Quilt Interior

Because this quilt features a diagonal set, setting and corner triangles must be used to fill in the outer edges of the quilt interior. See The Secret of the Setting Triangles, page 43.

CUTTING THE SETTING AND CORNER TRIANGLES

1. To make the setting triangles, cut eight 6-inch squares. Cut each square on both diagonals to yield 32 setting triangles.

2. For the four corner triangles, cut two 3¹/2-inch squares, and cut each square once diagonally.

ASSEMBLING THE DIAGONAL ROWS

1. Following **Diagram C**, lay the unit blocks out on a large flat surface or use a design wall, page 178. To develop the basket weave pattern, alternate block strips. Use the darker blocks around the outer edges of the quilt, then progressively lighter blocks, until the very center block is the lightest of all. Fill in edges with setting triangles as shown.

2. Diagram C shows the quilt divided into five sections. The corners look similar to the rows in the *Sticks and Stones On Point Basic Quilt*, page 40, and include all of the setting triangles and corner triangles. Sew setting triangles and unit blocks into place and complete the rows. Join the rows and add corner triangles to complete each corner.

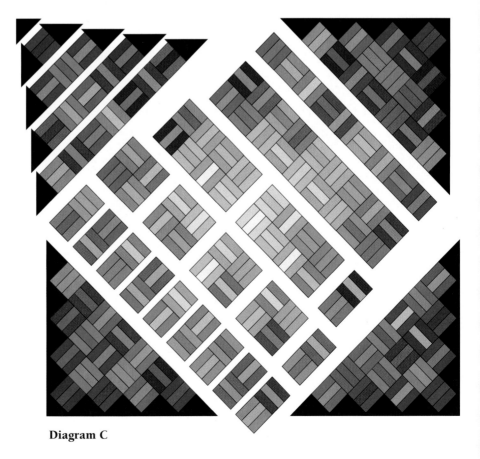

Diagram C

3. The nine center rows are easily assembled just like the pairs, pairs of pairs, etc. in the *Fence Rail Basic Quilt*, page 20. You can treat this part of the construction just like a straight set quilt. You could do long rows all the way across the quilt, but I have found the procedure diagrammed to be much easier to control.

4. When the five sections are complete and pressed, add the corners to the center section, being careful to match seams. Add any corner, then add its opposite, then the final two. Trim the excess fabric from the setting and corner triangles in order to square up the quilt interior before adding the borders, page 179.

The MCM for the assembled quilt interior is 38³/4 inches by 38³/4 inches from block point to block point. The photographed quilt has an additional ³/4 inch of float on each side; allow for a floating set on your quilt as desired.

Finishing the Quilt

The borders were cut 1³/4 inches, 1³/4 inches and 3¹/2 inches; binding strips were cut 2¹/8 inches. Each border features corner blocks. Read Finishing Your Quilt, page 179, for additional details.

On the Flip Side

Putting together the different fabrics to make unit blocks was fun, and suddenly there were more than 60 extra unit blocks. Clearly, there were enough extra blocks to piece together for a great vest, or make a fun addition to the back of the quilt. I only wavered briefly before deciding the quilt deserved the blocks. The width of the additional strips from the border fabrics was determined completely by the amount of each remaining fabric.

If piecing the quilt back for your quilt, allow extra yardage for each border fabric, and disregard the separate backing fabric requirement.

Bonus:

Mini Scrappy Basket Weave

Have fun with a mini Scrappy Basket Weave. *It's just like* Scrappy Basket Weave, *except:*

1. The quilt is 16$\frac{1}{2}$ inches square (42 cm).

2. You use a minimum of 30 fabrics, not 70.

3. The strips are cut 1 inch wide.

4. The strip sets are arranged without regard to value; light and dark fabrics are used in both positions of the strip sets.

5. While the larger wallhanging is assembled in five sections, this quilt can easily be assembled in rows, **Diagram D**.

6. The setting triangles are cut from six 3$\frac{3}{4}$-inch squares. Cut on both diagonals to yield 24 triangles.

7. Create corner triangles by cutting two 1$\frac{1}{2}$-inch squares in half diagonally.

8. A very narrow flap is added before the binding. See Flaps Add a Special Touch, page 182.

Read Tips for Making Mini and Miniature Quilts, page 177.

Mini Scrappy Basket Weave

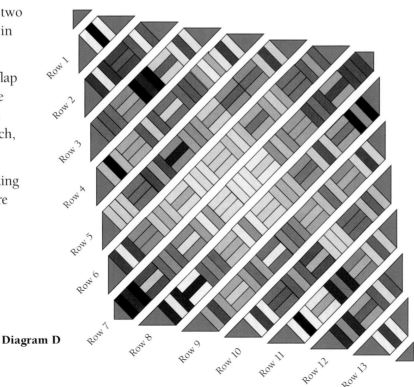

Row 1
Row 2
Row 3
Row 4
Row 5
Row 6
Row 7
Row 8
Row 9
Row 10
Row 11
Row 12
Row 13

Diagram D

53

Too Pretty to Be Called a Railroad Crossings Quilt

Snapshot

- Unit Blocks: 28
- Interior Arrangement: 8 diagonal rows with extra sub-units and setting and corner triangles, **Diagram H**, page 57
- Strip Widths: 9", random and 4" cut
- Borders: 6¹/8" and 5¹/2" cut ("Joseph's Coat")
- French-fold binding: ¹/2" finished

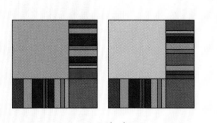

Unit Blocks

Queen Quilt Size:

90³/4" x 107³/4"
230.5 cm x 273.7 cm

Block Size:

12" square
30.5 cm square

Materials Required:

⁷/8 yard of ecru print fabric
   (12 squares)
1³/8 yards of ecru/plum print fabric
   (20 squares)
³/4 yard of medium plum floral fabric
   for small squares
⁷/8 yard of plum mosaic fabric for large
   setting and corner triangles
4 yards of assorted ecru, green and
   plum print scraps, including second
   border
2⁷/8 yards of green and plum printed
   stripe fabric for first border
7⁷/8 yards of fabric for backing
packaged batting larger than quilt
⁷/8 yard fabric for French-fold binding

In Railroad Crossings, the design which gives the quilt its name comes from the entire quilt, not just one block. The piecing is in the sashing; the quilt "block" is a large empty square. The diagonal set creates visual interest in the quilt.

Finding the Unit Block

The Railroad Crossings unit block is composed of the large unpieced square, two pieced sashing strips, and a small joining square, **Diagram A**. The *Too Pretty to Be Called a Railroad Crossings Quilt* incorporates 28 unit blocks, **Diagram A**, along with extra sub-units and setting and corner triangles to form the quilt interior. Additionally, the use of a second fabric for the large unpieced squares in 12 of the unit blocks creates a secondary pattern in the quilt, **Diagram B**, page 56.

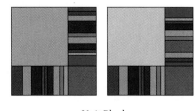

Unit Blocks
Diagram A

Selecting the Fabric

The green and plum printed floral stripe border fabric was selected first, and set the color scheme for the quilt. All other fabrics were chosen to blend with it; however, as with any scrap quilt, fabrics do not have to match. Approximately 24 additional fabrics were used to make the pieced sashing and border.

Cutting the Fabric

1. Cut thirty-two 9-inch squares; 20 from the ecru/plum print and 12 from the ecru print.

2. From the medium plum floral, cut eight strips 4 inches wide by 18 inches long.

3. For the pieced sashing, cut 18-inch long strips of random widths from ⁷/8 inch to 1¹/2 inches wide. Cut on the lengthwise grain and cut a minimum of approximately 10 strips from each of 24 fabrics.

Making the Strip Sets

Cut random width strips to make the pieced sashing. The smaller the joining square is going to be, the narrower the strips can be; however, a strip cut narrower than ⁷/8 inch will be barely usable once ¹/4-inch seam allowances are taken on each side. Even though the pieced sashing is made from strip sets, the casual observer of your finished quilt will think you have cut each piece individually and carefully selected its position. One of the potential problems with strip piecing is having the repeats become very obvious.

The classic
Railroad Crossings is so
named for the look of the overall
quilt design, not for the individual
block. Too Pretty to be Called a
Railroad Crossings Quilt incorporates
28 unit blocks with extra sub-units and
setting and corner triangles to form the quilt
interior. The use of a second fabric for the unpieced
squares creates an interesting secondary pattern.

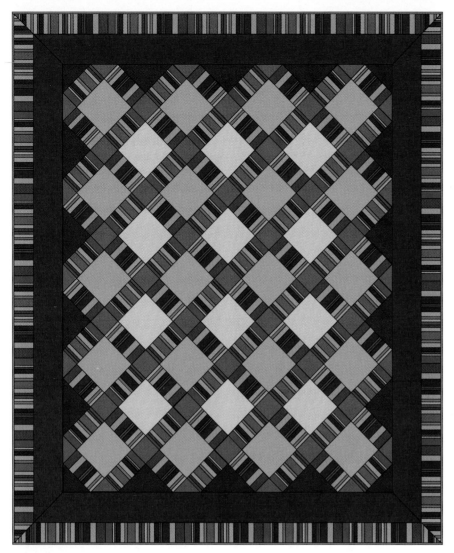

Diagram B

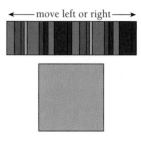

TIP ◆ ◆ ◆ ◆ ◆ ◆ ◆ ◆ ◆ ◆

*Although the strip sets need only be wide enough to fit the 9-inch unpieced squares, making the strip sets slightly wider (11 inches) will make it easier to camouflage the strip repeat, **Diagram E**. Sashing can be trimmed after it is sewn to the large square.*

←— move left or right —→

Diagram E

2. Make 20 sub-units of sashing and ecru print large squares by cutting across sashing strip sets to make 20 segments 4 inches long. Join these segments to the right side of 20 large squares, **Diagram F**. Four of these will be used as extra sub-units along the bottom of the quilt.

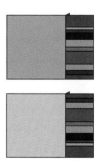

Diagram F

There are a few methods for camouflaging the repeat of the strips. It is easier to disguise several short subsets in different repeats than one long set. When you do cut matching sections, whether long or short, be sure to reverse the direction with some sets, or split the set apart and add several different strips to break the pattern, **Diagram C**.

Making the Sub-units

1. For the pieced sashing, complete 20 strip sets, a minimum of 11 inches wide by 18 inches long, **Diagram D**.

Make 12 sub-units of sashing and ecru/plum print large squares the same way.

3. Sew the strips for the small squares to eight sashing strip sets. Cut across the newly-created strip sets in 4-inch increments to make 31 sub-units of sashing and small squares, **Diagram G**. (Three will be combined with large setting triangles.)

reverse
direction:
add a short
set (3 strips)
for
transitions

split sections:
add a short set
(3 strips) for
transitions

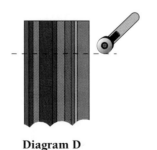

Diagram C

Diagram D

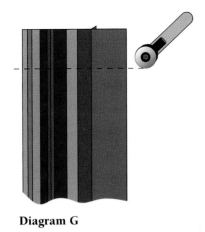

Diagram G

4. Cut across the remaining strip sets in 4-inch increments to yield 17 pieced sashing segments, **Diagram G**.

Making the Unit Block

Join the sashing and large square sub-units with the sashing and small square sub-units to make 28 unit blocks, **Diagram A**. The MCM for the completed blocks is 12½ inches square.

Assembling the Quilt Interior

The *Too Pretty to Be Called a Railroad Crossings Quilt* features a diagonal set that requires corner triangles and two sizes of setting triangles.

CUTTING THE SETTING AND CORNER TRIANGLES

1. To make the 14 large setting triangles, cut four 14-inch squares from plum mosaic fabric. Cut each square on both diagonals.

To make the 18 small setting triangles, cut five 7-inch squares from medium plum floral fabric. Cut each square on both diagonals.

2. To make the corner triangles, cut two 8½-inch squares from plum mosaic fabric. Cut each square on one diagonal to yield four corner triangles.

ASSEMBLING THE DIAGONAL ROWS

Using a large flat surface or a design wall, page 178, assemble the unit blocks and extra sub-units into rows. Fill in edges with setting triangles to complete the rows, **Diagram H**. In the diagram, the full unit blocks appear already joined in the rows to simplify the positioning of additional sub-units and setting triangles. Join the rows and add corner triangles to complete the quilt interior. Trim the excess fabric from the setting and corner triangles in order to square up the quilt interior before adding borders, (see page 179 for Squaring up the Quilt).

The MCM for the completed *Too Pretty to Be Called a Railroad Crossings Quilt* interior is 68½ inches by 85½ inches from block to block, with ¼ inch of additional float on all sides.

Adding the Borders

The first border was cut 6⅛ inches wide, a size determined by the fabric. Yours may be different.

PIECING THE JOSEPH'S COAT BORDER

1. The pieced outside border is frequently called a Joseph's Coat border. To piece it, cut approximately six strips from each of 24 assorted fabrics, 18 inches long, in widths ranging from 1½ inches to 2 inches.

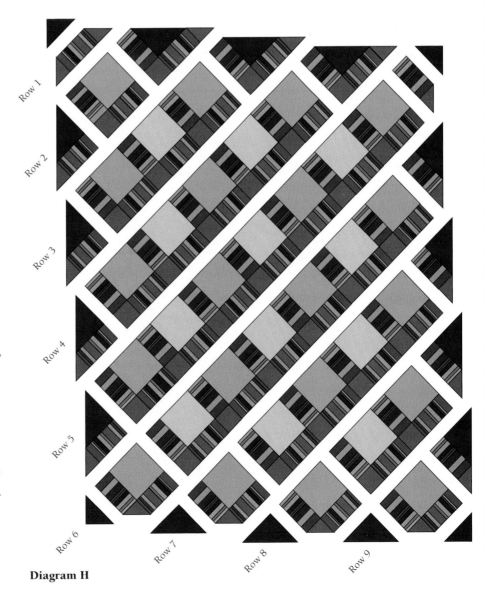

Row 1
Row 2
Row 3
Row 4
Row 5
Row 6
Row 7
Row 8
Row 9

Diagram H

57

2. Sew the pieces together into strip sets approximately 15 to 18 inches wide. Cut across the strip sets in 5½-inch increments.

3. Make strips for the second border by sewing the strip sets together end to end, camouflaging the repeats as described on page 56.

4. Add the border using mitered or mock-mitered corners.

Finishing the Quilt

The quilt was layered with batting and backing, and machine quilted in the ditch between the quilt blocks, using invisible thread. The plain squares were quilted using the Quilting Design to the right. A ½-inch-wide (strips cut 2⅝ inches wide) French-fold binding finishes the quilt. See Finishing Your Quilt, page 179, for further details.

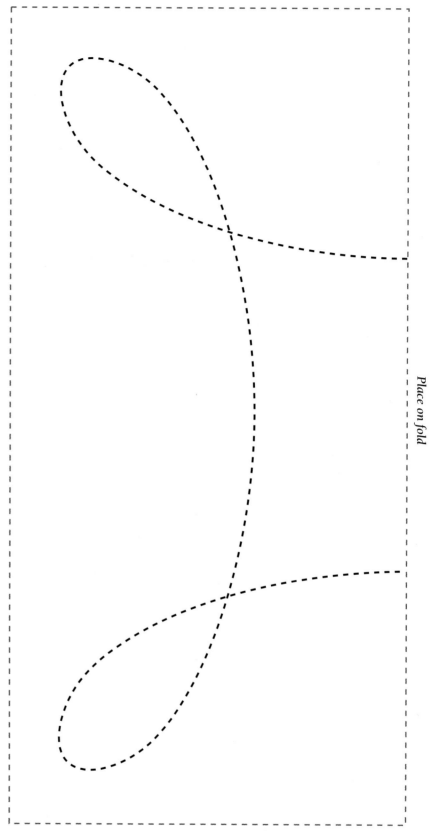

Place on fold

½ Quilting Design

More Railroad Crossings

Snapshot

- Sub-units: 24
- Interior Arrangement: 9 diagonal rows with setting and corner triangles, **Diagram A**, page 60

Black and Camel Quilt

- Strip Widths: $5^{1}/2$", random and 3" cut
- Borders: $1^{3}/4$", $1^{1}/2$" and $2^{3}/4$" cut
- Pieced French-fold binding: $3/4$" finished

Navy and Plum Quilt

- Strip Widths: $6^{1}/2$", random, $3^{1}/2$" cut
- Borders: $2^{1}/4$", $1^{3}/4$" and $3^{1}/2$" cut
- French-fold binding: $5/8$" finished

Black and Camel Quilt Size:
$31^{1}/2$" x $42^{1}/2$"
80 cm x 108 cm

Navy and Plum Quilt Size:
$38^{3}/4$" x $51^{1}/2$"
98.4 cm x 130.8 cm

Black and Camel Block Size:
$7^{1}/2$" square
19.1 cm

Navy and Plum Block Size:
9" square
22.9 cm

Materials Required for Black and Camel Quilt:

$1^{1}/8$ yards of camel print fabric, including third border

$1/2$ yard of black print fabric, including second border, cut crosswise

$1^{1}/4$ yards of assorted scraps, including pieced French-fold binding

$1/4$ yard of black and camel print fabric for first border, cut crosswise

$1^{3}/8$ yards of fabric for backing

1 yard of batting

Materials Required for Navy and Plum Quilt:

$1^{1}/4$ yards of pink print fabric, including third border

$3/8$ yard of navy blue floral fabric, including second border, cut crosswise

$3/4$ yard total of assorted scraps

$7/8$ yard of plum fabric for first border and French-fold binding

$1^{5}/8$ yards of fabric for backing

$1^{5}/8$ yards of batting

Reviewing the Variable Size Possibilities of the Grid System

Even though these Railroad Crossings quilts are different sizes, they are made with the same number of pieces. The pieces are proportionate. The two squares that determine the

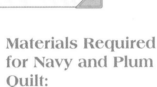

Even though these
More Railroad Crossings *quilts are made with the same number of pieces, the* Black and Camel Quilt, *top photo, is larger than the* Navy and Plum Quilt.

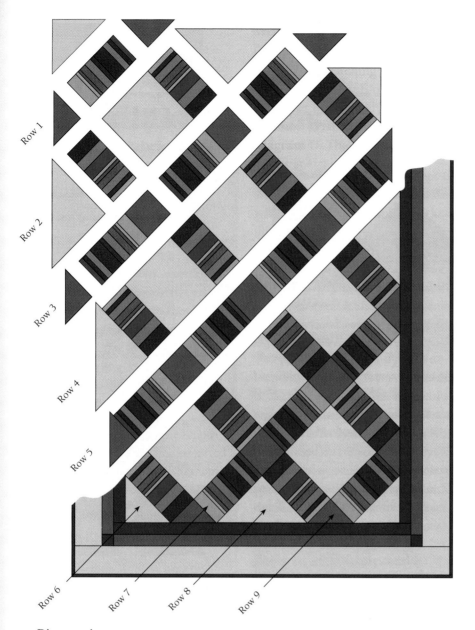

Row 1
Row 2
Row 3
Row 4
Row 5
Row 6
Row 7
Row 8
Row 9

Diagram A

quilt's final size (the small joining square and the large unpieced square) are cut 3 inches and 5¹/2 inches for the *Black and Camel Quilt*; for the *Navy and Plum Quilt*, the squares are cut 3¹/2 inches and 6¹/2 inches. These two measurements determine the size of everything except the borders. For a better comparison, the borders are also proportionate. The point is, by changing the squares' cut measurements only ¹/2 inch and 1 inch respectively, there results an MCM difference of 7¹/4 inches in width and 9 inches in length between the two quilts.

Selecting the Fabric

Railroad Crossings is really a scrap quilt. You may be able to make it from collected fabrics. If you are purchasing fabric, you may choose to buy only the dominant fabrics for the squares and borders, and make the pieced sashing from scraps. In both small quilts, the fabrics selected for the unpieced squares established the color scheme. Then 12 to 15 coordinating scrap fabrics were selected to make the pieced sashing. Make sure there is a good variety of light and dark fabrics, of colors, and of size and kind of design.

DIFFERENT FABRICS EQUAL DIFFERENT RESULTS

That may seem like an obvious statement, but please read on. The *Black and Camel Quilt* was made first. The *Navy and Plum Quilt* was then made to visually illustrate how enlarging the pieces only slightly would change the final size of the quilt dramatically. I was determined the quilts would have the same proportion, equivalent fabric arrangements, and the pieced binding. Equivalent fabric arrangement means that fabrics of the same value would be placed in the same positions in each quilt. I wanted to reduce the number of variables for the purpose of comparison.

But it wasn't that easy! When the *Navy and Plum Quilt* top was completed, something seemed wrong. Even when the quilt top was layered and ready for quilting, I kept stewing. Finally, I cut large setting triangles from the pink fabric and pinned them over the navy blue floral setting triangles. What a difference! Suddenly the pieced sashing stood out instead of being lost in the print fabric. Once I saw the improvement, the quilt was unpinned, the borders removed and the triangles replaced. It would have been easier to make a second quilt with pink setting triangles, but there was not enough pink fabric for two quilts. (For the first version of the *Navy and Plum Quilt*, see the photograph on page 61.)

Then, the strip-pieced binding, which is so effective on the *Black and Camel Quilt*, simply didn't work on the *Navy and Plum Quilt*.

TIP ◆ ◆ ◆ ◆ ◆ ◆ ◆ ◆

Don't be afraid to alter your plans. It is impossible to anticipate the exact finished look when you are working with so many different fabrics.

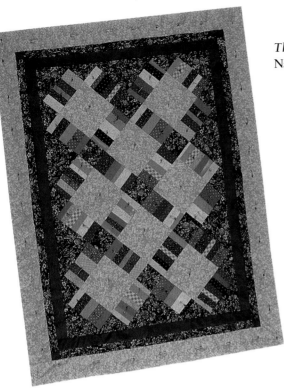

from one long edge. The other edge was placed right sides together with the quilt top and machine-stitched in place 1/4 inch from the quilt edge. Extra batting and backing was rolled into the binding as it was turned to the back and hand-stitched in place.

The borders for the *Plum and Navy Quilt* were cut 2 1/4 inches, 1 3/4 inches and 3 1/2 inches; the binding strips were cut 3 1/8 inches wide.

For more finishing information, see Finishing Your Quilt, page 179.

Making these small quilts is just like making *Too Pretty to be Called a Railroad Crossings Quilt*, except the sub-units are assembled in rows, **Diagram A**, instead of the larger unit block. When making either of these small quilts, there are only five complete unit blocks, with 39 additional sub-unit pieces. It is easier to forget the unit block, assemble the sub-units into the diagonal rows, and sew the rows together.

Finishing the Quilts

The borders for the *Black and Camel Quilt* were cut 1 3/4 inches, 1 1/2 inches and 2 3/4 inches wide. The binding was made just like the sashing. This pieced binding would be too bulky if made by the French-fold binding method described on page 188. After strip sets were made they were cut into pieces twice the desired finished width, plus 1/2 inch for seam allowances—in this case 2 inches. Pieces were sewn together end to end to make the binding strips, then stay-stitched 1/4 inch

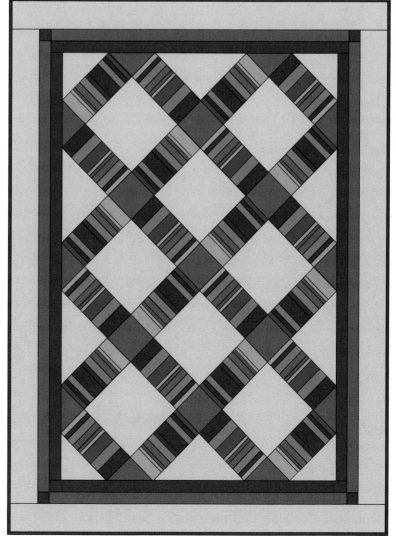

Diagram B

61

Introducing the Basic Four Patch

This is the basic technique for making the four-patch unit. Impress your friends with your speed and accuracy. Impress yourself with the ease and enjoyment of this method. The quilts that follow will refer to these instructions.

Four Patch is the name most commonly given to a unit that contains four squares of equal size. The most common configuration is alternating dark and light fabrics, **Diagram A**. The four patch unit is easy to make using two strips of fabric and the Sew-Before-You-Cut method of assembly.

Strip widths are chosen to be pleasing for the particular fabric and quilt; the cut strip width determines the length of the segments for the second cut. Four patch units are so easy to make and so easy to manipulate that endless combinations appear in quilt blocks.

Cutting the Fabric

As there are only two fabrics used in the typical four patch, one strip set combination is adequate if the fabrics are non-directional. A strip set must be made for each row if you are using directional fabrics, **Diagram B**.

Place light and dark fabrics right sides together before cutting. That will position them properly for

sewing. Cut strips on the lengthwise grain. The number and length of the strips are determined by the size of the quilt.

Making the Four Patch Unit

1. Using **Diagram B** as a guide, sew the strips together into strip sets. Press the seam allowances toward the dark fabric.

2. Place two strip sets right sides together with opposite fabrics touching, **Diagram C**.

3. Using the cut width of the individual strips as the increment length for the segments, make the second cut across the strip sets, **Diagram D**. Do not separate the pairs of segments: the ridges of the seam allowances almost grip each other as they face opposite directions, creating "automatic pinning" for the next step.

4. Sew each pair of segments together, chain piecing as in **Diagram E**.

After chain piecing, I like to leave the units connected while pressing. Press either way (half will be against the light fabric, half against the dark), but be consistent, especially if using a directional fabric.

Row 1
Diagram A   Row 2

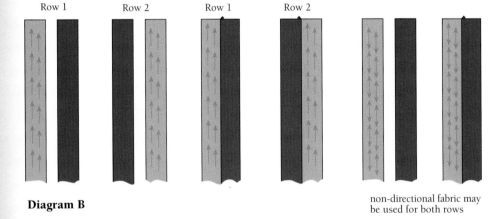

Diagram B

non-directional fabric may be used for both rows

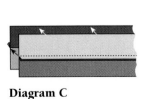

Diagram C

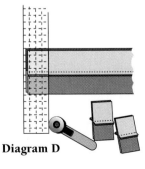

Diagram D

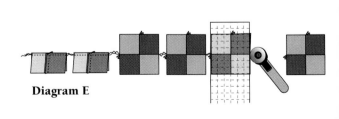

Diagram E

5. Check the units individually by aligning perpendicular marks on an acrylic ruler with the seam lines, so that the edge of the ruler matches the edge of the unit. Check each unit against the MCM, and trim edges or make minor cutting adjustments if needed.

Complete the four-patch units, **Diagram F**, by cutting the pairs of segments apart with the rotary cutter and acrylic ruler.

Diagram F

Isn't that slick? And it comes with the Four-Patch Guarantee: "You can spend more time making four patches and you can do it with more difficulty, but you can't be any more accurate."

No-Name Four Patch Duo

Snapshot

- Unit Block A: 8
- Unit Block B: 8
- Interior Arrangement: alternating blocks plus extra sub-units, **Diagram G**, page 66
- Strip Widths: 2" and 4¹/2" cut
- Borders (*Red and Ecru Wallhanging*): 5" cut
- Borders (*Peach and Seafoam Wallhanging*): 1" (flap), 1³/4" and 5¹/2" cut
- French-fold binding: ¹/2" finished

Unit Block A Unit Block B

Refer to Introducing the Basic Four Patch, page 62, if necessary. Although each of these quilts uses only two fabrics, the quilt that follows (page 67) uses four. Varying the proportions of the strips, mood of the fabrics and number of colors makes the same simple quilt design look completely different.

Selecting the Fabric

This pair of quilts dramatically illustrates the importance of fabric selection to the mood of the quilt. Even though the two quilts are assembled from pieces of identical shape and size, the red and ecru quilt is strong, graphic, high-contrast, country and masculine. The low contrast of the soft peach and seafoam colors, together with the large print, gives it a soft, romantic, wicker-garden-room look.

Finding the Unit Block

The *No-Name Four Patch* combines a single unpieced square with two vertical strips, two horizontal strips, and a four-patch sub-unit, all made from the same narrower-width strips. In the quilt, there are two unit blocks, identical except for the reversal of fabrics, **Diagram A**.

Red and Ecru Wallhanging Size:
42" by 42"
106.7 cm by 106.7 cm
as shown in color picture, page 64, and illustration in **Diagram H**, *page 66.*

Peach and Seafoam Wallhanging Size:
45¹/2" by 45¹/2"
115.6 cm by 115.6 cm
as shown in color picture, page 65, and illustration in **Diagram H**, *page 66.*

Block Size:
7" square
17.8 cm square

Materials Required*:
³/4 yard of light fabric
³/4 yard of medium or dark fabric
2⁵/8 yards of fabric for backing

1¹/2 yards of batting
⁵/8 yard of fabric for French-fold binding
* Fabric requirements for these two wallhangings are identical except for the borders.

Fabric Requirements for Red and Ecru Wallhanging Borders:
⁵/8 yard red print fabric for border

Fabric Requirements for Peach and Seafoam Wallhanging Borders:
¹/8 yard of white fabric for flap border
¹/4 yard of peach fabric for second border
1 yard of peach print fabric for third border

Making either quilt of this No-Name Four Patch Duo *is an easy way to become familiar with four-patch units.*

Unit Block A Unit Block B
Diagram A

This Red and Ecru Wallhanging *is strong, graphic, high-contrast, country and masculine.*

Making the Sub-units

Each sub-unit in the unit blocks begins with strips. Strip widths and proportions are chosen to be pleasing for the particular quilt, and can easily be changed, as you will see in *Yes! It's a No-Name Four Patch*, page 67. For this quilt, the four patch is made from strips cut 2 inches wide; the unpieced square is made from strips cut 4¹/₂ inches wide.

CUTTING AND SEWING THE NARROW STRIPS

1. With light and dark fabrics right sides together, cut ten pairs of strips, 2 inches wide by 27 inches long.

2. Sew the 2-inch strip sets together, **Diagram B**. Press seam allowances toward the dark strip. Do not cut into short pieces yet.

Diagram B

MAKING THE FOUR PATCHES

1. The 16 four patches are quickly assembled from four strip sets. Position the strip sets right sides together with opposite fabrics touching, and cut 16 pairs of 2-inch long segments.

2. Chain piece the pairs together. The MCM for these 16 four patches is 3¹/₂ inches square, **Diagram C**.

Diagram C Make 16

64

ADDING THE WIDE STRIPS

1. For the large unpieced squares, cut two lengthwise strips from both the light and dark fabrics, 4½ inches wide by 27 inches long. Do not cut these strips into squares. Cut one 4½-inch square from light fabric, to be used as an extra sub-unit.

The vertical narrow strips can be sewn to the strips for the squares before cutting, **Diagram D**. Anything that you can Sew-Before-You-Cut is quicker, easier and more accurate.

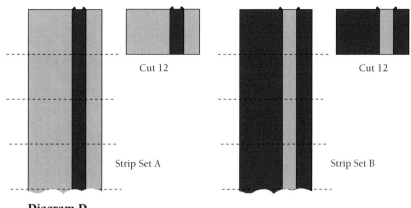

Cut 12

Strip Set A

Cut 12

Strip Set B

Diagram D

This Peach and Seafoam Wallhanging *shows how different a quilt with low-contrast fabrics can be from a high-contrast quilt like the* Red and Ecru Wallhanging. *The soft peach and seafoam colors, together with the large print, give it a soft, romantic, wicker-garden-room look.*

2. Make Strip Set A by sewing a wide light strip to the dark side of two narrow strip sets. Then make Strip Set B by sewing a wide dark strip to the light side of two narrow strip sets.

Cut across both strip sets in 4½-inch increments, making 12 strip and square combinations of each, **Diagram D**, page 65. Eight of each kind will be used to make unit blocks; the remainder will be used as extra sub-units.

JOINING THE FOUR PATCHES AND HORIZONTAL STRIPS

For the remaining sub-unit of each unit block, the narrow strip sets must be cut before they can be joined to the four patches.

1. Make the 16 horizontal strip sections by cutting across the remaining narrow strip sets in 4½-inch increments, **Diagram E**.

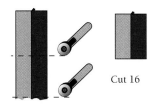

Cut 16

Diagram E

2. Join the horizontal strips to the four patches to make eight of each sub-unit, paying careful attention to the position of light and dark fabrics, **Diagram F**.

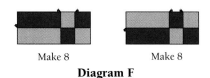

Make 8   Make 8

Diagram F

Assembling the Unit Blocks

Now sew the strip and square combinations to the strip and four patch combinations, making eight of each unit block, **Diagram A**, page 63. Pay special attention to the position of light and dark fabrics when assem-

bling the blocks. The MCM for the unit blocks is 7½ inches square.

The unit blocks alternate, and are combined with an extra row of sub-units across the right and bottom of the quilt, **Diagram G**. See The Rule of Matching Corners, page 37.

Refer to Putting Pairs Together, page 24, for assembly directions. The completed quilt interior MCM is 32½ inches by 32½ inches.

Finishing the Quilt

There are many finishing options. Please read Finishing Your Quilt, page 179, and make your choice before cutting. The border on the red quilt was cut 5 inches wide and the borders on the peach and seafoam quilt were cut 1 inch, 1¾ inches and 5½ inches wide. The binding strips were cut 2⅝ inches wide. These quilts were machine quilted in the ditch using invisible thread.

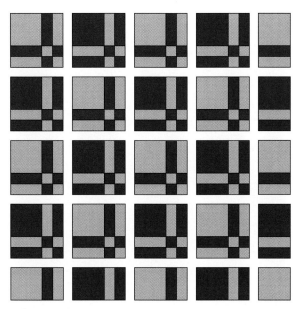

Diagram G

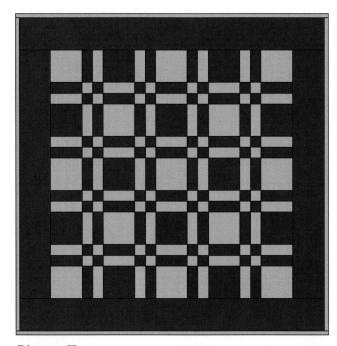

Diagram H

66

Yes! It's a No-Name Four Patch

Snapshot

- Unit Block A: 5
- Unit Block B: 4
- Interior Arrangement: alternating blocks plus extra sub-units, **Diagram G**, page 69.
- Strip Widths: 1¼" cut and determined by fabric panel
- Borders: 1¼", 2" and 3" cut
- French-fold binding: 5/8" finished

Unit Block A   Unit Block B

Wallhanging Size:

39¼" by 39¼"

99.7 cm by 99.7 cm

as shown in color picture, page 68, and illustration in **Diagram H**, *page 69.*

Block Size:

9" square

22.9 cm square

Materials Required:

½ yard of muslin (light) fabric for the unit blocks

½ yard of brown (dark) fabric for the unit blocks

¼ yard of gold (medium) fabric for the unit blocks

Five pre-printed fabric panels for the unit blocks, approximately 8" square

1¼ yards of fabric for backing

1¼ yards of batting

¼ yard of dark green print fabric for first border, cut crosswise

¼ yard of dark floral fabric for second border, cut crosswise

3/8 yard of gold print fabric for third border, cut crosswise

5/8 yard of fabric for French-fold binding

User-friendly panels and the No-Name Four Patch combine for a fresh idea. Please refer to Introducing the Basic Four Patch, page 62, and the No-Name Four Patch Duo, *page 63, for more complete directions.*

At first, it's hard to believe this quilt is also a No-Name Four Patch. Change the proportion of the strips, add two more fabrics and create a great way to show off a pre-printed fabric panel. Versatility is one benefit of pattern-free patchwork that can be activated very easily in a design this simple.

The size of the pre-printed fabric panel determined the width to cut the wide strips or large squares, and personal choice determined the small strip width. Although the printed panel used for this quilt is no longer available, fabric companies regularly print beautiful panel designs. Often, quiltmakers resist the temptation to buy these because they don't know how to use them. This quilt shows a very simple and effective way to let the fabric do more than its share of the work.

Cutting the Fabric

These measurements are applicable to panels that are 8 inches square. Make appropriate adjustments for other sizes.

1. Cut five 8-inch square panels of pre-printed fabric and four 8-inch squares of gold fabric.

2. With light and dark fabrics together, cut 16 pairs of lengthwise strips, 1¼ inches wide by 18 inches long.

Making the Unit Blocks

1. Sew the light and dark narrow strips together into 16 strip sets, **Diagram A**. Press seam allowances to the dark side. These strip sets are the same for both unit blocks.

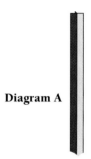

Diagram A

2. For Unit Block A, sew the pre-printed panels to the dark sides of three strip sets. For Unit Block B, sew gold squares to the light sides of two other strip sets. Refer to **Diagram B**.

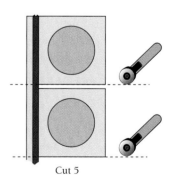

Cut 5

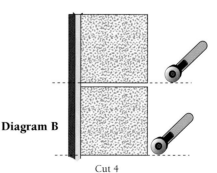

Diagram B

Cut 4

User-friendly panels and the No-Name Four Patch combine for a fresh idea, and Yes! It's a No-Name Four Patch. By changing the proportion of the strips and adding two more fabrics, you can create a wallhanging that shows off pre-printed panels.

Using the panels and gold squares as guides, cut in 8-inch increments across the strip sets, cutting five strip and square combinations for the Unit Blocks A and four for the Unit Blocks B, **Diagram B**.

3. Make 15 strip segments by cutting across the narrow strip sets in 8-inch increments, **Diagram C**.

4. To assemble the four patches, position the remaining strip sets right sides together with opposite fabrics touching, and cut 16 pairs of 1¼-inch segments, **Diagram D**. Chain piece the pairs together to make 16 four-patch sub-units. See Introducing the Basic Four Patch, page 62. The MCM for these sub-units is 2 inches square.

5. Join the 8-inch strip sections to 15 of the four patches, noting the alternating fabric positions shown in **Diagram E**.

Make 8

Make 7

Diagram E

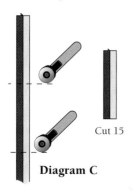

Cut 15

Diagram C

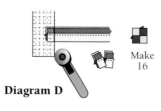

Make 16

Diagram D

6. Make five Unit Blocks A and four Unit Blocks B by sewing strip and four-patch combinations to the tops of the strip and square combinations, **Diagram F**. Pay careful attention to the alternating position of light and dark fabrics. The MCM for the unit blocks is 9¹/2 inches square.

Assembling the Quilt Interior

Assemble the unit blocks and extra sub-units according to **Diagram G**. The quilt interior MCM is 29 inches by 29 inches.

Finishing the Quilt

The borders for this quilt, **Diagram H**, were cut 1¹/4 inches, 2 inches and 3 inches wide; the binding strips were cut 3¹/8 inches wide. For more finishing information, see Finishing Your Quilt, page 179.

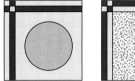

Unit Block A   Unit Block B

Diagram F

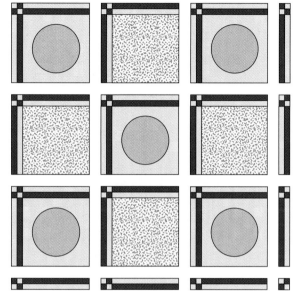

Diagram G

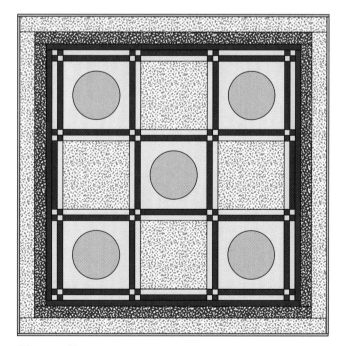

Diagram H

69

Cubic Turtles

Snapshot

- Unit Block A: 13
- Unit Block B: 12
- Interior Arrangement: alternating blocks plus extra sub-units, **Diagram H,** page 73

Pink Wallhanging
- First Strip Width: 1¹/₂" cut
- Borders: 1¹/₄" and 2" cut
- French-fold binding: ³/₈" finished

Blue Wallhanging
- First Strip Width: 2" cut
- Borders: 1⁵/₈", 3" and 1" (flap) cut
- French-fold binding: ¹/₂" finished

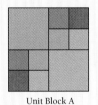

Unit Block A

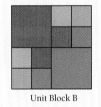

Unit Block B

Pink Wallhanging Size:
27¹/₄" by 27¹/₄"
69.2 cm by 69.2 cm

Blue Wallhanging Size:
41¹/₄" by 41¹/₄"
104.8 cm by 104.8 cm

Pink Wallhanging Block Size:
4" square
10.2 cm square

Blue Wallhanging Block Size:
6" square
15.2 cm square

Materials Required for Pink Wallhanging:
³/₈ yard of olive fabric #1
³/₈ yard of dark pink fabric #2, including second border
³/₈ yard of light pink fabric #3, including first border
³/₈ yard of beige fabric #4
⁷/₈ yard of fabric for backing
⁷/₈ yard of batting
³/₈ yard of fabric for French-fold binding

Materials Required for Blue Wallhanging:
1 yard of floral fabric #1, including second border
1 yard of blue fabric #2, including first border
1 yard of rust fabric #3, including corner blocks and French-fold binding
1 yard of gold fabric #4, including flap border
1³/₈ yards of fabric for backing
1³/₈ yards of batting

Cubic Turtles *is a fun variation of the Basic Four Patch. Instead of the typical two-fabric four patch, these quilts feature four fabrics. Please refer to Introducing the Basic Four Patch, page 62, and the* No-Name Four Patch Duo, *page 63, for further guidance.*

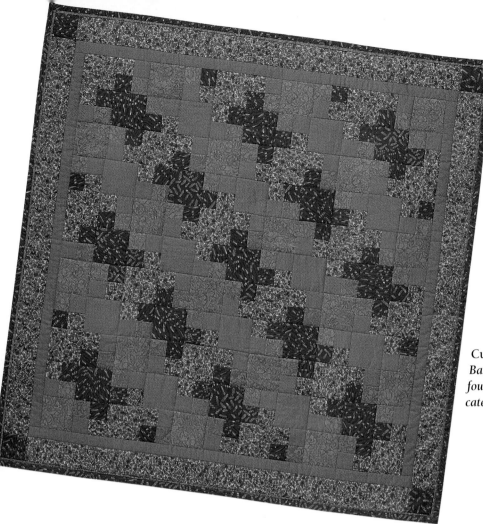

Cubic Turtles *is a fun variation of the Basic Four Patch. These quilts feature four fabrics to create a more sophisticated design.*

A common approach to designing is to ask, "what if?" Using that method with four patches, it is easy to create this unit block. What if two four-patch sub-units are set together with two alternate empty squares?

What if one alternate square matches one fabric, and one alternate square matches the other fabric? Using two colors, this looks like a tile pattern, **Diagram A**.

Using four colors creates a more sophisticated design. In Unit Block A, two four-patch sub-units are made from four different fabrics, and set with two alternate empty squares, made from two of the same fabrics. In Unit Block B, the same two four patches are rotated, then set with two alternate empty squares made from the other two fabrics, **Diagram B**. This project really could be called Tessellating Turtles, as the inlaid pattern does just that.

Diagram A

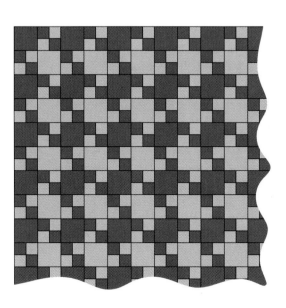

Two-color
Cubic Turtle
Unit Block

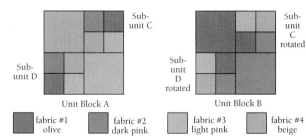

Diagram B

Selecting the Fabric

Choose any four non-directional fabrics, and purchase the same amount of each fabric, excluding border requirements. The pinks, beige and olive in the smaller wallhanging were part of a hand-dyed color group. The floral print set the color scheme used in the Blue Wallhanging; the tone-on-tone textured prints were selected to coordinate.

TIP

As designs become more complicated, it is a good idea to make a worksheet.

Book Illustration / My Quilt

Fabric #3 = Light Pink

Fabric #2 = Dark Pink

Fabric #4 = Beige

Fabric #1 = Olive

Making the Four Patches

The 60 four-patch sub-units are quickly assembled from the strip sets, **Diagram C**. The strip sets in Sub-units C and D are simply rotated to become Sub-units C-rotated and D-rotated. If you choose to use directional fabrics, however, it will be necessary to make separate strip sets.

1. On the lengthwise grain, cut eight 1¹/₂ inch-wide strips from each fabric for the Pink Wallhanging. These strips are only ³/₈ yard (13¹/₂ inches) long. For the Blue Wallhanging, cut four strips from each fabric, 2 inches wide by 32 inches long.

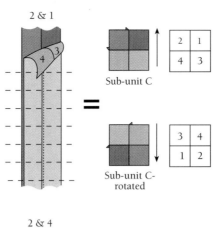

2 & 1

Sub-unit C

2	1
4	3

Sub-unit C-rotated

3	4
1	2

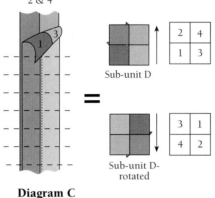

2 & 4

Sub-unit D

2	4
1	3

Sub-unit D-rotated

3	1
4	2

Diagram C

2. Join half of the strips into strip sets 1 & 2 and 3 & 4, **Diagram C**. Press the seam allowances toward the dark strips.

3. For Sub-units C and C-rotated, position strip sets right sides together, paying careful attention to fabric position. Cut 30 pairs of segments, 1¹/₂ inches long for the Pink Wallhanging, or 2 inches long for the Blue Wallhanging. Chain piece the pairs together. The MCM for these four-patch sub-units is 2¹/₂ inches square for the Pink Wallhanging, or 3¹/₂ inches square for the Blue Wallhanging. Fifteen of these sub-units will be used as C, and 15 as C-rotated.

4. Repeat step 3, joining strips 1 & 3 and 2 & 4 into sets and making 15 Sub-units D and 15 D-rotated.

Adding the Alternate Empty Squares

(If your strip sets are not the appropriate MCM, substitute your O&O measurement in every step of this section.)

1. Cut lengthwise strips for the alternate empty squares. For the Pink Wallhanging, cut four strips from each fabric, 2¹/₂ inches wide by 13 inches long. For the Blue Wallhanging, cut two strips from each fabric, 3¹/₂ inches wide by 33 inches long.

2. Chain piece 15 Sub-units C to the strips of fabric #4. Study **Diagram D** carefully: Keeping the wide strip right side up on the bottom, position sub-units right side down with the fabric #1 square in the upper left corner. Sew the sub-units to the wide strip, and press the seam allowances toward the wide strip. Cut across the strip sets in 2¹/₂- or 3¹/₂-inch increments. Also cut three unpaired squares from the wide strip of fabric #4.

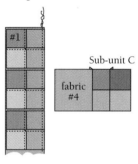

#1

Sub-unit C

fabric #4

Diagram D

TIP

When sewing pieced sub-units (or unit blocks) to a wide strip of fabric, always keep the wide strip on the bottom. Although this may mean that it will be necessary to rotate the sub-units, it will enable you to keep them properly aligned. Diagrams show the sub-units as "sewn," and "opened, rotated and ready to use."

3. Chain piece 13 Sub-units D to the strips of fabric #3, following **Diagram E** carefully. Cut across the strip sets in 2¹/₂- or 3¹/₂-inch increments.

4. Chain piece 15 Sub-units C-rotated to the strips of fabric #1, following **Diagram F** carefully. Cut across the strip sets in 2$\frac{1}{2}$- or 3$\frac{1}{2}$-inch increments. Also cut three unpaired squares from the wide strip of fabric #1.

5. Chain piece 12 Sub-units D-rotated to the strips of fabric #2, following **Diagram G** carefully. Cut across the strip sets in 2$\frac{1}{2}$- or 3$\frac{1}{2}$-inch increments.

Making the Unit Blocks

Join the unit block halves, making 13 Unit Blocks A and 12 Unit Blocks B. Follow **Diagram B** closely to keep fabrics in their proper positions. The

MCM for the completed unit blocks is 4$\frac{1}{2}$ inches square for the Pink Wallhanging, and 6$\frac{1}{2}$ inches square for the Blue Wallhanging.

The remaining sub-units complete the design of the quilt interior, **Diagram H**.

Assembling the Quilt Interior

Following the quilt layout, **Diagram H**, assemble the unit blocks into five rows of five blocks each, as well as the extra row of sub-units along the bottom and right side of the quilt. Refer to Putting Pairs Together, page 24, for instructions. The MCM for the assembled Pink Wallhanging interior is

22$\frac{1}{2}$ inches by 22$\frac{1}{2}$ inches. The MCM for the Blue Wallhanging is 33$\frac{1}{2}$ inches by 33$\frac{1}{2}$ inches. Press the quilt interior.

Finishing the Quilt

There are many finishing options. Please read Finishing Your Quilt, page 179, and make your choice before cutting. The borders on the pink quilt, **Diagram I**, were cut 1$\frac{1}{4}$ inches and 2 inches wide and on the blue quilt, 1$\frac{5}{8}$ inches and 3 inches wide; binding strips were cut 2$\frac{1}{8}$ inches wide for the pink quilt and 2$\frac{5}{8}$ inches wide for the blue quilt. Each wallhanging was machine quilted in the ditch using invisible thread.

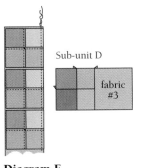

Sub-unit D

fabric #3

Diagram E

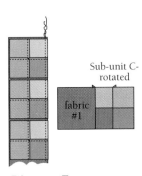

Sub-unit C-rotated

fabric #1

Diagram F

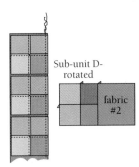

Sub-unit D-rotated

fabric #2

Diagram G

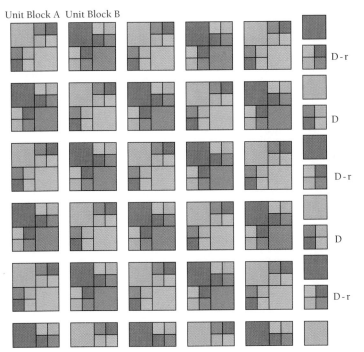

Unit Block A Unit Block B

D-r

D

D-r

D

D-r

Diagram H

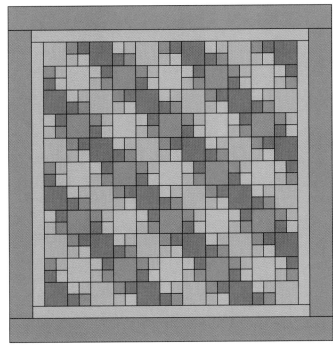

Diagram I

Bonus:
Look at This Card Trick

The traditional Card Trick block is made using a clever fabrication of an Ohio Star block, **Diagram A**. There are 28 pieces in each unit block.

Diagram A

Look closely in the center and you will see a four patch made with four fabrics, as in the *Cubic Turtles* quilts.

Add strips of the appropriate fabric on two opposite sides, cut the same width as the four patch strips, **Diagram B**.

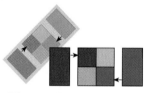

Diagram B

Then add pieced strips to top and bottom, **Diagram C**. The cut width of the middle strip should equal the width of the four patch.

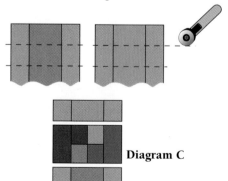

Diagram C

Rotate to an on-point position, **Diagram D**.

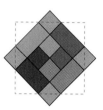

Diagram D

There are only 12 pieces in the new Card Trick unit block, and all of them can be created with strip techniques.

Set these blocks with plain alternate blocks and appropriate setting and corner triangles. Let the border "cut off" the outside corners of background fabric to minimize the amount of "float," **Diagram E**.

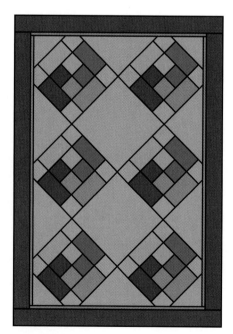

Diagram E

If you are putting more than six blocks together, you may want to add interest by substituting the simple pieced block in **Diagram F** for the plain alternate blocks.

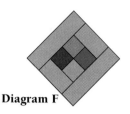

Diagram F

If the strips for the Card Trick are cut 2½ inches wide, the quilt in **Diagram E** would be approximately 28 inches by 39 inches.

Mosaic in Pink

Snapshot

- Unit Block A: 12
- Unit Block B: 20
- Interior Arrangement: 10 diagonal rows with setting and corner triangles, **Diagram K**, page 77
- First Strip Width: 1½" cut
- Borders: pieced border from four-patch sub-units; 1½" and 2½" cut
- French-fold binding: ½" finished

Unit Block A   Unit Block B

Crib Quilt Size:

36" by 40¾"
91.4 cm by 103.5 cm

Block Size:

4" square
10.2 cm square

Materials Required:

1¼ yards of pink print fabric, including setting and corner triangles and second border

¾ yard of muslin, including first border and French-fold binding

3½" by 22½" strips of at least eight pink fabrics (or the equivalent)

1¼ yards of backing fabric

1¼ yards of batting, or packaged crib-size batting

The basic unit block in Mosaic in Pink, *sometimes called Four Patch Combination, requires four four-patch sub-units. Please refer to Introducing* the Basic Four Patch, *page 62, for further guidance.*

Mosaic in Pink features two unit blocks alternating in a diagonal set, **Diagram K**, page 77. Unit Block A is a combination of four four-patch sub-units, while Unit Block B is a single empty square, **Diagram A** (page 76). The pieced border also uses the four-patch sub-unit, while introducing the idea of design by omission. By eliminating two of the four patches in the outside rows, a very effective border design is created. The best part is that you know it will fit perfectly.

Mosaic in Pink *features two unit blocks alternating in a diagonal set. Unit Block A is a four patch of four-patch sub-units; Unit Block B is a single square. The pieced border uses the four-patch sub-unit while introducing the idea of design by omission.*

Unit Block A   Unit Block B

Diagram A

Selecting the Fabric

Monochromatic color schemes seem very easy to select. In this quilt you can see a good example of just enough variety in the fabric used in the four patch and in the border to make the quilt sparkle rather than fade away.

Making the Four-patch Sub-units

Use strip sets to easily assemble the four patches. Refer to Introducing the Basic Four Patch, page 62, if necessary. Eighty-four sub-units are required to assemble the quilt.

1. Cut all fabric strips on the lengthwise grain. With muslin and assorted pink fabrics right sides together, cut 12 pairs of strips $1^1/2$ inches wide by $22^1/2$ inches long.

2. Sew into 12 strip sets.

Press seam allowances toward the pink fabrics, **Diagram B**.

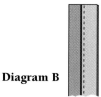

Diagram B

3. Pair matching strip sets right sides together with opposite fabrics touching. If necessary, cut long strip sets in half to create a pair of strips. Cut 84 pairs of $1^1/2$-inch long segments. Chain piece the pairs together, **Diagram C**. The MCM for these four patches is $2^1/2$ inches square.

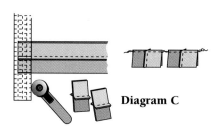

Diagram C

Making Unit Block A

For each of the 12 Unit Blocks A, choose four matching four-patch sub-units. Join these sub-units into pairs, then pairs of pairs, paying careful attention to fabric orientation, **Diagram D**. The MCM for the unit blocks is $4^1/2$ inches square.

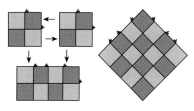

Diagram D

Joining Unit Blocks A and B

Unit Block B is an empty square of background fabric. Instead of cutting individual squares, sew Unit Blocks A to strips of background fabric. This streamlined approach results in perfectly-sized squares because Unit Block A is used as a guide when cutting Unit Block B. If your unit blocks are not $4^1/2$ inches square, substitute your O&O measurement.

1. Cut five strips of background fabric, $4^1/2$ inches wide by 20 inches long.

2. Chain piece 12 Unit Blocks A to three of these strips. Do not butt the unit blocks together when sewing; plan to trim top and bottom. Set aside the two remaining strips for use when making the pieced border.

3. Using Unit Blocks A and a ruler as guides, cut across the strips in $4^1/2$-inch increments to make 12 pairs of Unit Blocks A and B, **Diagram E**. Press seam allowances toward Unit Block B.

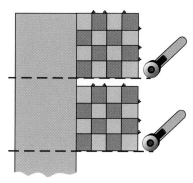

Diagram E

Making the Pieced Border

MAKING THE PIECED BORDER BLOCKS

Chain piecing is used to join four patches to strips of background fabric to make the 14 blocks for the pieced border. If your completed four patch is not $2^1/2$ inches, substitute your O&O measurement.

1. Cut four strips of background fabric, $2^1/2$ inches wide by 22 inches long.

2. Chain piece 28 four-patch sub-units to these strips. Use eight four patches (two per corner) to make the four corner units. If you choose to have matching pink fabrics in the corner units, as in the photographed quilt, set aside eight matching four patches now; non-matching corners would create a scrappier look.

3. Cut across the strips in $2^1/2$-inch increments to make 28 sets of four patches and empty squares, **Diagram F**. Press seam allowances toward the empty squares.

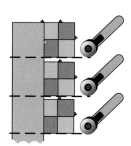

Diagram F

76

4. Join pairs of pairs to make 14 blocks for the pieced border, **Diagram G**. The MCM for the blocks is 4¹/₂ inches square.

Diagram G

MAKING THE FOUR CORNER UNITS

1. Sew the remaining four-patch sub-units into four pairs, matching fabric squares in the center, **Diagram H**.

Diagram H

2. Cut one strip of pink background fabric, 2¹/₂ inches wide (or your O&O) by 20 inches long.

3. Chain piece the four-patch pairs to the strip.

4. Cut across the strip in 4¹/₂-inch increments to make four corner units, **Diagram I**. Press seam allowances toward the background fabric.

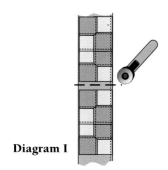

Diagram I

JOINING THE PIECED BORDER UNITS TO THE BACKGROUND FABRIC

Join the pieced border units to the remaining strips of background fabric cut for Unit Block B.

1. Chain piece one corner unit and seven of the border blocks to two background fabric strips. Be sure to follow the fabric orientation shown in **Diagram J**.

2. Cut across the strips in 4¹/₂-inch increments, **Diagram J**. Press seam allowances toward the background fabric.

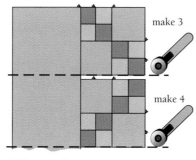

make 3

make 4

Diagram J

Assembling the Quilt Interior

Because this quilt features a diagonal set, setting triangles are used to fill in the outer edges of the quilt interior (see The Secret of the Setting Triangles, page 43). Corner triangles will be added after the first border.

CUTTING THE SETTING TRIANGLES

Cut five 7¹/₂-inch squares from pink background fabric. Cut each square on both diagonals to yield 20 setting triangles (only 18 will be used).

ASSEMBLING THE DIAGONAL ROWS

Lay out the pairs of blocks and pieced border units in diagonal rows on a large flat surface, or use a design wall, page 178. Fill in the edges with setting triangles to complete the rows, **Diagram K**. To achieve a comfortable scrap look, do not overplan the block placement.

Join the pairs of blocks and pieced border units together in each row. Add the setting triangles and join the rows to complete the quilt interior. Trim any excess fabric from the setting triangles and square up the quilt interior, page 179.

The completed quilt interior MCM is 28⁵/₈ inches by 34¹/₄ inches from block to block. The photographed quilt has an additional ¹/₄ inch of float outside the pieced border; allow for a floating set on your quilt as desired.

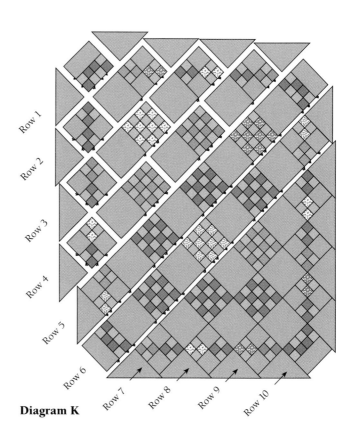

Row 1
Row 2
Row 3
Row 4
Row 5
Row 6
Row 7 Row 8 Row 9 Row 10

Diagram K

Layering and Quilting

The photographed quilt was layered with batting and backing, allowing $4^{1}/_{2}$ inches for the additional borders to be added, and machine quilted in the ditch between the unit blocks with invisible thread. The empty background squares create a perfect place to add a simple row of hand quilting, if desired.

Finishing the Quilt

The quilt top could be pieced traditionally and then quilted, but this Modified Quilt-As-You-Sew method accentuates the crisp design line and completes the quilting simultaneously. See Finishing Your Quilt, page 179.

ADDING THE FIRST BORDER

Before the corner triangles are added, the quilt interior is octagonally-shaped. Adding a simple contrasting border before the corner triangles accents this unusual shape, **Diagram L**. Cut these muslin border strips $1^{1}/_{2}$ inches wide.

1. Add the corner strips for the narrow border first. Place 7-inch long strips right sides down on the quilt corners, aligning each strip with the edge of the corner block, **Diagram M**. Stitch in place and flip away from the quilt interior. Press very lightly.

2. Add the additional narrow muslin border strips, **Diagram N**. Trim excess fabric from the border strips now.

ADDING THE REMAINING BORDER AND BINDING

The unusual element of adding the corner triangles *after* the first border actually makes them a part of the second border. Cut two 7-inch squares from background fabric. Cut both squares once diagonally to yield four corner triangles. With right sides together, sew the corner triangles to the muslin border, through all layers, **Diagram O**. Open out and press lightly.

Cut the final Modifed Quilt-As-You-Sew borders $2^{1}/_{2}$ inches wide and finish with a $1/_{2}$-inch (strips cut $2^{5}/_{8}$ inches) wide French-fold binding.

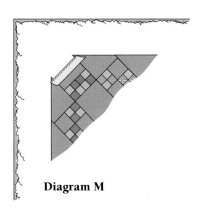

Diagram M

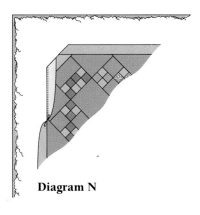

Diagram N

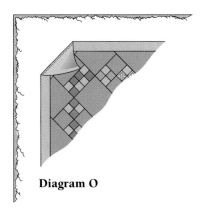

Diagram O

Diagram L

Just Alike, But Different!

One of the tricks to relaxed quiltmaking for people who still don't have time to quilt is being comfortable with a technique. Once you know how to make a quilt, it's fun to make it again—especially when it is barely recognizable as the same quilt! Benefiting from practice, you can also make a second quilt faster using the same design. Refer to Mosaic in Pink, *page 75, for details when making the next quilt.*

Look at the diagram for the full-size *Mosaic in Blue* quilt on this page, **Diagram C**, and compare it to the diagram of the *Mosaic in Pink* crib-sized quilt shown in **Diagram L** on page 78. They are just alike, except:

1. The selection of the fabrics for Unit Block A, **Diagram A**, is different. The pink quilt uses two fabrics: light and medium. The blue quilt uses three fabrics: light, medium, and a large, but generally dark, print.

Unit Block A   Unit Block B

Diagram A

2. The orientation of the fabrics is different, **Diagram B**.

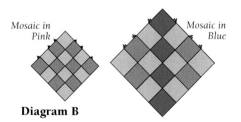

Mosaic in Pink   *Mosaic in Blue*

Diagram B

3. The first strip for the pink quilt is cut 1½ inches wide; for the blue quilt it is 2½ inches wide.

4. There are only 12 Unit Blocks A in the pink quilt; 35 are required for the blue quilt.

5. The pink quilt uses scraps, muslin and background fabric in the pieced border. The pieced border in the blue quilt is made with only two fabrics: the background fabric and a constant, contrasting fabric. I had originally intended to use scrap blocks in the blue quilt's border, but decided that plan made the quilt too busy. It needed a calmer, controlling factor in the border.

6. The blue quilt doesn't have the contrasting narrow border around the blocks. Instead, it features a narrow flap border.

Otherwise, the two quilts are just alike!

Diagram C

Mosaic in Blue

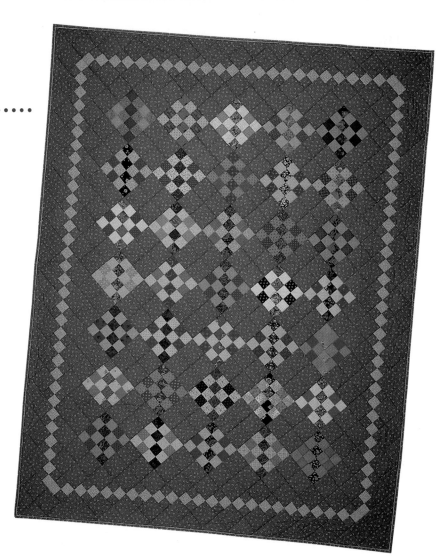

Double Quilt Size:

81¾" by 104¼"
207.6 cm by 264.8 cm

Block Size:

8" square
20.3 cm square

Materials Required:

1½ yards of assorted light scraps
¾ yard of assorted medium scraps
¾ yard of assorted dark scraps
6 yards of blue print background fabric, including setting and corner triangles and French-fold binding
1⅛ yards of ecru print fabric for pieced border and flap border
6 yards of backing fabric
6 yards of batting

Fabric Selection

If you are a fabric collector like me, you will enjoy putting together 35 different combinations, one for each block. First choose a large print or theme print for each block, and then a light fabric for the background squares and a medium or accent fabric. That means you will be cutting little pieces from 105 different fabrics. While you have them out, you may want to cut for one or two other scrap quilts.

You could probably do a reasonably good rendition with 12 to 15 fabrics in each category. Just mix the combinations up and then scatter the blocks with the same fabrics when positioning the blocks for assembly.

Making and Joining Unit Blocks A and B

For each Unit Block A, cut four strips 2½ inches wide by 11 inches long. Cut two from the light fabric, one from the medium, and one from the dark fabric. Make two light/medium four-patch sub-units, and two light/dark sub-units.

Assemble into 35 unit blocks, paying careful attention to fabric orientation, **Diagram A**. The MCM for the unit blocks is 8½ inches square.

1. Chain piecing is used to join the Unit Blocks A to strips of background fabric. If your unit blocks are not 8½ inches square, substitute your O&O measurement. Cut 16 strips of background fabric, 8½ inches wide by 27 inches long.

In this full-size Mosaic in Blue quilt, 105 different fabrics were used. There were 35 different fabric combinations—one for each block. You could probably do a reasonably good rendition of this quilt with 12 to 15 fabrics by mixing up the combinations and scattering the blocks with the same fabrics.

2. Chain piece 35 Unit Blocks A to 12 of these strips. (The remaining four are used later.) Cut across the strips to make 35 pairs of Unit Blocks A and B, **Diagram D**. Cut one single Unit Block B.

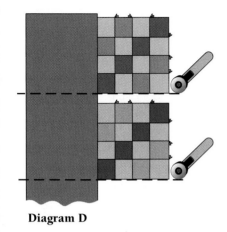

Diagram D

◆ TIP ◆ ◆ ◆ ◆ ◆ ◆
Whenever possible, press seams toward non-pieced units. In this quilt you can consistently press toward the background fabric.

Making the Pieced Border

MAKING THE FOUR-PATCH SUB-UNITS

The pieced border requires 48 four-patch sub-units for the border blocks and eight for the corner units.

On the lengthwise grain, cut 12 strips each from background and ecru print fabrics, 2$\frac{1}{2}$ inches wide by 27 inches long. Make 12 strip sets. Press. Complete 56 four patches.

MAKING THE PIECED BORDER BLOCKS

Four-patch sub-units are chain-pieced to strips of background fabric to make the blocks for the pieced border. Be sure to follow light/dark fabric orientation as shown in diagrams. If your four patches are not 4$\frac{1}{2}$ inches square, substitute your O&O throughout this section.

1. Cut 12 strips of background fabric, 4$\frac{1}{2}$ inches wide by 22 inches long.

2. Chain piece 48 four patches to these strips. Press. Cut across the strips to make 48 sub-unit pairs, **Diagram E**. Join pairs of pairs to make 24 blocks with an MCM of 8$\frac{1}{2}$ inches square, **Diagram F**, for the pieced border. It is important for your finished Unit Block A and the pieced border blocks to be the same size!

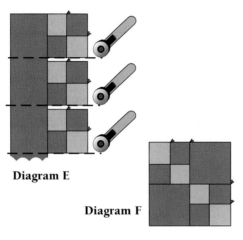

Diagram E

Diagram F

MAKING THE FOUR CORNER UNITS

1. Sew the remaining four-patch sub-units into four pairs, matching fabric squares in the center, **Diagram G**.

Diagram G

2. Cut two strips of background fabric, 4$\frac{1}{2}$ inches wide by 20 inches long.

3. Chain piece the four-patch pairs to the strip. Press. Cut across the strips in 8$\frac{1}{2}$-inch increments to make four corner units, **Diagram H**.

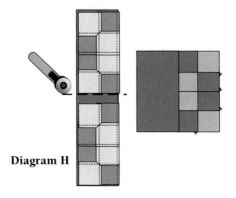

Diagram H

JOINING THE PIECED BORDER COMPONENTS TO BACKGROUND FABRIC

1. Chain piece 12 border blocks to the four remaining background fabric strips. Press. Cut across the strips in 8$\frac{1}{2}$-inch increments, **Diagram I**.

2. Join one corner unit to the remaining single Unit Block B, **Diagram J**.

Assembling the Quilt Interior

Because this quilt features a diagonal set, setting and corner triangles are used to fill in the outer edges of the quilt interior, page 43.

1. To make the setting triangles, cut seven 13$\frac{3}{4}$-inch squares from background fabric. Cut each square on both diagonals to yield 28 large setting triangles.

For the four corner triangles, cut two 8-inch squares, and cut each square once diagonally.

2. Lay out pairs of blocks and pieced border units in diagonal rows, filling in the edges with setting triangles, **Diagram K**. Join the units in each diagonal row. Join the rows, and add the corner triangles to complete the quilt top. Trim the excess fabric from the setting and corner triangles in order to square up the quilt interior.

The quilt top MCM is 79$\frac{1}{4}$ inches by 101$\frac{3}{4}$ inches from block corner to block corner. The photographed quilt has an additional 1 inch of float on each side.

Finishing the Quilt

There are many finishing options. Please read Finishing Your Quilt, page 179, and make your own choice. This quilt was machine quilted in the ditch using invisible thread. The flap border (strips cut 1 inch wide) was added just before the binding.

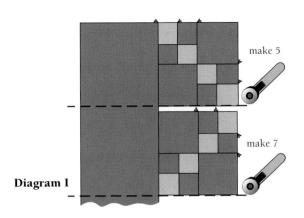

make 5

make 7

Diagram I

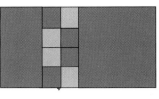

Diagram J

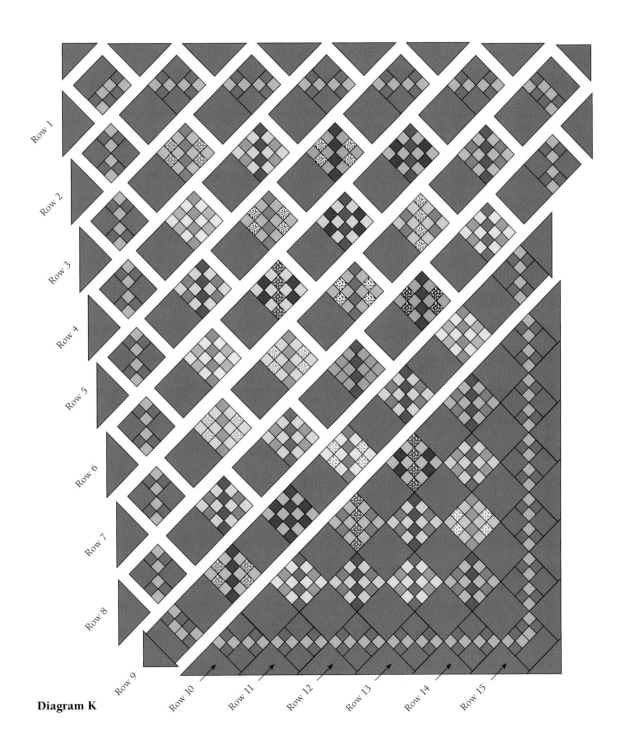

Row 1

Row 2

Row 3

Row 4

Row 5

Row 6

Row 7

Row 8

Row 9

Row 10

Row 11

Row 12

Row 13

Row 14

Row 15

Diagram K

Where's Elvis?

Double Quilt Size:
82" by 102"
208.3 cm by 259.1 cm

Block Size:
8" square
20.3 cm square

Materials Required:
1 1/2 yards pink polka-dot fabric for
  background
1 1/2 yards assorted black print fabrics
1 1/2 yards assorted white print fabrics
1 3/4 yards black fabric for sashing
  strips and narrow border strips
thirty-five 2 1/2" squares cut from print
  fabric, for sashing squares
1 yard black and white checkerboard
  print fabric for first border **or**
  3/4 yard each black and white fabrics
  to make pieced border
3/8 yard black and pink check
  fabric for border corner blocks
2 1/2 yards multi-colored print
fabric for second border and
  French-fold binding
queen-size packaged batting
6 yards fabric for backing (or see On
  the Flip Side, page 89)

If the unit block for Where's Elvis?
*looks familiar, it is with good reason. It
has already appeared in the* Cubic
Turtles *wallhangings and the borders of
both* Mosaic *quilts. If it doesn't look
familiar, that's good, because that
demonstrates the ability to disguise a
shape by simply rearranging or recolor-
ing. Refer to Introducing the Basic Four
Patch, page 62, for further instructions.*

*Alternate some four patch blocks
with plain squares to make larger
four patches, rotate them appropriately
and set with sashing and sashing blocks.
You'll have an easy-to-make, but complicated-looking quilt, called Banded
Irish Chain. This quilt, however, is
affectionately called* Where's Elvis?

Selecting the Fabric

If you happen to have hot pink polka-
dots, assorted black and white prints
including a giant checkerboard
design, a fabric featuring 2 1/2-inch
squares of the Andy
Warhol Elvis, and a
retro 1950s multi-col-
ored album cover
print, you can dupli-
cate this quilt. Some
people might consider
it scary that I actually
owned and had pur-
chased at different times
all of the fabrics used in
the front of the quilt (see
photo, right). To me, it validates the
theory that sometimes you just have

to buy fabrics you don't have any plan
for, but might need. Mind you, this
did not start out to be an Elvis quilt.
The original plan was to use my collected black and white prints to make
the four patches in a much more dramatic and contemporary way. But the
completed four patches just didn't
look right with anything but the hot
pink, and once I saw that, the quilt
turned into a 1950s thing. Then I
remembered the Elvis fabric I had
bought on a remnant table. As they
say, one thing led to another!

Although you might not choose to
make a quilt from this combination
of fabrics (or even be able to find
them!), the point is that this quilt is
so easy to make, you can make it to fit
any theme. This quilt was made for
fun, not forever! Just imagine, however, if it should survive a hundred
years. Wouldn't it be fun to eavesdrop
as future quilt historians figure out
who Elvis was and let their imagina-
tions run wild about the person who
made this quilt?!

Just one black and one white fabric
could be used in the four-patch
positions for the entire quilt. From
a distance the quilts would look
very similar. The white or light fabric
would create a strong diagonal line,
and the black or dark fabric would
make boxes at every other intersection. But remember, I'm a fabric collector and it's hard for
me to use only two
fabrics when I could
use, and already
own, 48! When
interpreting this
quilt in other fab-
rics, just keep the
relationship of
light and dark
in mind.

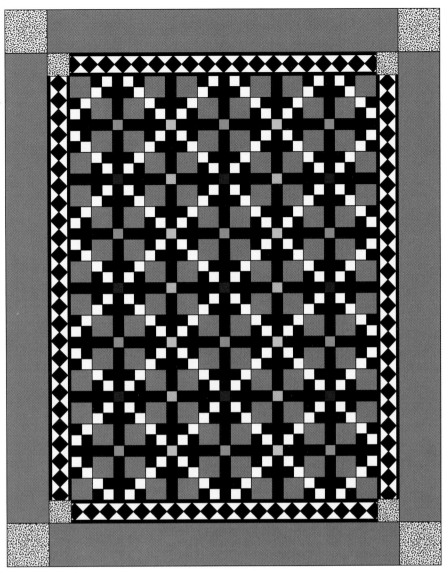

Where's Elvis? *quilt layout*

Finding the Unit Block

In each unit block, two four-patch sub-units are set alternately with two unpieced squares, **Diagram A**. Then the 48 unit blocks are straight set with sashing and sashing squares. If only one black and one white fabric had

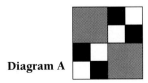

Diagram A

been used, the unit blocks would be identical. However, the actual layout and piecing of *Where's Elvis?* was complicated by the decision to make four four-patch sub-units of each black and white combination, and then to make each set of four meet at a sashing intersection (see **Diagram B**, page 87). That plan positioned each four patch of a set of four in a different unit block, which was the end of efficient chain piecing for this

quilt. Instead the quilt pieces were positioned on a design wall and moved in an orderly fashion back and forth to the machine.

Random placement of the sub-units, or the use of only two fabrics in the black and white positions, would make for a much easier sewing process. The quilt instructions are written for either of those layouts. If you are organizing sets, adjust accordingly.

This quilt, affectionately called Where's Elvis?, is an easy-to-make, but complicated-looking quilt where four patch blocks alternate with plain squares and are set with sashing and sashing blocks.

In **Diagram B**, the circles in the top half represent the tight circles of design created with sets of four matching sub-units in *Where's Elvis?* The circles in the lower half of the quilt suggest a way that sets of eight sub-units could be arranged. The construction is simplified because the sub-units in each unit block match!

Making the Unit Block

MAKING THE FOUR PATCHES

1. Cut 20 strips each from selected black prints and white prints, 2¹/₂ inches wide by 27 inches long. Cut on the lengthwise grain. If you want a specific number of certain combinations, make the appropriate adjustment now.

2. Make 20 black and white strip sets, pressing seam allowances toward the dark fabric, **Diagram C**.

3. Pair matching strip sets right sides together with opposite fabrics touching, and cut 96 pairs of 2¹/₂-inch - long segments. Chain piece the pairs together to make the 96 four-patch sub-units, **Diagram D**. The MCM for the four patches is 4¹/₂ inches square.

JOINING THE FOUR PATCHES TO THE ALTERNATE PLAIN SQUARES

Chain piecing is used to join the four patches to strips of pink fabric. If your sub-units are not 4¹/₂ inches square, substitute your O&O measurement in every step of this section.

1. Cut 16 lengthwise strips from pink fabric, 4¹/₂ inches wide by 27 inches long.

2. Chain piece the four-patch sub-units to the pink strips. Using the sub-units and a ruler as guides, cut across the strips to create 96 four patch and square combinations, **Diagram E**.

COMPLETING THE UNIT BLOCK

Make 48 unit blocks by chain piecing four patch and square combinations together, opposite sides touching. The MCM for the unit blocks is 8¹/₂ inches square, **Diagram A**, page 85.

Adding the Sashing

There are 82 sections of sashing. They are added to the unit blocks in two ways. If your unit blocks are not 8¹/₂ inches square, substitute your O&O measurement in every step of this section.

JOINING THE BLOCKS AND SASHING STRIPS

1. For the sashing pieces, cut 24 lengthwise strips from black fabric, 2¹/₂ inches wide by 27 inches long.

2. Chain piece 20 of the unit blocks to seven of the sashing strips as shown in **Diagram F**. Chain piece remaining sashing strips to opposite side of remaining 20 unit blocks. Pay careful attention to the block orientation. Use the unit blocks as a guide to cut across the sashing fabric, making 40 sets of blocks and sashing, **Diagram F**.

Diagram B

Diagram C

Diagram D

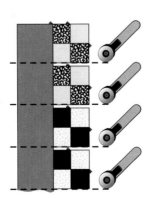

Diagram E

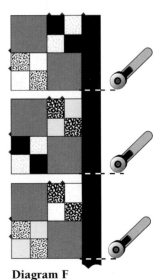

Diagram F

Chain piece 20 unit blocks as shown and 20 with unit blocks reversed

MAKING THE SASHING STRIP-AND-SQUARE COMBINATIONS

1. Cut across the remaining sashing strips in 8½-inch increments to make 42 sashing pieces.

2. For the 35 sashing squares, cut 2½-inch squares from print fabric.

3. Join sashing squares to sashing strips to make 35 sashing strip-and-square combinations, **Diagram G**. Press seam allowances toward the sashing.

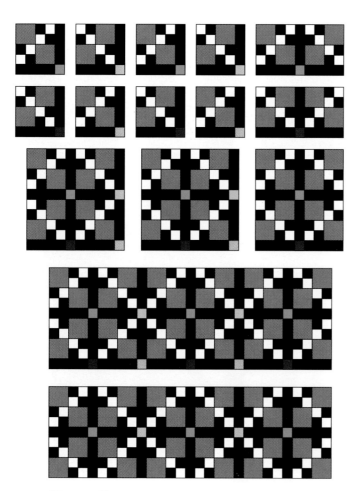

Diagram G

4. Carefully matching the pressed seams, add these 35 combinations to the bottom of the appropriate unit block sections, **Diagram H**. Add the remaining seven plain sashing strips to the bottom of seven of the remaining blocks.

Assembling the Quilt Interior

Following **Diagram H**, assemble the unit blocks into eight rows of six blocks each. Assemble the quilt interior, referring to Putting Pairs Together, page 24. The assembled quilt interior MCM is 58½ inches by 78½ inches.

Finishing the Quilt

There are many finishing options. Please read Finishing Your Quilt, page 179, and make your choice before cutting. The first border on the photographed quilt (see also quilt layout, page 85) is actually bias strips cut from a printed black and white checkerboard fabric with 2-inch squares. Border strips were cut 3⅜ inches wide. A strip of black fabric, cut 1¼ inches wide on the straight grain, was added on each side. Piece the fabric to make the

border strips, and cut to fit the quilt. Add corner blocks (cut 4⅞ inches x 4⅞ inches). The second border was cut 7½ inches wide. The binding strips were cut 2⅝ inches wide.

This quilt was machine quilted in the ditch between the quilt blocks, using invisible thread. The outside border was free-motion quilted with variegated rayon decorative thread.

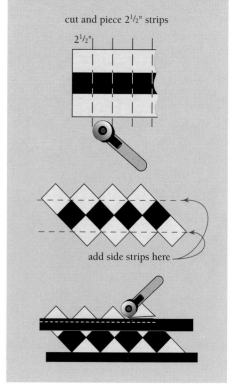

TIP

A Pieced Checkerboard Border:

If you love the checkerboard enough to piece it, it could be done with Seminole strips or squares and setting triangles in true diagonal set style. I would recommend the Seminole technique, because it is much faster, and the checkerboard section has narrow straight grain stabilizing strips on both sides.

cut and piece 2½" strips

2½"

add side strips here

Diagram H

On the Flip Side

This quilt has a wonderful pieced back (photo, right and **Diagram I**). While I owned all of the fabric on the front of the quilt, I must admit to searching out fabric for the backing, including the additional Elvis prints, but there was no real plan. Once I had the panel print of Elvis, skewing it seemed much more pleasing than just centering it. Then the skewed center block was elongated with strips to get the rectangular proportion needed. Additional borders, determined simply by how much of which fabric was available, were added.

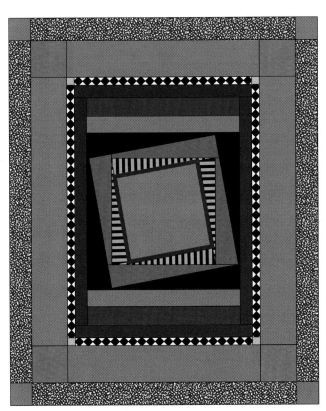

Diagram I

 TIP

One Way to Skew a Square:

Estimate the angle, the height and the length of the new border. I just laid the Elvis square (including piano keys) on top of the gray and black stripe fabric at an angle I liked, and measured. Cut two rectangles an inch taller than the widest point and as long as the new square will be. It is better to allow extra and trim off excess, than to not have enough. There is probably a geometric formula somewhere, but this works just fine!

With both rectangles right side up, cut diagonally from one corner to the other. Sew the cut edge of the first triangle to one side of the center square. Stop just short of the edge and finish that seam later. Work counter-clockwise, allowing space at each end for overlapping. Trim away any excess fabric and square up the unit after each skewed border is added.

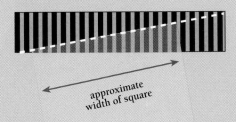

approximate width of square

Framed Four Patch Quilts Provide Tips for Grid Design

In spite of the fact that this book has instructions and diagrams for endless quilts, there are probably other design ideas floating in your mind. Please allow me to use the next two quilts to explain some of the thought processes I have gone through on nearly every project in this book. I hope it will help you manipulate the ideas in this book or any patchwork design source.

This discussion of design is simplified by being directed exclusively at quilts that can be drawn on a grid. Even then, designing quilts can look and sound complicated, especially when I try to write down my thoughts. With a little practice, the whole thing quickly becomes an automatic problem-solving thought process. For the purpose of discussion, let's assume I have decided to work with the *Framed Four Patch*, **Diagram A**.

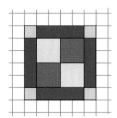

Diagram A

People usually have some size in mind when they start a quilt. That doesn't mean the quilt will finish at that size, but it is a starting point. Generally, the smaller the end use, the smaller the pieces will be. So looking at the *Framed Four Patch* and thinking of making a large bed quilt, I figured, if the smallest strip is cut 1½ inches wide and finishes 1 inch wide, the finished block will be 6 inches square. To make an 84-inch by 100-inch quilt with a straight set, I

would need 14 rows across (84 divided by 6) and 17 rows down (100 divided by 6). Multiplying 14 by 17, I find I would need 238 blocks. Wow, that's a lot of blocks! But, wait, this block would look good set with alternating plain blocks, so that would mean approximately half as many, or 119 pieced blocks. If I put fairly wide

borders around the quilt, I could dramatically reduce the number of blocks. **Diagram B** shows the quilt pared down to 59 pieced blocks. This seems like a nice design with a realistic amount of piecing that would look good in the new indigo and ecru fabrics I just bought.

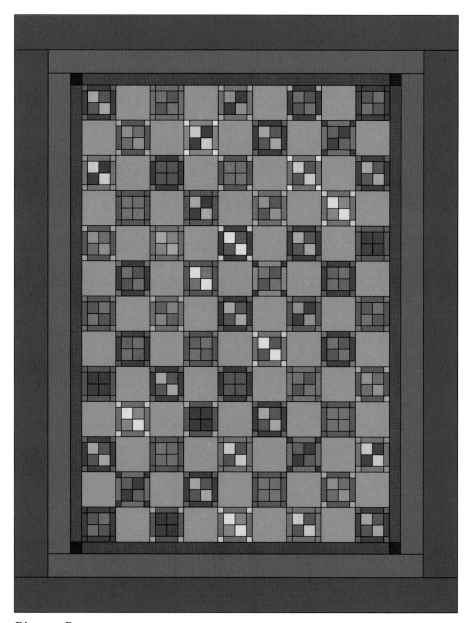

Diagram B

90

The only thing I'm worried about is that the border looks very wide and plain for that much patchwork in the interior. I could make the blocks a little larger and reduce the border width without increasing the amount of piecing. If I just cut the smallest strip 1¾ inches wide, the block would end up 7½ inches square, and the interior of the quilt would be 13½ inches wider and 19½ inches longer. I need to mull that over. It's really too much bigger to still add borders and yet not big enough to go without them. I can't just drop a row because of The Rule of Matching Corners, page 37. Mmmm?

A funny thing is happening. The more I mull this over, the more I keep seeing the *Framed Four Patch* made in a group of hand-dyed, color-blended fabrics I had been thinking of for a wallhanging. How many blocks would I need to make a wallhanging version?

Look at **Diagram C**. That looks great; only 13 pieced blocks—they can be made in an evening! But wait, what if I put those blocks on point, **Diagram D**? It's only three more pieced blocks and I think I like it better. It really isn't necessary to decide now. I'll make 16 blocks and when they are made, I can decide for sure on the set. The worst that could happen would be that I would have three extra blocks.

And so the decision was made to make the *Framed Four Patch* wallhanging with a diagonal set. But a few years later, that other layout was still lurking in my mind. The indigo and ecru fabric was gone, but instead, the homespun I had been collecting seemed perfect for a straight set quilt for a twin bed; see *Framed Four Patch in Homespun*, page 94.

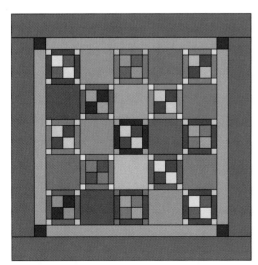

Diagram C

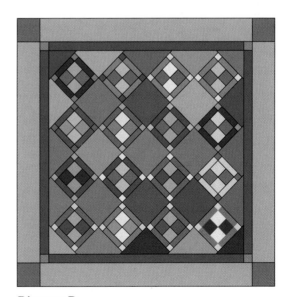

Diagram D

Framed Four Patch

Snapshot

- Unit Block A: 16
- Unit Block B: 9
- Interior Arrangement: 7 diagonal rows with setting and corner triangles; pieced blocks are set 4 across by 4 down, **Diagram D**, page 93
- Strip Widths: 2¹/2" cut for four patches; 1¹/2" and 4¹/2" cut for frames and 6¹/2" cut for Unit Block B
- Borders: 2" and 4¹/2" cut
- French-fold binding: ¹/2" finished

Unit Block A   Unit Block B

Wallhanging Size:

47¹/2" by 47¹/2"
120.7 cm by 120.7 cm

Block Size:

6" square
15.2 cm square

Materials Required:

¹/2 yard each of 8 hand-dyed fabrics, including borders and corner blocks
1³/4 yards of batting
1¹/2 yards of 60"-wide fabric for backing
³/4 yard of fabric for French-fold binding

The pieced unit block for the Framed Four Patch *is made up of a classic four patch with borders and corner blocks. Traditionally, each square in the four*

patch is twice as wide as the strips that create the frame. In other words, the whole block should be six times the finished width of the strip used to make the frame. The proportion is arbitrary, but this design is one of the few blocks for which the larger pieces are cut and sewn first.

Selecting the Fabric

The fabrics were hand-dyed in a blending gradation from a pale khaki to a dark blue. A similar range of eight fabrics could be chosen from commercially-dyed fabrics. My plan was to use the fabrics randomly; I wanted to see each color in each position, if possible, and play with the relative values.

Making Unit Block A

There are eight fabrics and 16 Unit Blocks A, **Diagram A**. Follow the basic four-patch instructions, page 62, to make two four-patch sub-units from each of eight combinations, then add different frames so no two blocks are alike. Although the blocks are made in random combinations, strip techniques are still used to some advantage.

Unit Block A   Unit Block B
Diagram A

FRAMING THE FOUR PATCHES

If your four patches are not 4¹/2 inches square, substitute your O&O measurement in every step of this section. Because there are so few

blocks and random fabric placement, only a minimal amount of chain piecing is used.

In the following steps, try cutting extra pieces of certain colors instead of struggling to make two of each; the results will be more random and pleasing.

1. To make the first frame strips, cut four lengthwise strips from each fabric, 1¹/2 inches wide by 4¹/2 inches long. Piece a strip from each fabric to opposite sides of two different four patches, **Diagram B**.

Diagram B

2. To make the remaining frame strips, cut one 4¹/2-inch-wide by 7-inch-long piece from each fabric.

For the frame corner blocks, cut pairs of strips 1¹/2 inches wide by 3¹/2 inches long; a total of 16 strips are needed. Instead of cutting an equal number from each fabric, cutting more of these from the light and bright fabrics and fewer from the dull or dark ones will make the pattern sparkle.

3. Continue to create the random results by piecing one pair of corner block strips to each 4¹/2-inch by 7-inch piece. Cut across the pieced strips to create two frame and corner blocks strips for a unit block, **Diagram C**.

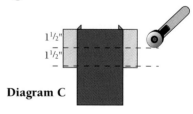

1¹/2"
1¹/2"

Diagram C

4. Complete the unit block by joining the frame and corner blocks strips to the four patches, **Diagram A**.

Repeat to make 16 unit blocks.

1. To make setting triangles, cut at least four 10½-inch squares. Cut each square on both diagonals to yield 16 setting triangles (you'll use 12).

2. For corner triangles, cut two 6-inch squares. Cut each square once diagonally to yield four corner triangles.

3. Lay out the quilt blocks and fill in edges with setting triangles as shown, **Diagram D**. Join pieces into diagonal rows. Join the rows and add corner triangles to complete the quilt interior. Trim the excess fabric from the setting and corner triangles in order to square up the quilt interior, page 179.

The MCM for the assembled quilt interior is 34½ inches by 34½ inches from block to block. The photographed quilt has an additional ¾ inch of float on each side.

Finishing the Quilt

There are many finishing options. Please read Finishing Your Quilt, page 179, and make your choice before cutting. The borders on this quilt were cut 2 inches and 4 inches wide; the binding strips were cut 2⅝ inches wide. This quilt, **Diagram E**, was machine quilted in the ditch between the quilt blocks, using invisible thread.

This Framed Four Patch *was made with fabrics hand-dyed in a blending gradation from a pale khaki to a dark blue. The fabrics were used randomly with each color in each position.*

Making Unit Block B

The MCM for Unit Block A is 6½ inches square. If your unit blocks are not 6½ inches square, substitute your O&O in this section.

From each fabric, cut one 6½-inch square for the alternate blocks. From one fabric, cut two. Or you may prefer to double up on the light and medium fabrics for the alternate squares and reserve the darker fabrics for the setting and corner triangles.

Assembling the Quilt Interior

Because this quilt features a diagonal set, setting and corner triangles must be used to fill in the outer edges of the quilt interior, page 43.

Diagram D

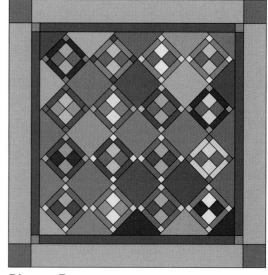

Diagram E

Framed Four Patch in Homespun

Twin Quilt Size:
60" by 96"
152.4 cm by 243.8 cm

Block Size:
6" square
15.2 cm square

Materials Required:
scraps or fat quarters of at least 20 homespun and prairie vintage-look fabrics

3 yards of background fabric

³/₄ yard of fabric for border

Twin-size packaged batting

4¹/₄ yards of fabric for backing

³/₄ yard of fabric for French-fold binding

Remember, all of our material requirements are for 45-inch wide fabrics. Many homespun fabrics are 60 inches wide, so you can buy a little less.

While the straight set Framed Four Patch *plan had been around several years (see pages 90 to 91), the original border plan still didn't seem appropriate. Instead,* **this** *plan evolved. The first border is a relatively narrow contrasting band that crosses at the corners and*

extends to the edge of the quilt. The second border actually continues the pieced interior design. Read the Framed Four Patch *section to see how strip techniques are still used to advantage, page 92.*

Selecting the Fabric

Currently, homespun fabrics are very popular and readily available. I had been collecting and using them for a few years so I had a good selection of leftovers. A few new fabrics were added to the scraps to expand the variety, and the border and background fabrics were purchased to complement the homespun collection. The quilt could be made entirely of homespun and checks, but I like the relief of a few vintage-looking small prints.

Making Unit Block A

Unit Block A, **Diagram A**, is the same size as the Framed Four Patch block featured in the previous quilt. Again, random fabrication was used to make the block. The center four-patch sub-units need to have a light pair of

squares and a dark pair. All of the small corner blocks in the frames are from lighter fabrics.

Unit Block A   Unit Block B
Diagram A

Make 68 Framed Four Patch unit blocks. Follow the instructions in the *Framed Four Patch*, page 92, except, assuming you have enough of each fabric, cut proportionately longer strips and make more blocks from each fabric.

The quilt is laid out with all of the light blocks in the four patch going in the same diagonal direction. If you have any one-way plaids or print designs, be very careful with the alignment of fabrics when making those blocks.

Adding Unit Block B

If your unit blocks are not 6¹/₂ inches square, substitute your O&O in this section.

1. From the background fabric, cut nine strips 6¹/₂ inches wide by 54 inches long.

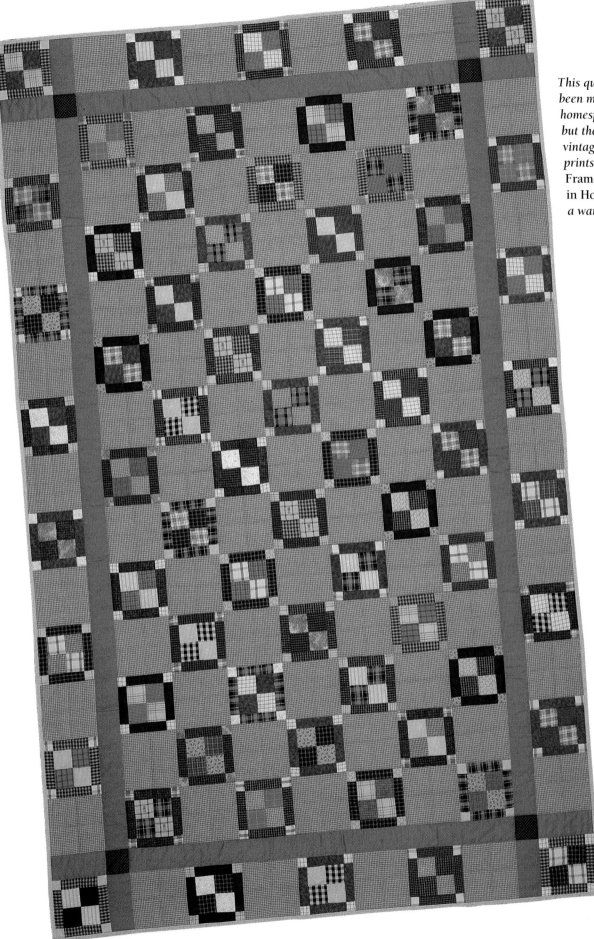

This quilt could have been made entirely of homespun and checks, but the relief of a few vintage-looking small prints truly gives Framed Four Patch in Homespun a warm, cozy feel.

2. The unit blocks will be joined into horizontal rows. Chain piece 45 framed four patch blocks to six Unit Block B strips. Make sure the light/dark orientation of the four patches is the same as you chain piece. Press seam allowances toward the Unit Blocks B.

3. Cut across the strips to create 45 pairs of Unit Blocks A and B. Cut across the remaining strips (in 6$\frac{1}{2}$-inch increments) to create 22 single Unit Blocks B.

Assembling the Quilt Interior

Assemble 39 of the pieced Unit Block A/B pairs, seven single Unit Blocks A and six single Unit Blocks B as shown in **Diagram B**. Pay careful attention to fabric orientation. Lay out the quilt blocks and fill in the ends of the rows with the appropriate individual unit block. Sew pieced pairs and single blocks into place to complete the rows. Join the rows, carefully matching seams. All seam allowances should be pressed toward the background fabric, creating automatic pin-

ning. Square up the quilt interior; see page 179.

The MCM for the assembled quilt interior is 42$\frac{1}{2}$ inches by 78$\frac{1}{2}$ inches.

Finishing the Quilt

There are many finishing options. Please read Finishing Your Quilt, page 179, and make your choice before cutting.

1. Cut the first border 3 inches wide and add it with corner blocks, **Diagram C**, referring to page 182.

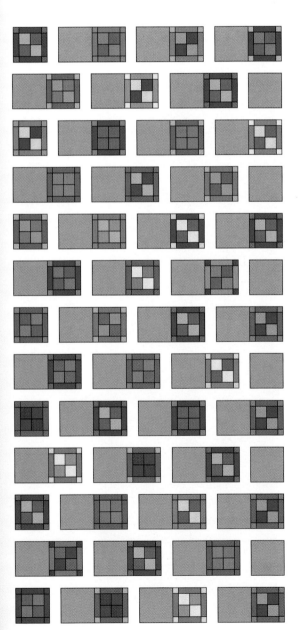

Diagram B

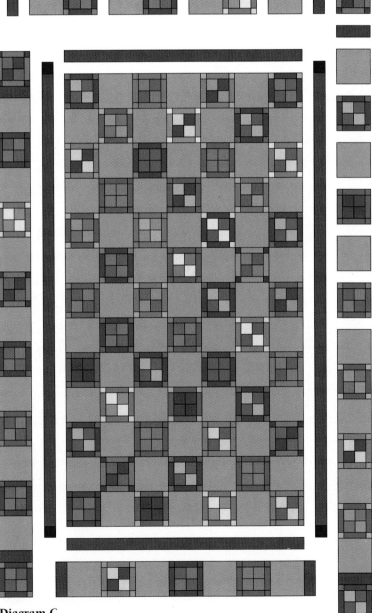

Diagram C

2. The pieced quilt continues in what could be called a second border. It is pieced from Unit Blocks A and B, with strips that continue the first border. Pay careful attention to fabric orientation as you assemble this section, both for directional fabric designs, and for the diagonal design line created with the light squares in the four patches.

Cut additional 3-inch-wide strips from fabric used for the first border. Use six Unit Block A/B pairs, two single Unit Blocks B, and four border extension strips to piece the top and bottom strips for the second border, **Diagram C**.

Use 16 Unit Blocks A, 14 Unit Blocks B, and four border extension strips to piece the side strips for the second border, **Diagram C**.

Add these final sections to the quilt, matching seams carefully.

This quilt was machine quilted in the ditch between the quilt blocks, using invisible thread. A $1/2$-inch (strips cut $2^5/8$ inches wide) French-fold binding completes the quilt, **Diagram D**.

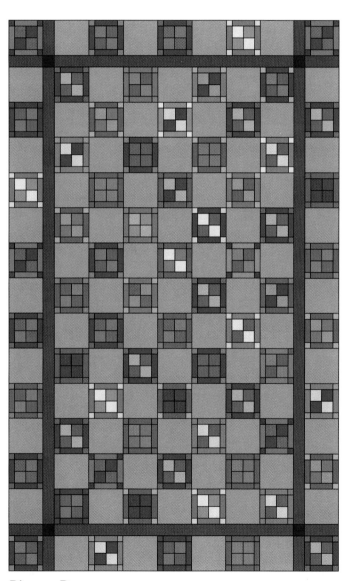

Diagram D

Introducing the Basic Nine Patch

This is the basic technique for making nine patch blocks. Quilts that follow will refer to these instructions.

*Now that you know how to make four patches, you know how to make nine patches, too, **Diagram A**. One more row of strips is added in each direction. Nine patches can be made into great quilts or used as zippy accents. As you look through quilt books, you'll start seeing the nine patch unit repeat everywhere.*

Diagram A

Cutting the Fabric

Simply put, to make the nine patch, make a set of strips for each row, **Diagram B**. Typically, Rows 1 and 3 are identical and one strip set can be used for both. If they do not match, a strip set must be made for each row. If you are using directional fabrics, it is also a good idea to make three complete strip sets. There is a more complete discussion of directional fabrics and nine patch blocks on page 108 (*Fenced-In Chickens*).

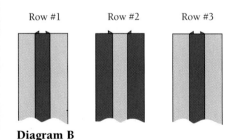

Row #1	Row #2	Row #3

Diagram B

Place alternating light and dark fabrics right sides together before cutting the lengthwise strips. The number and length of strips is determined by the size of the quilt.

Making the Nine Patch Unit

1. Using **Diagram B** as a guide, sew the strips together into strip sets. Plan your pressing to create automatic pinning, pages 24 to 25. When making nine patch units, press seam allowances toward the darkest fabric.

2. Place the strip sets for Rows 1 and 2 right sides together. Using the cut width of the individual strips as the increment length for the segments, make the second cut across the strip sets, **Diagram C**. Do not separate the pairs of segments after cutting: the seam allowances create automatic pinning for the next step.

3. Sew each pair of segments together, chain piecing as in **Diagram D**. I like to leave

Diagram C

the units connected while pressing. Press either way, toward Row 1 or toward the center row, but try to be consistent.

4. Cut the last strip set into the same length segments for Row 3. Check and double-check that you are actually sewing the top of Row 3 to the bottom of Row 2! Then complete the nine patch unit by chain piecing the third row to the pairs, **Diagram E**. Remember, check and check again—it is really maddening to sew Row 3 to Row 1, **Diagram F**.

5. I check the units individually by aligning perpendicular marks on an acrylic ruler with the seam lines, so that the edge of the ruler should match the edge of the unit. I check each unit against the MCM, and trim edges and threads and make minor cutting adjustments if needed.

When you start making nine patch unit blocks this quick and accurate way, you will love finding quilt designs that take advantage of your skills.

Diagram D

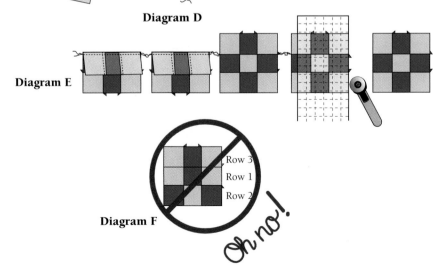

Diagram E

Diagram F

Oh no!

98

Floral Bouquet Nine Patch

Snapshot

- Unit Block A: 9
- Unit Block B: 4
- Interior Arrangement: Unit Blocks A are set 3 across by 3 down, with sashing strips accented by Unit Block B, **Diagram D**, page 100
- Strip Widths: 1¹/₂" cut
- Borders: 1¹/₄" (flap), 1⁷/₈" and 5" cut
- French-fold binding: ⁷/₈" finished

Unit Block A

Unit Block B

Yes, It's a No-Name Four Patch! demonstrated the effective use of four-patch units in combination with printed panels. Here, triple sashing strips appear to weave together and create the nine-patch units at every intersection. Refer to Introducing the Basic Nine Patch, page 98, for further instructions.

Wallhanging Size:

49¹/₂" by 49¹/₂"
125.7 cm by 125.7 cm

Unit A Block Size:

10" square
25.4 cm square

Unit B Block Size:

3" square
7.6 cm square

Materials Required:

nine panel prints for Unit Blocks A, approximately 10¹/₂" square

1¹/₄ yards of blue fabric, including third border

*fat quarter of white fabric

*fat quarter of floral stripe fabric

1¹/₂ yards of 60" fabric for backing

¹/₄ yard of light rose fabric for flap border, cut crosswise

¹/₄ yard of dark rose fabric for second border, cut crosswise

⁷/₈ yard of fabric for French-fold binding

3 yards of batting or twin-size packaged batting

*These pieces can often be cut from the printed panel fabric and additional fabrics will not need to be bought.

Triple sashing strips appear woven together around floral pre-printed panels and create nine-patch units at every intersection in Floral Bouquet Nine Patch.

Selecting the Fabric

When time is at a premium, printed panels are a perfect way to let the fabric do most of the work. The next time you see a printed fabric panel that portrays a friend's hobby or pastime, see how quickly you could create a special gift. Printed panels usually have two or more designs in the same yardage, creating the opportunity for different arrangements. The squares shown are $10\frac{1}{2}$ inches, but the idea is just as applicable to other sizes. (This particular print is no longer available, but new ones are being introduced regularly.)

When the panel background is light, the triple sashing strips will look best with dark strips on the outside. Conversely, should you choose to work with panels that have a dark background, the two outside sashing strips should be light.

Making the Unit Blocks

1. Trim nine panel prints to make the Unit Blocks A, **Diagram A**. The blocks shown are $10\frac{1}{2}$ inches square.

2. Unit Blocks B, **Diagram A**, are nine patches made from strips sets, **Diagram B**. See Introducing the Basic Nine Patch, page 98. Make sure you have planned the dark and light arrangement correctly for your quilt. The strips shown were cut $1\frac{1}{2}$ inches wide by 7 inches long. The MCM for these four nine-patch units is $3\frac{1}{2}$ inches square.

Unit Block A

Diagram A

Unit Block B

> **TIP**
> *The quilt displays an illusion of difficulty because of the small nine-patch units, yet there are only four! The high-contrast small pieces attract enough attention in the center of the quilt to disguise the ease of the project.*

Assembling the Quilt Interior

1. Sashing strips are cut the same width as the strips for the nine patches. The size of the printed panel determines the length of the strip. Using strips that match the fabrics in Row 2 of the nine patches, make enough strip sets for 12 sashing strip positions. Join a sashing strip set to the right edge of six Unit Blocks A, **Diagram D**.

2. Select four sashing strip sets and join a nine-patch Unit block to one end of each, **Diagram C**.

Assemble the quilt blocks with sashing strips, as shown in **Diagram D**. The completed quilt interior MCM is $36\frac{1}{2}$ inches by $36\frac{1}{2}$ inches.

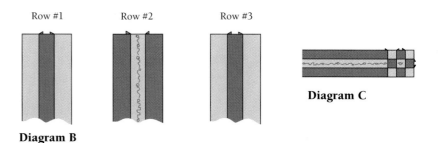

Row #1   Row #2   Row #3

Diagram B

Diagram C

Diagram D

Finishing the Quilt

There are many finishing options. Please read Finishing Your Quilt, page 179, and make your choice before cutting. In addition to $1^{7}/8$-inch and 5-inch cut borders, the quilt is accented with a narrow flap. This quilt was machine quilted in the ditch between the quilt blocks, using invisible thread. The continuous-line butterfly design found on page 102 was machine quilted in the border, **Diagram E**. Some rather open free-motion quilting in the printed blocks completed the quilting. A $^{7}/8$-inch-wide (strips cut $4^{1}/8$ inches wide) French-fold binding finishes the quilt, **Diagram F**.

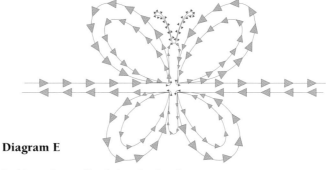

Diagram E

In this continuous-line design, the direction of arrows indicates the direction of sewing.

Diagram F

101

Bonus: Crib Quilt

1. You don't have to use printed panels to take advantage of triple sashing and nine patch sashing blocks! Any fabric with motifs big enough to make a statement works just as well. So, pick your favorite juvenile print for a cute crib quilt, as shown, or use pink flamingos as a novelty, because this is a project you can easily do in an evening.

Replace the printed panel unit block with a large square of your selected fabric. Use it and one contrasting fabric for the sashing strips and nine patch units, or select two new fabrics.

2. Not all of the sashing blocks have to be nine patch units. If I had not been out of the white background fabric after store hours, I might not have thought to try a few unpieced squares.

3. Think about tying. In addition to being quick to piece, this quilt was quick to finish because it was tied. The rainbow variegated yarn often used in afghans was the perfect choice for random ties in this quilt.

Crib Quilt, as shown:
35¼" by 49¾"
89.5 cm by 126.4 cm
• Strip Widths: 10½" and 2" cut
• French-fold binding: ⅞" finished

My typical speculative purchase is usually ¾ yard of any fabric. When these fabrics were purchased, however, I was just going to make a square with triple sashing and four nine patch corner blocks as a sample for a class, so I bought only ½ yard of each fabric. After the first block, it looked so cute I decided to make two blocks,

and then four and, you got it: "Why not make a crib quilt?" By the time I had reached that point the stores had closed. The moral of the story is that you can make this quilt with ½ yard of each fabric, but it will be a lot easier if you buy ⅝ yard, or splurge on ¾ yard each and have some scraps left.

Butterfly Quilting Pattern

Twice as Much Fun

Nine patch units usually have five squares of one color and four of another in a checkerboard design. Both blocks in **Diagram A** fit that definition. Which one is the real nine patch? They both are, of course, and when you start using both styles of nine patch blocks you can expect twice as much fun.

Diagram A

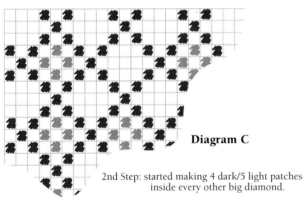

Diagram B

1st Step: Doodling with 5 dark/4 light nine patches alternating with empty squares

Sometimes called Single Irish Chain.

Is it okay, then, to incorporate more than two colors in a block? You bet! There is nothing that requires nine patch blocks to be made with just two fabrics. You might say that increasing the number of fabrics is Twice as Much Fun, Doubled! Just look at this example. While playing around with the nine patch on graph paper, I started doodling with the five dark/four light nine patch, alternating it with empty squares; the result is sometimes called a Single Irish Chain, **Diagram B**. Then I started adding the opposite nine patch (four dark/five light) inside every other big diamond, **Diagram C**.

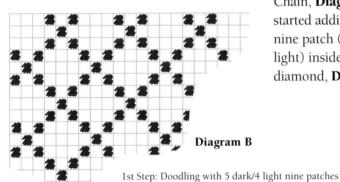

Diagram C

2nd Step: started making 4 dark/5 light patches inside every other big diamond.

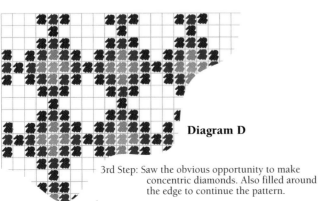

Diagram D

3rd Step: Saw the obvious opportunity to make concentric diamonds. Also filled around the edge to continue the pattern.

The obvious thing to do next was to make a concentric diamond in a third color and add a contrasting center, **Diagram D**. I liked what I saw. I liked the design, but most of all, I liked the fact that it looked complex, but the construction would be easy! Then it was tempting to create another diamond by filling in the blank square, **Diagram E**. Nice, but it seemed like too much, so it was back to **Diagram D**.

There are similar quilts with recognized names, but unaware of a common name for this particular design, I've named it Twice as Much Fun, **Diagram F**, even though both quilts shown that are made from this design also have individual names. The first quilt I made using this pattern was *Victorian Posy*.

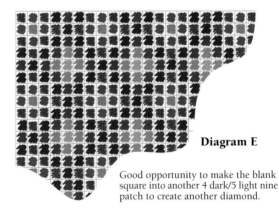

Diagram E

Good opportunity to make the blank square into another 4 dark/5 light nine patch to create another diamond.

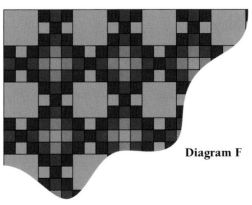

Diagram F

Victorian Posy

Wallhanging Size:
53¹/4" by 53¹/4"
135.3 cm by 135.3 cm

Block Size:
9" square
22.9 cm square

Materials Required:
scraps of gold for center contrasting square*
scraps of rose*
⁷/8 yard of green print fabric (not including binding)
⁷/8 yard of brown print fabric
⁷/8 yard of muslin print background fabric
1³/8 yards of print stripe fabric for first border
1 yard of floral print fabric for second border
3¹/4 yards of fabric for backing
60" square of batting
⁵/8 yard of fabric for French-fold binding

*can be all one fabric, but quilt shown has several different fabrics

Seeing this strong diagonal design in a straight set nine patch arrangement made me very anxious to move from paper to fabric. The use of non-directional fabrics, the nine patch unit blocks and a straight set made it easy to accomplish.

Selecting the Fabric

It is hard to remember whether it was the color of the pencils I was doodling with or the border fabric that made me select the pink, green and brown color combination. Regardless, the quilt quickly bloomed into assorted pink flowers with gold centers and green leaves, with the dark brown diamond, beige background and the very Victorian look. The fabrics chosen for the patchwork are all non-directional; these instructions are for non-directional fabrics.

Finding the Unit Block

The alternate empty square makes it easy to find the repeat that defines the unit block, **Diagram A**. It may take a minute to see that the unit block is made from three different sub-units, not four. The sub-units are named A, B and C for easier identification. Rotate the nine-patch Sub-unit B to see the match. Both nine-patch sub-units are made with three colors of fabric, not just two.

Diagram A

Making the Nine Patches

1. In *Victorian Posy* there are 16 unit blocks, and therefore 16 Sub-units A. Two different gold prints were mixed with seven different rose fabrics to create a scrappy effect. While that is not very conducive to strip techniques, it only affects the center row of this sub-unit and even there, short strips can be used advantageously. Rows 1 and 3 match in each Sub-unit A, with the same green print used in all the sub-units, and most of the rose fabrics used in several blocks, so these strip sets are not as short.

Cut six green strips, 2 inches wide by 31¹/2 inches long. Cut short 2-inch wide strips of rose and gold fabrics. Cut all strips on the lengthwise grain. Assemble the strip sets for each row. Placing the strip sets for Rows 1 and 2 right sides together, cut 16 pairs of 2-inch segments. Chain piece the pairs together. Cut and add the sixteen 2-inch segments for Row 3 to complete the 16 Sub-units A. Review Introducing the Basic Nine Patch, page 98, if necessary. The MCM for Sub-unit A is 5 inches square.

2. For the 40 Sub-units B, cut the following number of 2-inch by 31¹/2-inch strips on the lengthwise grain: 15 brown, six green and six background fabric strips. Assemble the strip sets for each row, and complete 40 B Sub-units, as above. The MCM for these sub-units is 5 inches square.

Victorian Posy has a strong diagonal design in a straight set nine patch arrangement. The fabric choices made this quilt bloom into assorted pink flowers with gold centers, green leaves and dark brown diamonds.

Adding Sub-unit C

(If your Sub-units A and B are not the appropriate MCM, substitute your O&O measurement in every step of this section.)

1. For Sub-unit C, cut five strips 5 inches wide by 27 inches long from the background fabric.

Chain piece 24 Sub-units B to the strips, making sure they are positioned so that one of the background squares in Sub-unit B is on the seam line, **Diagram B**. Press seam allowance toward the strip for Sub-unit C.

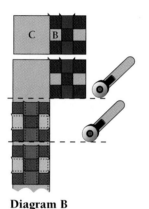

Diagram B

2. Using Sub-unit B as a guide, cut across the strip in 5-inch increments, making 24 strip and square combinations. Sixteen of these will be used to make unit blocks; the remainder will be used as extra sub-units. Also cut one 5-inch square from one strip, to be used as an extra sub-unit.

Making the Unit Block

1. Chain piece the 16 remaining Sub-units B to the Sub-units A, **Diagram C**. Pay careful attention to fabric position when joining the sub-units: the background fabric in Sub-unit B should *not* be on the seam line. Press the seam allowance toward Sub-unit A.

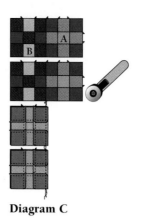

Diagram C

2. Complete the 16 unit blocks just as if you were making a four patch. Check the position of the pairs of sub-units carefully as you work. The C/B Sub-units should be right sides together with the B/A Sub-units, respectively. Chain piece the pairs of pairs together. Trim threads and press half of the seam allowances up and half down. The MCM for the completed unit block is 9¹/₂ inches square, **Diagram A** (page 104).

Assembling the Quilt Interior

Lay out the unit blocks so the direction of the pressed seams alternates, and add the extra sub-units down the right side and across the bottom of the quilt, **Diagram D**. Assemble using the Putting Pairs Together, page 24. The completed quilt interior MCM is 41 inches by 41 inches.

Finishing the Quilt

There are many finishing options. Please read Finishing Your Quilt, page 179, and make your choice before cutting. The borders on this quilt were cut 2¹/₂ inches and 4¹/₂ inches wide. The stripe was worth a mock-mitered corner. The quilt was machine quilted in the ditch using invisible thread. Free-motion quilting was added to the outside border. A ³/₈-inch-wide (cut 2 inches wide) French-fold binding finishes the quilt, **Diagram E**.

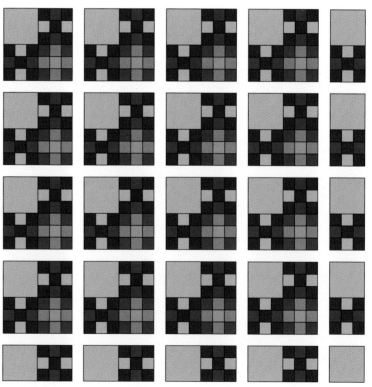

Diagram D

106

Diagram E

Bonus: Another View

It wasn't long after *Victorian Posy* was finished that it occurred to me it might be nice to omit the last row of Sub-units B where they are positioned next to the border. The diagonal design is a completed shape, as in **Diagram F**, rather than appearing to reach out for something as it does in the original, **Diagram E**. I didn't want to make another quilt so similar to the first, but when I was visiting and teaching in Iceland a few weeks later, an opportunity arose to have someone else make the quilt according to my new design idea. My friend and hostess Guðfinna Helgadóttir wanted to make something new for her classes, so I deviously suggested Twice as Much Fun. She chose to make her version with directional fabrics; see *Fenced-In Chickens*, next. We ended up with a great lesson on using directional fabrics with strip techniques.

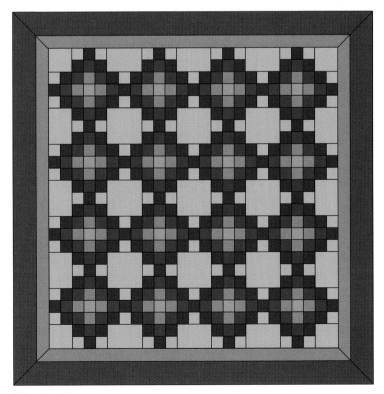

Diagram F

107

Fenced-In Chickens

Wallhanging Size:
37¹/₄" by 37¹/₄"
94.6 cm by 94.6 cm

Block Size:
9" square
22.9 cm square

Materials Required:
assorted scraps of print fabrics for Sub-unit A*
³/₄ yard of novelty print (chicken) fabric
³/₄ yard of green print ("chicken wire") fabric, including fourth border
³/₄ yard of green check fabric, including third border
¹/₄ yard of tan print fabric for first border, cut crosswise
¹/₄ yard of rust fabric for second border, cut crosswise
1¹/₄ yards of batting
1¹/₄ yards of fabric for backing
¹/₂ yard of fabric for French-fold binding

*can be all one fabric, but quilt shown has several different fabrics

The wonderful chicken print set the mood as well as created the lesson in using directional prints with strip techniques. Refer to Victorian Posy, *page 104, for further guidance.*

Selecting the Fabric

Some of the most wonderful fabrics, like the chicken print here, are directional. Some fabrics have a very subtle directional overtone that you don't even notice until you spot one or two squares out of 50 that are "different!" Actually, the green print in this quilt is one of those. You probably can't tell it in the picture, and I won't dwell on it in the discussion, but this fabric has a subtle chicken wire look. Even though it is obvious that it would add to the confusion, the fabric was just too perfect for the quilt to substitute something else.

This discussion is not meant to say, "Don't use directional fabrics when using strip techniques." It is written with the goal of saying, "Know what you are doing when you choose directional fabrics." Clearly the inference is, "When you need real speed and the benefit of strip techniques, don't select directional fabrics."

Making the Sub-units

The actual pieces are made just like *Victorian Posy*, except for the fabric variations and the number of sub-units needed. The chart, on page 110, tells the story of directional versus non-directional fabrics for making the unit block, **Diagram A**.

Diagram A

Unit Block

Finishing the Quilt

There are many finishing options. Please read Finishing Your Quilt, page 179, and make your choice before cutting. The borders are cut 2 inches, 1¹/₂ inches and 2 inches wide. There is a narrow flap (cut 1¹/₂ inches wide) between the second and third borders. This quilt was machine quilted in the ditch using invisible thread. A ³/₈-inch-wide (strips cut 2 inches wide) French-fold binding finishes the quilt, **Diagram B**.

Diagram B

*The wonderful chicken print in Fenced-In Chickens by Guðfinna Helgadóttir,
set the mood as well as created the lesson in using directional prints with strip techniques.*

Non-Directional Fabric		Directional Fabric
	Sub-unit A 9 scrap 9-patch centers	
	Sub-unit A 9 scrap 9-patch centers	
	Sub-unit B 12 connecting 9-patch just alike	
	Sub-unit B 6 connecting 9-patch	
		6 connecting 9-patch
	Sub-unit C 4 large unpieced squares	
	Sub-unit C 4 large unpieced squares	
	8 unpieced rectangles	
	4 unpieced rectangles	
		4 unpieced rectangles
	4 smaller corner squares	
	4 smaller corner squares	
	12 Rows 1 & 2 of connecting 9-patch	
	3 Top Units of connecting 9-patch	
	3 Bottom Units of connecting 9-patch	
	3 Left Units of connecting 9-patch	
	3 Right Units of connecting 9-patch	

Bonus:
....
Twice as Much Fun

If you would like to start with a smaller version of Twice as Much Fun, here is another project you can easily do in an evening. The unique feature in this version is the narrow background border that allows the center design to float. A first border of the background fabric on either of the other versions would do the same thing for them.

Sticks and Stones and Nine Patches

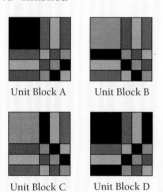

Double Quilt Size:
82¹/4" by 100¹/4"
208.9 cm by 254.6 cm

Block Size:
9" square
22.9 cm square

Materials Required:
3¹/4 yards of black floral fabric (dark)
1¹/4 yards of black print fabric (dark)
1 yard of red fabric (medium dark)
1¹/2 yards of green fabric (medium)
1³/4 yards of tan floral fabric (light)
1⁷/8 yards of tan print fabric (light)

6 yards of fabric for backing
6 yards of batting, or queen-size packaged batting
³/4 yard of fabric for French-fold binding

Although the look of *Sticks and Stones and Nine Patches* is complicated, the construction combines three familiar and easy blocks. The three-strip fence rail, nine patch, and solid blocks combine to create an illusion of two sets of circles on the quilt top. One of the goals of this book

is to maximize the interaction of strip techniques.

Selecting the Fabric

The illusion of circles depends upon the fabric placement and contrast. Select fabrics in four tonal ranges: dark (black), medium dark (red), medium (green), and light (tan). The darkest fabric is used for the dominant circle pattern; the medium fabric for the second set of less prominent circles. The greater the contrast of these fabrics to the lighter fabrics, the more the "circles" will stand out. Although the photographed quilt features two fabrics in both the light and the dark ranges, only one of each is necessary.

Finding the Unit Block

The four unit blocks in this quilt are each constructed from one unpieced square, one nine-patch sub-unit, and two three-strip fence rail blocks, **Diagram A**. The unit blocks are lettered A through D, and the sub-units are lettered E through I. The four unit blocks together form one master unit, **Diagram B**. The quilt interior is assembled from 12 master units set three by four. An extra row of sub-units along the right and bottom sides of the quilt allows for matching corners (see **Diagram G**, page 114).

Making the Sub-units

First, assemble three-strip fence rail and nine-patch sub-units, using strip techniques. After completion, measure these sub-units to determine whether you will be using the MCM or your O&O when cutting the next components (strips for the stones).

THREE-STRIP FENCE RAIL— SUB-UNIT E

1. On the lengthwise grain, cut 13 strips each from the light, medium and medium dark fabrics, 2 inches wide by 27 inches long.

2. Assemble the strips into three-strip sets according to **Diagram C**. Press the seam allowances toward the darker strips. The MCM for the finished strip sets is 5 inches wide.

3. The sub-unit is created with the second cut. (If your strip sets are not 5 inches wide, use your O&O for the second cut.) Cut across the strip sets in 5-inch increments, **Diagram C**, creating 62 Sub-units E.

THREE-STRIP FENCE RAIL— SUB-UNIT F

1. The second three-strip fence rail sub-unit is made in the same manner, using different fabrics. On the length-wise grain, cut ten strips each from the dark print, light print and medium fabrics, 2 inches wide by 27 inches long.

2. Referring to **Diagram D**, sew the strips into three-strip sets. Cut across the strip sets in 5-inch increments, creating 48 Sub-units F. The MCM for Sub-unit F is 5 inches square.

NINE PATCH—SUB-UNIT G

1. Cut the following lengthwise strips, 2 inches wide by 36 inches long: nine strips of tan floral, six strips of tan print, six strips of red, and six strips of black print fabrics.

2. Sew the strips into three-strip sets, **Diagram E**, and complete 48 nine patches, referring to **Diagram F** and page 98 if necessary. The MCM for Sub-unit G is 5 inches square.

STONES—SUB-UNITS H AND I

If the MCM of your Sub-units E, F and G is not 5 inches square, use your O&O for Sub-units H and I.

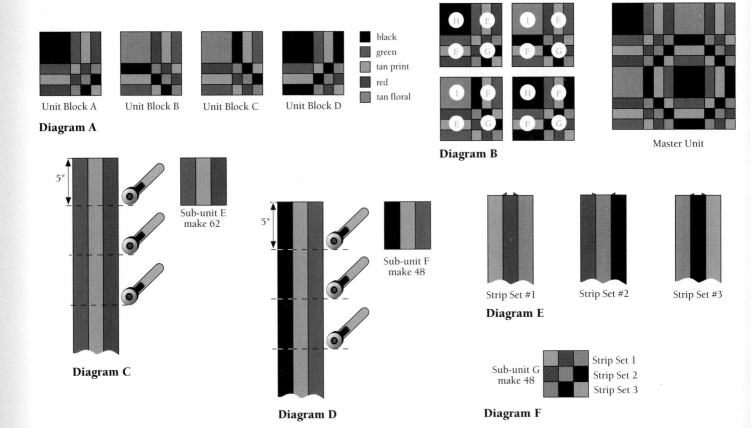

Unit Block A Unit Block B Unit Block C Unit Block D

Diagram A

black
green
tan print
red
tan floral

Diagram B

Master Unit

5"

Sub-unit E
make 62

Diagram C

5"

Sub-unit F
make 48

Diagram D

Strip Set #1 Strip Set #2 Strip Set #3

Diagram E

Sub-unit G
make 48

Strip Set 1
Strip Set 2
Strip Set 3

Diagram F

Although the look of Sticks and Stones and Nine Patches is complicated, the construction combines three familiar and easy blocks. The three-strip fence rail, nine patch and solid blocks combine to create an illusion of two sets of circles on the quilt top.

1. For Sub-unit H, cut six strips of dark floral fabric, 5 inches wide by 31 inches long. Cut across the strips in 5-inch increments to make 32 squares.

2. For Sub-unit I, cut six strips of tan floral fabric, 5 inches wide by 31 inches long. Cut across the strips to make 31 squares.

Assembling the Unit Blocks

1. Join the sub-units to make 12 of each unit block, **Diagram A**. Pay careful attention to the alignment of the sub-units during assembly. The MCM for completed unit blocks is 9½ inches square. Remaining sub-units will be used when assembling the quilt interior.

2. Join one of each Unit Block A through D to make the Master Unit, **Diagram B**. The MCM for a completed master unit is 18½ inches square. Repeat for a total of 12 Master Units.

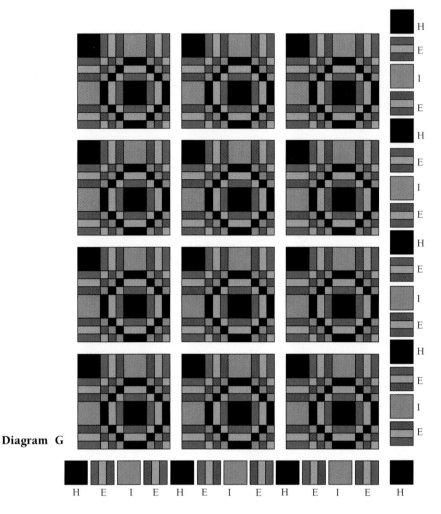

Diagram G

On the Flip Side

The backing for *Sticks and Stones and Nine Patches* (see photo, left) is a quick and easy idea for a pieced backing. Cut a center panel as wide as the available fabric and a proportionate length. Then add borders, any width and any style, to make the backing as large as needed.

114

Assembling the Quilt Interior

Study the quilt layout carefully, and assemble the quilt interior into four rows of three master units each, **Diagram G**. Sew the extra sub-units along the right and bottom sides of the quilt. The MCM for the assembled quilt interior is 59 inches by 77 inches.

Finishing the Quilt

There are many finishing options. Please read Finishing Your Quilt, page 179, and make your choice before cutting. The borders and appropriate corner blocks on this quilt were cut 1³/₄ inches, 1¹/₈ inches, 3¹/₄ inches and 7¹/₄ inches wide; the binding was cut 2⁵/₈ inches wide. This quilt interior and narrow borders were machine quilted in the ditch using invisible thread. The large floral border was finished with free-motion quilting; ¹/₂-inch-wide French-fold binding finishes the quilt, **Diagram H**.

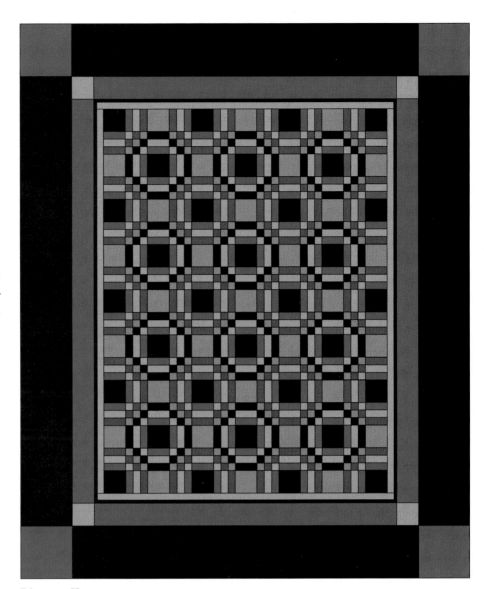

Diagram H

MAKING A "FLIP SIDE" CENTER PANEL PROPORTIONATE TO THE QUILT TOP

1. Measure the quilt top. Let's say it is 82 inches by 102 inches.

2. Measure the width of the fabric you plan to use for the center panel. Let's say it is 42 inches wide.

3. Subtract that width from the quilt width.
   82 inches - 42 inches = 40 inches

4. Subtract the answer in Step 3 from the length of the quilt top.
   102 inches - 40 inches = 62 inches

5. The size of the center panel for the hypothetical quilt should be 40 inches by 62 inches.

PLANNING THE BORDERS

Now the hypothetical quilt backing needs 20 inches of borders. Anything goes. The quilt back shown required close to 20 inches. That width was accomplished with a triple rose and white border (each cut 2 inches wide) with appropriate nine-patch corner blocks, a plain 7-inch cut border with corner blocks, and a final border with corner blocks.

While the final border needed to finish at about 8¹/₂ inches, it was cut 11 inches wide to allow a little extra when layering. Even though the quilt back has corner blocks in the final border, I wouldn't recommend them. Look again and you can see that they aren't square, an obvious give-away that the quilt top wasn't perfectly centered when it was layered. A plain final border would camouflage that problem.

115

Bonus:

Sticks and Stones and Nine Patches Quilts

In expounding on strip techniques, I often say, "Anything designed on a grid can be made larger or smaller by making each square in the grid represent larger or smaller pieces."

With the *Sticks and Stones and Nine Patches* bonus quilts, a more obvious concept is applied. Make the same size block, but make more or fewer of them, to make different size quilts.

Would You Prefer a King-Size Quilt?

This quilt is very easy to alter. To make a king-size quilt, just make one more vertical row of master units before adding the borders. When selecting fabrics, buy 1/4 to 3/8 yard more of the sub-unit fabrics and the third border fabric, and buy 1/2 yard more of the fourth border fabric.

Would You Prefer a Twin-Size Quilt?

An easy way to make a twin-size quilt is to follow the instructions for this queen/double quilt, but make one fewer vertical row of master units. When selecting the fabrics, buy 1/4 to 3/8 yard less of the sub-unit fabrics and the third border fabric, and 1/2 yard less of the fourth border fabric.

Diane Hicks and I belong to the same quilt guild. When she showed her twin-size variation of *Sticks and Stones and Nine Patches* at Show and Tell, I leapt from my chair and asked if we could photograph it for this book. The quilt, appropriately called *Bats and Balls*, was made for her grandson.

Diane's variation is more complicated to describe verbally, but easy to see in diagrams. **Diagrams I**, **J** and **K** show the makeup of the unit blocks, and **Diagram L**

Unit Block A   Unit Block B   Unit Block C   Unit Block D

Fabric Key
☐ Red/White
■ Red
■ Blue/White
■ Dark Blue Baseballs

Diagram I

Sub-unit E   Sub-unit F   Sub-unit G   Sub-unit H

Diagram J

Bats and Balls *by Diane Hicks*

shows the interior layout. Using the same size strips (2 inches cut) as the original quilt, the MCM before borders is 32 inches by 68 inches. Add borders as desired. You can see in the photo that Diane added a strong border around the interior and then incorporated some extra sub-units into the "outfield." Aim for close to 14 inches of borders to make a finished 60-inch by 90-inch twin-size quilt.

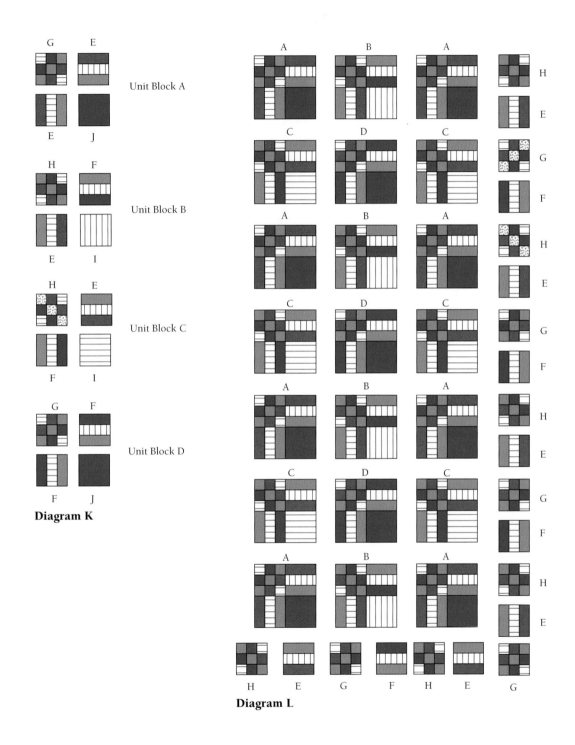

Diagram K

Diagram L

117

Would You Prefer a Wallhanging?

Once again, start with 2-inch cut strips for a nice wallhanging (see photo, right) approximately 49½ inches square. When selecting fabric, a fat quarter (18 inches by 22 inches) of fabric is plenty for every position but one. Buy 1¾ yards of the fabric used in the background, largest border and binding.

Follow **Diagrams M**, **N** and **O** for unit blocks and layout. If you think the unit blocks and layout resemble Diane Hicks' *Bats and Balls*, you are correct. The first three rows of unit blocks are identical, finished off with the same bottom and side rows of subunits. Notice that the arrangement on both of these quilts pushes the "circles" that are created right into the corners of the quilt interiors, while the original quilt layout did not.

The borders were cut 2 inches, 2 inches, and 6 inches wide.

Fabric Key

■ Light Floral
□ Light Print
■ Medium
■ Medium Dark
■ Dark Floral

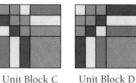

Unit Block A   Unit Block B   Unit Block C   Unit Block D

Diagram M

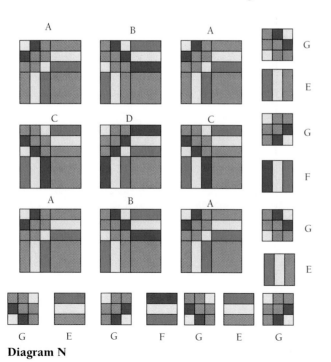

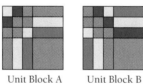

G   E   G   F   G   E   G

Diagram N

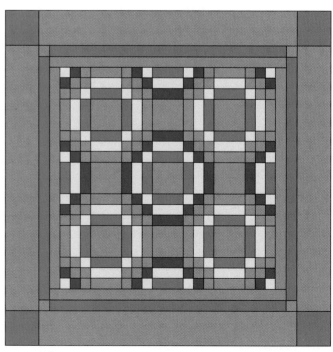

Diagram O

118

Would You Prefer a Smaller Wallhanging?

If so, it is hard to beat a miniature (see photo, right). Therefore, lest I dwell too long on the topic of making more or fewer blocks to change the size of a quilt, let us return to smaller strips for smaller quilts. This 20-inch square miniature *Sticks and Stones and Nine Patches* was made using 1-inch cut strips. (See **Diagram P**.) The MCM for each sub-unit is 2 inches. The three borders were cut 1 inch, 1 inch and 1$\frac{1}{2}$ inches wide. What appears to be a final wide border is actually a $\frac{3}{4}$-inch wide (cut 3$\frac{1}{8}$ inches wide) French-fold binding.

The nine green "circles" seem to dominate because the fabric chosen for the second circle is very low contrast. Scraps or fat quarters should be adequate for all fabrics required except the backing; purchase $\frac{5}{8}$ yard for backing.

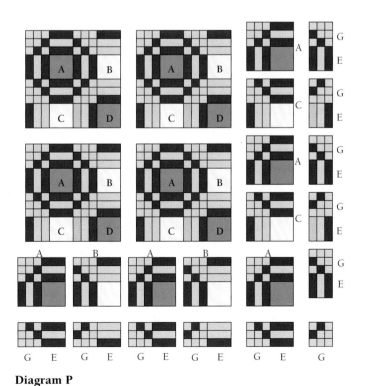

Diagram P

Nine Patch on Point

Nine Patch Chain

Snapshot

- Unit Block A: 12
- Unit Block B: 6
- Interior Arrangement: alternating blocks set in 6 diagonal rows with setting and corner triangles, **Diagram B**, page 121
- First Strip Width: 1¹/₂" cut
- Borders: ⁷/₈", ⁷/₈" and 2" cut
- French-fold binding: ¹/₄" finished

Unit Block A   Unit Block B

Wallhanging Size:
18¹/₄" by 22¹/₂"
46.4 cm by 57.2 cm

Block Size:
3" square
7.6 cm square

Materials Required:
³/₈ yard of navy print fabric, including corner and setting triangles
fat quarter of white print fabric, including border
¹/₈ yard of navy fabric for border, cut crosswise
³/₄ yard of red fabric for border, backing and French-fold binding
scrap of batting larger than finished size

Refer to Introducing the Basic Nine Patch, page 98, and Introducing Diagonal Set Quilts, page 40.

The high contrast of navy blue and white creates a strong chain in Nine Patch Chain.

Selecting the Fabric

It is easier to create a strong chain if the five squares (corners and center) of the nine patch are fairly high contrast to the background. Red, white and blue quilts are always popular; these fabrics seemed like a natural choice.

120

Making Unit Block A

1. On the lengthwise grain, cut seven navy and eight white strips, 1½ inches wide by 13½ inches long.

2. Using **Diagram A** as a guide, assemble the 12 Unit Blocks A. The MCM for completed unit blocks is 3½ inches square.

Unit Block A   Unit Block B
Diagram A

Adding Unit Block B

If your Unit Blocks A are not 3½ inches square, substitute your O&O measurement in the following steps.

1. Cut two lengthwise strips of navy fabric, 3½ inches wide by 13 inches long.

2. Chain piece six Unit Blocks A to these strips. Then using the Unit Blocks A and a ruler as guides, cut across the strips in 3½-inch increments to make six pairs of Unit Blocks A and B.

Assembling the Quilt Interior

Because this quilt features a diagonal set, setting and corner triangles must be used to fill in the outer edges of the quilt interior (see The Secret of the Setting Triangles, page 43).

1. To make the setting triangles, cut three 5¾-inch squares from the navy fabric. Cut each square on both diagonals to yield 12 setting triangles; ten are needed.

2. For the corner triangles, cut two 3-inch squares. Cut both squares once diagonally to yield four corner triangles.

3. Assemble the rows and square up the quilt interior, **Diagram B**. The MCM for the assembled quilt interior is 13¾ inches by 18 inches. The photographed quilt has an additional ¼ inch of float on each side; allow for a floating set on your quilt as desired.

Diagram B

Finishing the Quilt

The borders were cut ⅞ inch, ⅞ inch and 2 inches wide; the binding strips were cut 1⅝ inches wide. The quilt interior was machine quilted in the ditch using invisible thread, and hand-quilted in a cable pattern (below) on the final border. Mark the cable design, starting at the corners. As you progress toward the center of a border, measure before marking to determine whether the design fits. If not, squeeze or stretch the length of several cables; don't try to make the correction in only one.

You might look at this small quilt and wonder why I didn't hand quilt all of it, as it wouldn't have taken more than a couple of hours. But in two hours I could make two more small quilts, trying out other colors or fabrics. Besides, the prints are so busy that, even with the hand-quilted border, you really don't miss seeing hand quilting in the interior.

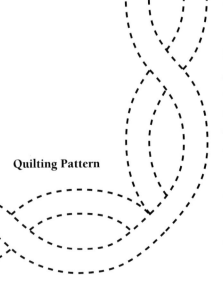

Diagram C

Quilting Pattern

Nine Patch Delight

Snapshot

- Unit Block A: 12
- Unit Block B: 8
- Interior Arrangement: alternating blocks set in six diagonal rows with setting and corner triangles, **Diagram J**, page 126

Wallhanging
- Strip Widths: 1¹/2" and 4¹/2"cut
- Borders: 4¹/2" cut
- French-fold binding: ¹/2" finished

Doll Quilt
- Strip Widths: 1" and 2¹/2" cut
- Borders : 1¹/8" and 2¹/4" cut
- French-fold binding: ¹/4" finished

Unit Block A   Unit Block B

Wallhanging Size:
34¹/2" by 43"
87.6 cm by 109.2 cm

Doll Quilt Size:
18" by 22¹/4"
45.7 cm by 56.5 cm

Wallhanging Block Size:
6" square
15.2 cm square

Doll Quilt Block Size:
3" square
7.6 cm square

Materials Required for Wallhanging:
1⁵/8 yards of dark fabric, including border
1¹/4 yards of light fabric, including French-fold binding
1¹/4 yards of fabric for backing
1 yard of batting

Materials Required for Doll Quilt:
¹/2 yard of dark fabric, including border and French-fold binding
¹/2 yard of light fabric
¹/8 yard of red fabric for first border, cut crosswise
⁵/8 yard of fabric for backing
⁵/8 yard of batting

The two quilts shown are made with exactly the same number of interior pieces and in the very same way, illustrating, once again, that when a design can be drawn on a grid, you can easily change the finished size just by changing the size of the strips.

Selecting the Fabric
Fabrics with directional designs are undesirable for *Nine Patch Delight* because the quilt design incorporates both strip techniques and a diagonal set. Classic blue and white fabrics were chosen to emulate antique doll and baby quilts.

TIP ♦ ♦ ♦ ♦ ♦ ♦

There Are More Ways than One to Piece a Quilt

Most quilts can be pieced in different ways; this quilt is a perfect example. Just remember, different methods are usually not right or wrong, just different.

The next several paragraphs and diagrams deal with analyzing a design and making choices. If you just want to make the quilt, skip to Cutting and Sewing the Strips, page 124, where the actual instructions begin.

Finding the Unit Block(s)

The two most obvious choices for unit blocks are shown in **Diagrams A** and **B**. It would be easy to say the unit blocks are those in **Diagram B**. However, if the quilt is assembled from those unit blocks, the four-patch intersection, which is the most obvious place for poorly-aligned seams to show, is created from four unit blocks, as shown in **Diagram C**. That means matching the seams on the four patch is more likely to be a challenge. Also, the setting triangles would all have to be pieced individually, allowing no time-saving strip techniques.

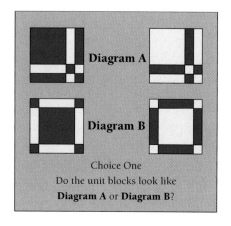

Diagram A

Diagram B

Choice One
Do the unit blocks look like
Diagram A or **Diagram B**?

Shift the rows so the four patch section is together and the unit blocks would look like **Diagram A**, which is my choice. If you have read this book from the beginning, you may be thinking there is something familiar

These two quilts are made with exactly the same number of interior pieces and in the very same way, illustrating that when a design can be drawn on a grid, you can easily change the finished size just by changing the size of the strips. Classic blue and white fabrics, with this diagonal setting, make each quilt a Nine Patch Delight!

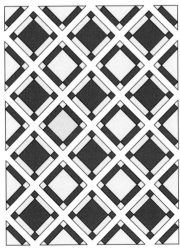

Diagram C

about this unit block. The next choice should clear up the mystery. The **Diagram A** unit block could be assembled like **Diagram D** or **Diagram E**. The method used for the *No-Name Four Patch Duo*, page 63, was **Diagram D**. Yes, the unit block is identical, but that quilt was straight set, and the first one I made included a directional fabric that specifically needed the method in **Diagram D**. For these quilts I chose **Diagram E**, because I had no directional fabrics and the method is a little quicker.

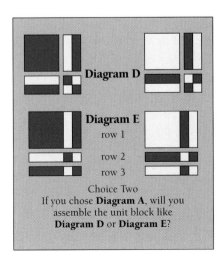

Diagram D

Diagram E
row 1

row 2

row 3

Choice Two
If you chose **Diagram A**, will you assemble the unit block like **Diagram D** or **Diagram E**?

The point is that most quiltmaking decisions are not right or wrong, but simply a choice; your decision on the same basic design may vary with different quilts.

Even though the first quilt using this block was called *No-Name Four Patch*, I call this quilt *Nine Patch Delight* to emphasize the technique and point out that all nine patch units don't need to be symmetrical. The techniques are just the same for making an asymmetrical nine patch block. Cut strips are sewn together into light and dark sets as shown in **Diagram E**. Every sub-unit of the quilt, except the setting triangles, is cut from these two sets of strips; the second cuts across the strip sets are different widths, and the combination of strip sets varies.

Choices When Piecing the Setting Triangles

CUTTING SETTING TRIANGLES FROM SQUARES

In the *Nine Patch Delight* quilts, pieced setting and corner triangles are introduced. Instead of the empty setting triangles that have completed the patchwork rows on previous diagonal set quilts, the patchwork pattern is continued. This brings us to still more choices. The pieced setting triangles can be made several different ways. Are you going to use the techniques and tricks taught in The Secret of the Setting Triangles, page 43? If so, you would cut individual squares and cut triangles with the hypotenuse on straight grain and piece each setting and corner triangle individually, **Diagram F**. This method is the most time consuming, but does avoid any bias along the outside of the quilt.

CUTTING SETTING TRIANGLES FROM STRIP-PIECED UNIT BLOCKS

Another common option is to strip-piece complete unit blocks, let them extend beyond the edge of the quilt,

and cut away any excess after the first border is added, **Diagram G**. Waiting to cut the nine patch blocks until the first border has been added will help stabilize the edge of the quilt and minimize stretching. This is important because the newly-cut edge of the nine patch unit will be on the bias.

MAKING SETTING TRIANGLES THE HYBRID WAY

Then, there is the hybrid decision—a little bit of both techniques—that I chose for this quilt, **Diagram H**. The large triangular section of the finished setting triangle is cut so that the hypotenuse is on the straight grain, and the strips and squares are pieced with strip techniques. Only the two small squares will have bias edges when the excess is cut away.

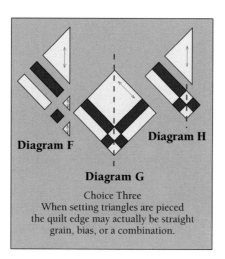

Diagram F

Diagram H

Diagram G

Choice Three
When setting triangles are pieced the quilt edge may actually be straight grain, bias, or a combination.

DECIDING QUILT BY QUILT

How to piece the setting triangles is a decision I make, weighing the pros and cons of each method, for each quilt. Sometimes, bias along the quilt's edge doesn't bother me. If a quilt is small and will not be handled a lot, it is easier to strip-piece nine patch unit blocks, sew over the edges when adding borders, and trim. Sometimes, however, a bias edge simply will not work. For example, if the pieces are large and may stretch easily, or when using stripes or other fabrics in which the bias would be visible and distract-

ing, it is necessary to piece each large triangle individually.

Because your method for making setting triangles will affect how many unit blocks are made, the decision should be made before beginning to cut the fabric. A decision has been made for every quilt in the book and that decision is reflected in the instructions. However, you may choose to override my decision, and you'll need to decide for yourself on some other quilts. For most of the quilts in this book, full blocks were strip-pieced, and excess fabric cut away unless the bias edge would be unusually long. Sometimes it is still necessary to combine pieced blocks with small single triangles to properly complete a diagonal row.

Cutting and Sewing the Strips (Both Sizes)

In case you skipped to here, the actual construction diagrams for these instructions are **Diagrams A, E, H, I** and **J**. The others have to do with the choices discussed above. When cutting the narrow width dark and light strips, put the two fabrics right sides together before cutting. When the strips are cut, they are in the proper position to sew. Cut all strips on the lengthwise grain.

1. For the wallhanging, cut nine narrow strips each from light and dark fabrics, 1½ inches wide by 22½ inches long. Also cut five wide strips from dark fabric and four from light fabric, 4½ inches wide by 22½ inches long.

For the doll quilt, cut seven narrow strips each from light and dark fabrics, 1 inch wide by 18 inches long. Also cut four wide strips from dark fabric and three from light fabric, 2½ inches wide by 18 inches long.

2. Sew the strips into sets, **Diagram I**. For the wallhanging, assemble five dark and four light strip sets; the MCM for the strip sets is 6½ inches wide. For the doll quilt, make four dark and three light sets; the MCM for these strip sets is 3½ inches wide. Press seam allowances toward the dark fabric.

3. When making the second cuts across the strip sets, cut in increments according to the following strip set cutting chart. Also refer to **Diagram I**.

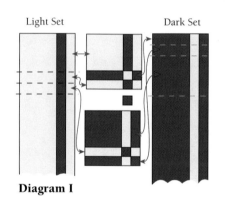

Diagram I

Making the Unit Block

Join the strip sections to make 12 Unit Blocks A and eight Unit Blocks B, **Diagram A** and **Diagram E**. The MCM for the assembled wallhanging blocks is 6½ inches square; for the doll quilt blocks it's 3½ inches square.

Making the Setting Units

Because this quilt features a diagonal set, setting and corner triangles must be used to fill in the outer edges of the quilt interior, page 43. Six of the setting triangles are joined with strip sections to extend the design to the quilt edge, **Diagram H**. Refer to Making Setting Triangles the Hybrid Way, page 124. Additionally, three four-patch sub-units are required.

MAKING THE SETTING AND CORNER TRIANGLES

Refer to the following cutting chart to cut the squares for making the setting and corner triangles. Cut the squares from light fabric.

1. To make setting triangles, cut the squares on both diagonals.

Combine six of the setting triangles with six strip sections, paying careful attention to fabric orientation, **Diagram H**. Three will fit along the left side of the quilt, and three along the right side of the quilt, **Diagram J** (page 126). The two single setting triangles will be used along the lower edge of the quilt.

2. For the four corner triangles, cut both squares once diagonally.

MAKING THE FOUR PATCHES

Remove the wide strips from the remaining strip sets. Position the narrow strip sets with right sides together, opposite fabrics touching, and cut three pairs of 1½-inch long segments for the wallhanging, or 1-inch long segments for the doll quilt. Join the pairs to make three four-patch sub-units. Refer to page 62, if necessary. The MCM for these four patches is 2½ inches square for the wallhanging, or 1½ inches square for the doll quilt.

STRIP SET CUTTING CHART				
	Wallhanging		**Doll Quilt**	
increments	wide - 4½"	narrow - 1½"	wide - 2½"	narrow - 1"
dark strip set	cut 12	cut 28	cut 12	cut 28
light strip set	cut 8	cut 28	cut 8	cut 28

SETTING AND CORNER TRIANGLES CUTTING CHART		
	Wallhanging	**Doll Quilt**
setting triangles	(2) 7¾" squares	(2) 5" squares
corner triangles	(2) 6" squares	(2) 3" squares

Assembling the Quilt Interior

Lay out the quilt blocks, filling in edges with four patches, single strip sections, and pieced and plain setting triangles as shown, **Diagram J**. Join the blocks in each diagonal row first. Then sew setting units into place to complete the rows. Join the rows and add corner triangles to complete the quilt interior. Square up the quilt interior. Mark what will be the cutting lines, but do not trim away excess yet. The marked cutting line, which is 1/4 inch outside the stitching line, will be the guide for the edge of the first border.

The MCM for the wallhanging interior is 26 inches by 34 1/2 inches; for the doll quilt it's 13 1/4 inches by 17 1/2 inches.

Finishing the Quilt

There are many finishing options. Please read Finishing Your Quilt, page 179, and make your choice before cutting. The wallhanging border was cut 4 1/2 inches wide and the doll quilt borders were cut 1 1/8 inches and 2 1/4 inches wide; the binding was cut 2 5/8 inches wide for the wallhanging and 1 5/8 inches wide for the doll quilt.

Trim excess fabric from the underside of the quilt after sewing the first border in place.

These quilts, **Diagrams K** and **L**, were machine quilted in the ditch using invisible thread.

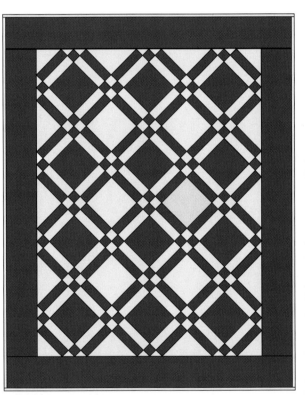

Diagram K

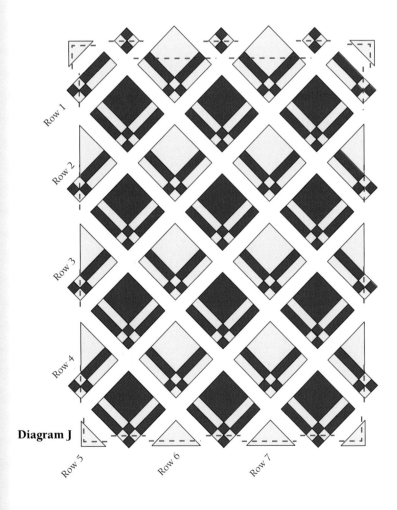

Diagram J

Row 1
Row 2
Row 3
Row 4
Row 5
Row 6
Row 7

Diagram L

Introducing the Magic Nine Patch

The Magic Nine Patch design expands the concept introduced in Twice as Much Fun, page 103. Two alternating nine-patch unit blocks, made from contrasting fabrics, **Diagram A**, are set diagonally to develop a new, larger pattern. Unit Block A is usually made in the typical, high-contrast five-and-four-squares arrangement. In our example, the lighter fabric is used in the five-square position in Unit Block A, but could be used in either position. Unit Block B is made with three fabrics. The fabric in the corners of Unit Block B must match the fabric in the four-square position of Unit Block A. The center square will have a strong contrast, and the remaining four squares should contrast with both the center and corners. What looks difficult is actually quite simple. Pieced setting and corner triangles continue the pattern all the way to the border.

Unit Block A   Unit Block B

Diagram A

What Makes the Magic Nine Patch "Magic"?

Most magic is an illusion, often a sleight of hand that makes the observer believe something has happened, when, in fact, it has not.

To find the magic in the Magic Nine Patch, look at the photo of the *Amish Magic Nine Patch Basic Quilt*, page 129. Most people see the bright blue grid of squares and the squares they contain, and think that is the quilt block. The unit just described is, in fact, a popular quilt block pattern called an Album or Friendship block, **Diagram B**. It contains 25 pieces: 13 squares on point, eight setting triangles and four corner triangles.

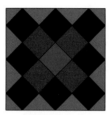

Diagram B

Put nine of those Album blocks together in three rows of three, **Diagram C**. Logic would say that nine blocks times 25 pieces equals 225 pieces; but, like magic, the setting and corner triangles from the individual blocks touch and become squares. The new arrangement has 145 squares, 32 setting triangles and four corner triangles, or 181 total pieces; 44 pieces have magically disappeared. In addition, look closely and you can see that the new design is actually

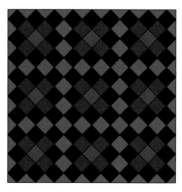

Diagram C

created by alternating two different nine-patch combinations (the unit blocks in **Diagram A**) in a diagonal set. The nine-patch repeat carries through to the first border seam by incorporating pieced setting triangles.

Different Setting Triangle and Edge Treatments

Now look at **Diagram C** and compare it with the quilt photograph on page 129 or with **Diagram D** on page 128. Does the blue on the outside edge look the same? That brings up another interesting thing about the Magic Nine Patch quilts. There are several different edge treatments created by the pieced setting triangles, or actually created by "ending" the quilt at different places in the last nine-patch unit block. In the actual *Amish Magic Nine Patch Basic Quilt*, the full square of blue is used to advantage, **Diagram D**, instead of cut in half as shown in the nine Album blocks, **Diagram C**.

Even though some of the magic of the Magic Nine Patch design results from reducing the number of pieces, in some cases, using more pieces is actually easier. In the case of the pieced setting triangles, when the squares are small, one option is to chain piece an entire nine patch with the intention of cutting away the extra pieces later, instead of individually cutting and positioning lots of little squares and triangles. Making extra nine patches is the method I have chosen for the quilts in this section.

TIP

Please read the discussion, Choices When Piecing the Setting Triangles (page 124), for a more complete review of choices in pieced setting triangles.

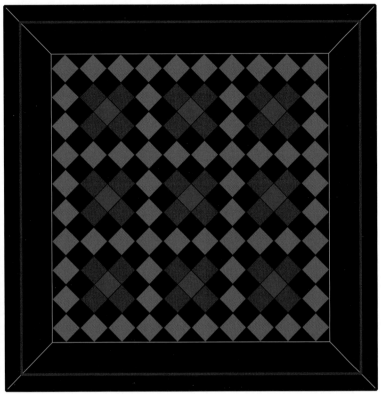

Diagram D

PREVIEW OF EDGE TREATMENTS

In the four Magic Nine Patch quilts shown, three different edge treatments are used. The decisions were based purely on what seemed right for each quilt. As you are making your own quilts, the fabric selection or desired finished size may indicate that one of the other edge treatments is better for your quilt.

Also note that when you extend the interior design of the quilt past the center of the nine patch, additional triangles are needed to fill in the edge. Those small fill-in setting triangles can usually be cut with the hypotenuse on straight grain to increase the stability of the edge. You would not want to cut the fill-in triangles with the hypotenuse on the straight if the fabric looks considerably different than in the nine-patch unit.

For most of the quilts in this section, nine-patch blocks were strip pieced, and combined as needed with small fill-in triangles to make the large pieced setting and corner triangles. Excess fabric was trimmed from the nine-patch units after the first border was added.

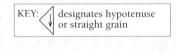

KEY: designates hypotenuse or straight grain

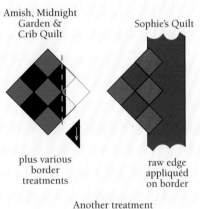

Amish, Midnight Garden & Crib Quilt

Sophie's Quilt

plus various border treatments

raw edge appliquéd on border

Another treatment not shown

first border matches small triangles

Amish Magic Nine Patch Basic Quilt

Wallhanging Size:
19¹/₄" by 19¹/₄"
48.9 cm by 48.9 cm

Block Size:
3" square
7.6 cm square

Materials Required:
³/₄ yard of black fabric, including first border and French-fold binding
fat quarter of royal blue fabric
¹/₂ yard of red fabric, including flap border
1¹/₂" by 15" strip of green fabric
³/₄ yard of fabric for backing
³/₄ yard of batting

The unit blocks are simple nine-patch unit blocks, set diagonally. Refer to Introducing the Basic Nine Patch, page 98, and Introducing Diagonal Set Quilts, page 40, for more complete instructions, if necessary.

In the Magic Nine Patch, two alternating nine-patch unit blocks, **Diagram A**, are set diagonally to develop an allover pattern. What looks difficult is actually quite simple. One fabric is used in both blocks to develop the background for the chain effect.

Pieced setting and corner triangles continue the patchwork repeat all the way to the border.

Unit Block A   Unit Block B

Diagram A

Simple nine-patch unit blocks set diagonally with plain blocks, and the use of solid-colored fabrics, make this Amish Magic Nine Patch Basic Quilt an easy, yet elegant quilt to make.

The pieced setting triangles are actually made by adding small, individually-cut triangles to nine-patch unit blocks which have been partially cut away. Refer to the discussion of Different Setting Triangle and Edge Treatments, page 127. Yes, there will be short bias sections, but this small wallhanging will not get strenuous use or much washing, so the bias will not be very susceptible to stretching.

Selecting the Fabric

The black, red, royal blue and bottle green are typical Amish colors that create a dynamic combination. This quilt, however, is suitable for nearly any color combination, as you will see in the variations.

Making Unit Block A

These instructions are written for strip piecing 16 Unit Blocks A, of which only four are used in their entirety. Parts of the other 12 are trimmed away after the first border is added.

1. For the 16 Unit Blocks A, cut ten blue and eight black lengthwise strips, $1\frac{1}{2}$ inches wide by 15 inches long.

2. Sew the strips into the appropriate three-strip sets for a nine-patch block. Press the seam allowances toward the shared background fabric (black).

3. Place strip sets for Rows 1 and 2 right sides together, and cut 16 pairs of $1\frac{1}{2}$-inch long segments. Chain piece the pairs together. Cut and add Row 3 to complete 16 Unit Blocks A, **Diagram A**. The MCM for the unit block is $3\frac{1}{2}$ inches square.

TIP ◆ ◆ ◆ ◆ ◆ ◆ ◆ ◆
Look again at **Diagram B**. *You could choose to make eight "eight-patch" blocks for the outside edges of the quilt. Just eliminate the appropriate strip on one row. On this small quilt, it isn't worth keeping track of the different blocks, but imagine a bed quilt with 30 or 40 nine-patch blocks around the edge, and the idea of eight patches is worthwhile.*

Making Unit Block B

1. For the nine Unit Blocks B, cut four red, one green and four black lengthwise strips, $1\frac{1}{2}$ inches wide by 15 inches long.

2. Arrange the strips for the three rows, and sew into three-strip sets. Complete nine Unit Blocks B, **Diagram A**. The MCM for the unit block is $3\frac{1}{2}$ inches square.

Assembling the Quilt Interior

As discussed, this quilt features a diagonal set. The pieced setting and corner triangles are pieced primarily from 12 of the Unit Blocks A already made. However, small triangles must be used to fill in the outer edges of the quilt interior, **Diagram B**.

1. Cut three 3-inch squares from black fabric. Cut each square on both diagonals to yield 12 small setting triangles.

2. Join the quilt blocks into rows. Add one small setting triangle at each end of Rows 1, 2, 3, 5, 6 and 7, as in **Diagram B**.

3. Assemble the quilt interior. To minimize stretching on the edges of the quilt, do not yet trim excess fabric from the large pieced setting and corner triangles.

Adding Borders to an Untrimmed Quilt Interior

The first border was cut $2\frac{1}{2}$ inches wide with the flap border cut 1 inch wide; the binding strips were cut $3\frac{1}{8}$ inches wide.

Now you are ready to add the first border and the instructions say, "Don't cut away excess fabric yet." Here is a new dilemma: the fabric edges you need to sew together don't match.

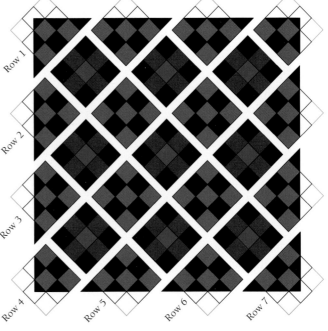

Diagram B

1. Use the same acrylic ruler you use for cutting strips to mark an edge on the quilt interior, **Diagram C**.

If you were going to trim away the excess, you would line up the ruler on the patchwork so that the 1/4-inch mark would consistently pass through the patchwork where you want a seam, **Diagram D**. Then you would cut off the excess and leave a 1/4-inch seam allowance.

Instead, line up the ruler the same way, but mark where you plan to cut. The MCM for the newly-marked quilt interior is 14 1/2 inches by 14 1/2 inches.

2. Place border right side down on the quilt, with its raw edge aligned with the drawn line. In this particular case the border has a mock-mitered corner. Hence, do not stitch across the seam allowance at the end of each seam. See Adding a Mitered Border, page 182, for details.

3. Trim excess fabric from the large pieced setting and corner triangles from the underside of the quilt.

4. The red border is a flap cut 1 inch wide; see Flaps Add a Special Touch, page 182 to 183, for instructions.

5. This quilt, **Diagram E**, was machine quilted in the ditch using invisible thread and finished with a 5/8-inch-wide (strips cut 3 1/8 inches wide) French-fold binding.

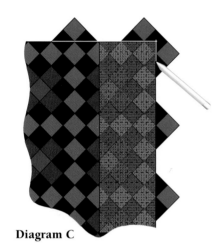

Diagram C

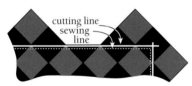

cutting line
sewing line

Diagram D

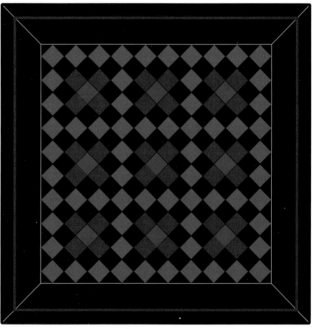

Diagram E

131

Bonus:
Magic Nine Patch Variations

These pictures show two other Magic Nine Patches made following the same diagrams and general directions as the *Amish Magic Nine Patch Basic Quilt*.

The difference is that these two wallhangings are approximately 25 inches square. The nine-patch unit blocks were made with 2-inch strips. Because I like to cut my borders on the lengthwise grain, I would make sure I had 3/4 yard of the border fabric for a quilt similar to *Midnight Garden*. Requirements for the other fabrics are basically a fat quarter or less of each.

Midnight Garden

The first border on *Midnight Garden* is a narrow black border that matches the background squares in the patchwork and gives the floral squares an embedded appearance.

Sophie's Wallhanging

Using an elinor peace bailey clown pattern (Yobo the Clown), I made a doll I called "Sophie Scissorhands." She seemed outrageous enough to need her own wallhanging. The unusual finish was meant to be in keeping with the doll.

The red and purple print blocks on the edge of the patchwork actually have exposed raw edges. Instead of nine-patch blocks, the edge units were made with six squares and the corners only four. After the interior was pieced, it was centered on a square of hot pink fabric approximately 5 inches bigger than the patchwork. The interior was stitched in place with angular, irregular top stitching that would later blend into the surface machine quilting.

The pink fabric was trimmed from underneath the quilt interior, as is often done in appliqué, to avoid the stiffness of several layers of fabric together.

The quilt was layered again, this time on top of a square of purple fabric approximately 5 inches bigger than the pink square. The same type of angular, irregular stitching was used to secure the quilt to the purple fabric. Excess fabric was trimmed from underneath the quilt. After layering and trimming batting and backing even with the purple fabric, most of the interior was quilted.

Approximately 60 assorted red and purple 2-inch squares were wrapped diagonally around the raw edge. These edges were left raw and the whole border was machine quilted to hold all the points in place. Additional irregular quilting was added over the entire surface of the quilt.

Midnight Garden

Sophie's Wallhanging

Marti's colorful doll, Sophie Scissorhands, is an adaptation of elinor peace bailey's Yobo the Clown design.

Magic Nine Patch with Shirred Border

Snapshot

- Unit Block A: 12
- Unit Block B: 6
- Interior Arrangement: alternating blocks set in 6 diagonal rows, **Diagram B**, page 134
- Strip Width: 3" cut
- Borders: 1½", 1½", 4", 1½" and 2" cut
- French-fold binding: ½" finished

Unit Block A   Unit Block B

Crib or Lap Quilt Size:
39½" by 50"
100.3 cm by 127 cm

Block Size:
7½" square
19.1 cm square

Materials Required:

⅞ yard of peach mini dot fabric, cut crosswise

1 yard of turquoise floral fabric, including French-fold binding, cut crosswise

⅛ yard of peach and turquoise floral fabric, cut crosswise

¾ yard of white print fabric

1½ yards of fabric for backing

1½ yards of batting or packaged crib-size batting

¾ yard of peach check fabric for first and final borders, cut crosswise

1⅛ yards of floral fabric for pieced shirred border, cut crosswise

This Magic Nine Patch features a shirred border perfect for a baby or an elegant lap quilt. Please refer to Introducing the Magic Nine Patch, page 127, for further guidance.

The Magic Nine Patch with Shirred Border is a simple variation of the Amish Magic Nine Patch Basic Quilt, page 129. Because the blocks are larger, not as many are required.

Selecting the Fabric

All of the fabrics conform to the peach and turquoise color scheme planned for the quilt. Study the photo to see how the contrast between the light background and the nine-patch unit blocks makes the design stand out.

*This **Magic Nine Patch** features a shirred border perfect for a baby or an elegant lap quilt. Notice how well color contrast can be achieved, even in pastels.*

133

Making Unit Block A

These instructions are written for strip piecing 12 Unit Blocks A, of which only two are used in their entirety. Parts of the other ten are used to make the large pieced setting and corner triangles, and are trimmed after the first border is attached (see **Diagram B,** below). Please refer to Choices When Piecing the Setting Triangles, page 124, before cutting the fabric.

1. For the 12 Unit Blocks A, cut seven white and eight turquoise floral strips lengthwise, 3 inches wide by 27 inches long.

2. Sew the strips into three-strip sets, and press the seam allowances toward the common background fabric (white). Assemble 12 Unit Blocks A, **Diagram A.** Refer to Introducing the Basic Nine Patch, page 98, if necessary. The MCM for the unit block is 8 inches square.

Making Unit Block B

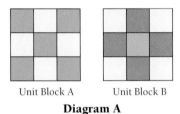

Unit Block A	Unit Block B

Diagram A

1. For the six Unit Blocks B, cut one peach and turquoise floral, four peach and four white lengthwise strips, 3 inches wide by 27 inches long.

2. Assemble the strip sets and complete six Unit Blocks B, **Diagram A.** The MCM for the unit block is 8 inches square.

Assembling the Quilt Interior

In addition to the Unit Blocks A, small triangles must be used to fill in the outer edges of the quilt interior (see Preview of Edge Treatments, page 128).

1. Cut three 5½-inch squares from white fabric. Cut each square on both diagonals to yield 12 setting triangles; ten are required.

2. Add one small setting triangle at each end of Rows 1, 2, 5 and 6. Add one at the appropriate end of Rows 3 and 4, as in **Diagram B.**

3. Assemble the quilt interior. Mark the cutting line for the setting and corner triangles, page 131, but do not trim the excess fabric yet.

The MCM for the marked quilt interior is 25 inches by 35½ inches.

Finishing the Quilt

1. The borders were cut 1½ inches, 1½ inches, 4 inches, 1½ inches and 2 inches; binding strips were cut 2⅝ inches. The cut width for the second and fourth border strips allows one ¼-inch seam allowance and one ½-inch seam allowance; allow length for mock mitering. The cut width for the center shirred strip allows two ½-inch seam allowances, which make gathering easier and neater; length is twice as long as the first pieced strip, plus length for mock mitering. Mark the centers on each strip.

2. Layer the quilt with batting and backing, allowing width for borders if using the Modified Quilt-As-You-Sew method. Refer to Finishing Your Quilt, page 179, for finishing details.

3. Add the first border to the quilt interior, sewing over the edges of the pieced setting and corner triangles. Trim the excess fabric from the setting and corner triangles. (Refer to Adding Borders to an Untrimmed Quilt Interior, page 130.)

4. Sew two rows of stitching along each long edge of the 4-inch-wide

Diagram B

center strips (third border), $1/4$ inch and $3/8$ inch from the strip edges. Gather each edge of the strips, adjusting the gathers to be perpendicular to the strip edges.

5. Match the marked centers on the inner strip (second border) and shirred center strip, and sew together using a $1/2$-inch seam allowance. The shirred border will extend 3 inches beyond each end of inner strip, **Diagram C**.

6. Match the marked centers on the outer strip (fourth border) and center strip. Reduce the gathers, but not completely, along the last 3 inches of length on each end of the center strip. (Too much fullness in the gathers at the ends makes the next step difficult.) Sew the strips together using a $1/2$-inch seam allowance, **Diagram D**.

7. Add the pieced border to the quilt interior and mock miter the corners, page 182.

8. Add the final border to the quilt interior using blunt corners (refer to page 181).

9. This quilt, **Diagram E**, was finished with a $1/2$-inch-wide (strips cut $2^5/8$ inches wide) French-fold binding, and machine quilted in the ditch using invisible thread.

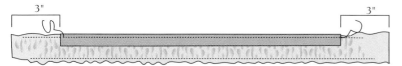

Diagram C

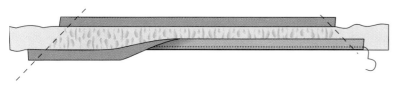

Diagram D

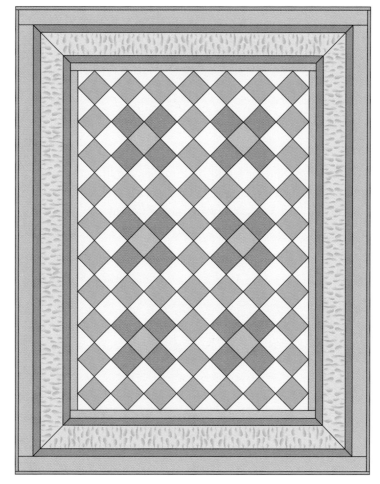

Diagram E

Introducing the 25 Patch

If two rows of two pieces make a four patch, and three rows of three make a nine patch, then five rows of five must be a 25 patch. This is the basic technique for making a 25 patch unit. Any quilts that have a unit block five rows high by five squares wide will refer to these instructions.

Five rows of five make a 25-patch unit; fabrics can be in any arrangement. The illustrated block has a pattern where each fabric moves over one position in each subsequent row, **Diagram A**.

Unit Block
Diagram A

Cutting the Fabric

After determining that the repeat is five rows of five squares, cut a strip for each square in each row, **Diagram B**. In the illustrated block, each row is different. The required number and the length of the strips will be determined by the quilt size.

Making the 25 Patch Unit

1. Using **Diagram B** as a guide, sew strips together into sets for the five rows. Create automatic pinning by alternating the direction to which the seam allowances are pressed (see Directional Pressing, page 16).

2. Place strip sets for Rows 1 and 2 right sides together. Using the cut width of the individual strips as the increment length for the segments, make the second cut across the strip sets, **Diagram C**. Do not separate the pairs of segments after cutting: the seam allowances create automatic pinning for the next step.

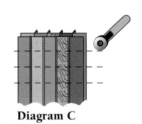

Diagram C

3. Sew each pair of segments together, chain piecing as in **Diagram D**. Make sure you are sewing the bottom of Row 1 to the top of Row 2. When the strip sets are not symmetrical, this is a potential problem on every seam.

Row 1
Row 2

Diagram D

4. Pair Rows 3 and 4, and cut and chain piece in the same manner.

5. Chain piece pairs of pairs together (Rows 1&2 and Rows 3&4). Be sure you are sewing the bottom of Row 2 and the top of Row 3 together in this step!

6. Cut the strip set for Row 5 into the same length segments. Stitch the top of Row 5 to the bottom of Row 4 to complete a 25-patch unit, **Diagram A**.

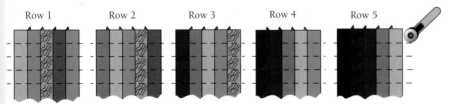

Row 1   Row 2   Row 3   Row 4   Row 5

Diagram B

Double Irish Chain Basic Quilt

The Double Irish Chain Basic Quilt has a strong diagonal pattern which looks much more complex than it really is.

Queen/Double Quilt Size:

84$^{3}/_{4}$" by 104$^{3}/_{4}$"
215.3 cm by 266.1 cm

Block Size:

10" square
25.4 cm square

Materials Required:

1$^{5}/_{8}$ yards of dark fabric

4$^{1}/_{8}$ yards of medium fabric, including third border

4$^{3}/_{8}$ yards of light fabric, including second border

$^{1}/_{2}$ yard of muslin for first border (cut crosswise and pieced)

7$^{1}/_{2}$ yards of fabric for backing

6 yards of batting, or king-size packaged batting

$^{5}/_{8}$ yard of fabric for French-fold binding

The Double Irish Chain is probably the most frequently made quilt with a 25-patch unit block, making it the appropriate first quilt in this section. Please refer to Introducing the 25 Patch, page 136, if necessary.

The strong diagonal pattern of the Double Irish Chain makes it an easily-recognized design. It may be the same thing that makes it a very popular quilt design. What I love most about the Double Irish Chain is that it looks much more complex than it is. What looks like an allover pattern is made by alternating two basic blocks across the quilt.

Selecting the Fabric

For many people, the nicest thing about Double Irish Chain is the ease of selecting fabrics. While the quilt shown is a classic monochromatic, with light, medium and dark rose and ecru fabrics, you will discover that nearly every three fabrics that look good together can be used.

Finding the Unit Blocks

Finding the two basic blocks is the first step in making the *Double Irish Chain Basic Quilt*. In this quilt, Unit Block A is made of twenty-five 2-inch squares; and Unit Block B appears to be made of a 10-inch square, with a 2-inch square appliquéd in each corner, **Diagram A**. People who *still* don't have time to quilt will appreciate being able to strip piece both unit blocks, no appliqué.

Unit Block A   Unit Block B

Diagram A

Making Unit Block A

TIP ◆ ◆ ◆ ◆ ◆ ◆ ◆ ◆ ◆
When fabric requirements include border fabric with fabric used elsewhere in the quilt, be sure to cut and reserve a strip of fabric along the lengthwise grain for the borders, before making any other cuts in your fabric.

1. On the lengthwise grain, cut 27 dark, 36 medium and 12 light strips, 2½ inches wide by 29 inches long.

2. Sew the strips together into sets for the rows, **Diagram B**. Rows 1 and 5, and Rows 2 and 4 are identical. Careful directional pressing of seam allowances, resulting in automatic pinning, contributes greatly to the ease of making this block.

3. Place strip sets for Rows 1 and 2, and for Rows 3 and 4, right sides together. Cut 32 pairs of 2½-inch long segments from each pair of strip sets. Chain piece the pairs together, and then join pairs of pairs.

4. Cut and add Row 5 to complete 32 Unit Blocks A, **Diagram A**. The MCM for the unit block is 10½ inches square.

Making Unit Block B

One technique for making Unit Block B is to cut a square the MCM of Unit Block A, and then appliqué a 2½-inch square in each corner. However, strip piecing is recommended.

1. Two different strip widths are used to make Unit Block B, **Diagram C**. The strips for the corner squares are the same width used in Unit Block A. The MCM for the width of the center strip is 6½ inches. That is the MCM

of the finished width of the three center squares in Unit Block A, plus two ¼-inch seam allowances. It is very important to measure the finished squares in your own Unit Block A and to substitute your O&O measurement, if necessary.

Cut all of the following strips 29 inches long, on the lengthwise grain:

For Rows 1 and 3, cut 12 strips of medium fabric, 2½ inches wide; and six strips of light fabric, 6½ inches wide.

For Row 2, cut 16 strips of light fabric, 2½ inches wide; and eight strips of light fabric, 6½ inches wide. I really am telling you to cut the same fabric apart and then sew it back together. The block looks more balanced when you have these seam lines, plus there are now "ditches" for stitching if you plan to machine quilt.

TIP ◆ ◆ ◆ ◆ ◆ ◆ ◆ ◆ ◆
If your friends are already wondering why you cut all that fabric up into little pieces and sew it back together, cutting apart and immediately sewing together the same fabric is something you might want to do when no one is watching.

2. Sew the strips together into sets for the rows, **Diagram C**.

3. Cut across the strip sets for Rows 1 and 3 to make 62 segments, 2½ inches long. Cut 31 segments 6½ inches long, from the strip sets for Row 2.

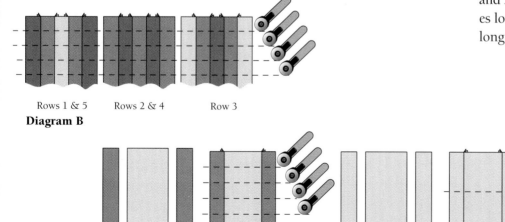

Rows 1 & 5   Rows 2 & 4   Row 3
Diagram B

Diagram C   Rows 1 & 3   Row 2   Row 1   Row 2   Row 3

4. Join the strip sets to complete 31 Unit Blocks B, **Diagram A**. Press the seam allowances away from the center of the block. The MCM for the unit block is $10^{1}/_{2}$ inches square.

Finishing the Quilt

Following the quilt illustration, **Diagram D**, assemble the blocks into nine rows of seven blocks each, referring to page 24 for the pairs method. The MCM for the assembled quilt interior is $70^{1}/_{2}$ inches by $90^{1}/_{2}$ inches.

The borders were cut $1^{3}/_{8}$ inches, $2^{3}/_{4}$ inches and 4 inches wide; the binding strips were cut $3^{5}/_{8}$ inches wide. This quilt was machine quilted in the ditch using invisible thread.

Diagram D

Glendale Gardens Double Irish Chain

Snapshot

- Unit Block A: 18
- Unit Block B: 17
- Interior Arrangement: alternating blocks set 5 across by 7 down, **Diagram C**, page 141
- First Strip Width: 3" cut
- Borders: $2^5/8$" and $7^1/2$" cut
- French-fold binding: 1" finished

Unit Block A   Unit Block B

Queen/Double Quilt Size:

$82^3/4$" by $107^3/4$"
210.2 cm by 273.7 cm

Block Size:

$12^1/2$" square
31.8 cm square

Materials Required:

$2^1/4$ yards of dark fabric
$1^5/8$ yards of medium fabric
3 yards of light fabric
1 yard of fabric for first border*
$2^5/8$ yards of fabric for second border*
$6^1/4$ yards of fabric for backing
$6^1/4$ yards of batting, or king-size packaged batting
$1^1/2$ yards of fabric for French-fold binding, cut crosswise and pieced

* These borders were cut to take advantage of printed designs on the lengthwise grain.

The Glendale Gardens Double Irish Chain quilt is practically the same size as the Basic Quilt on page 137, but by using wider strips, you need only 35 unit blocks—far fewer than the 63 unit blocks needed for the previous quilt.

Having studied strip techniques, you already realize that the Double Irish Chain can be any size just by changing the size of the squares. Conversely, if you leave the size of the quilt the same and change the size of the square, you will need to make more or fewer blocks depending on the change. This queen/double-size quilt requires only 35 unit blocks, while the previous quilt needed 63 unit blocks. Please refer to the Double Irish Chain Basic Quilt, page 137, if necessary.

Quilt Comparison

The two Double Irish Chain quilts shown in **Diagram B** are practically the same size, but the number of pieces and amount of work is amazingly different. The interior patchwork of the Basic Quilt requires 1,079 pieces; *Glendale Gardens* demands only 603. Even though both quilts were made using the quicker strip techniques in this book, Glendale Gardens needs 22 fewer strips.

> **TIP** ◆ ◆ ◆ ◆ ◆ ◆ ◆
> *No matter how fast you are, if you can reduce the number of pieces in a quilt without sacrificing design, you will be faster!*

Selecting the Fabric

Three inches doesn't seem "big," but in Double Irish Chain patchwork, it is pushing the limits of looking klutzy. To help disguise the larger-size blocks, select lower-contrast fabrics.

Making the Unit Blocks

1. For the Unit Blocks A, cut 18 medium, 24 dark and eight light lengthwise strips, 3 inches wide by 29 inches long.

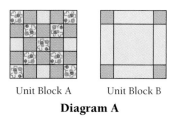

Unit Block A   Unit Block B
Diagram A

Sew the strips together into sets for the rows. Assemble 18 Unit Blocks A, **Diagram A**. Refer to Introducing the 25 Patch, page 136, if necessary. The MCM for the unit block is 13 inches square.

2. For the Unit Blocks B, cut 12 dark and 18 light lengthwise strips, 3 inches wide by 19 inches long. Also cut 15 light strips, 8 inches wide by 19 inches long.

Sew the strips into sets and assemble 17 Unit Blocks B, **Diagram A**. The MCM for the unit block is 13 inches square.

Finishing the Quilt

Follow the quilt layout in **Diagram C**, to assemble the blocks into seven rows of five blocks each. Refer to page 24 for the pairs method. The MCM for the quilt interior is 63 inches by 88 inches.

The borders were cut $2^5/8$ inches and $7^1/2$ inches wide—the width of the final border being determined by the printed fabric. The binding strips were cut $4^5/8$ inches wide.

There are many finishing options. Please read Finishing Your Quilt, page 179, and make your choice before cutting. This quilt was machine quilted in the ditch using invisible thread.

Double Irish Chain Basic Quilt

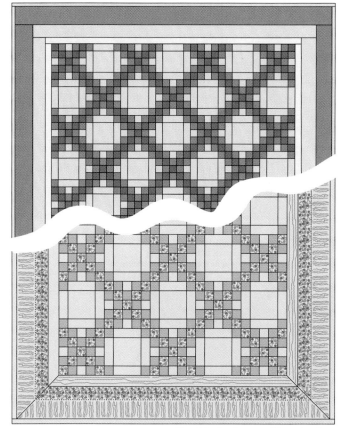

Diagram B   Glendale Gardens Double Irish Chain

Diagram C

141

Double Irish Chain Wallhanging Trio

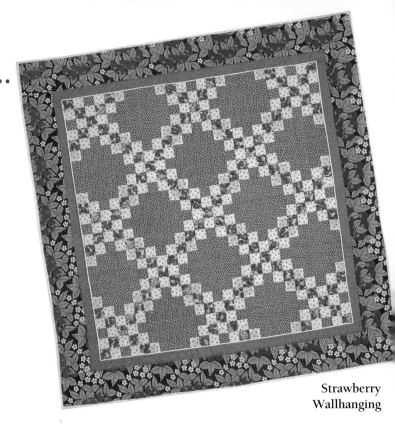

Strawberry
Wallhanging

Snapshot

- Unit Block A: 13
- Unit Block B: 12
- Interior Arrangement: alternating blocks set 5 across by 5 down
- First Strip Width: 2" cut
- Borders: as desired
- French-fold binding: as desired

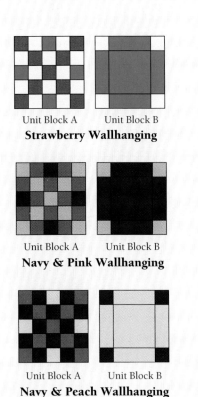

Unit Block A   Unit Block B
Strawberry Wallhanging

Unit Block A   Unit Block B
Navy & Pink Wallhanging

Unit Block A   Unit Block B
Navy & Peach Wallhanging

Strawberry Wallhanging Size:
49³/4" by 49³/4"
126.4 cm by 126.4 cm

Navy & Pink Wallhanging Size:
46¹/2" by 46¹/2"
118.1 cm by 118.1 cm

Navy & Peach Wallhanging Size:
49³/4" by 49³/4"
126.4 cm by 126.4 cm

Block Size:
7¹/2" square
19.1 cm square

Materials Required:
³/4 yard of fabric #1
³/4 yard of fabric #2
1¹/2 yards of fabric #3
fabric for borders as desired, minimum of ¹/2 yard for each border
approximately 54-inch square of fabric for backing
approximately 54-inch square of batting
³/4 yard of fabric for French-fold binding

These three Double Irish Chain *wallhangings are made with identical measurements, excluding the borders. These quilts prove that the placement of light, medium and dark values in the unit blocks can be as important as the selection of the values. Please refer to the* Double Irish Chain Basic Quilt, *page 137, if necessary.*

Selecting the Fabric

In the *Double Irish Chain Basic Quilt*, I said that nearly every three fabrics that look good together can be used to make a Double Irish Chain quilt. Well, I really prefer three fabrics with a recognized light, medium and dark relationship. Once selected, they can go in nearly any arrangement. These three wallhangings are proof. They are all different, and they all look great.

Making the Quilts

1. Refer to **Diagram A** and the Strip Cutting Chart on the next page to cut the fabric strips. Cut all strips on the lengthwise grain.

1	2	3	2	1
2	1	2	1	2
3	2	1	2	3
2	1	2	1	2
1	2	3	2	1

2	3	2
3	3	3
2	3	2

Diagram A

Navy & Pink
Wallhanging

2. Assemble 13 Unit Blocks A, **Diagram B**. Refer to Introducing the 25 Patch, page 136, if necessary. The MCM for the unit block is 8 inches square.

3. Assemble 12 Unit Blocks B, **Diagram B**. The MCM for the unit block is 8 inches square.

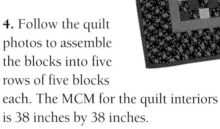

Navy & Peach
Wallhanging

4. Follow the quilt photos to assemble the blocks into five rows of five blocks each. The MCM for the quilt interiors is 38 inches by 38 inches.

5. See Finishing Your Quilt, page 179, for finishing options.

Unit Block A   Unit Block B
Strawberry Wallhanging

Unit Block A   Unit Block B
Navy & Pink Wallhanging

Unit Block A   Unit Block B
Navy & Peach Wallhanging

Diagram B

STRIP CUTTING CHART

| | Unit Block A | Unit Block B | |
	cut 2" x 27"	cut 2" x 27"	*cut 5" x 27"
fabric #1	9 strips	-----	-----
fabric #2	12 strips	4 strips	-----
fabric #3	6 strips	6 strips	*5 strips

Do not cut these strips until Unit Block A has been completed. This strip is the same width as the three finished center squares in Unit Block A, plus two 1/4-inch seam allowances.

Bonus:

Identifying Single, Double and Triple Irish Chains

These three Irish Chain illustrations are provided to compare the three quilt designs. To help compare effort and results, the number of pieces in each section of nine unit blocks is shown and the smallest square in each illustration is the same size.

The Single Irish Chain is often called a Double Nine Patch, for obvious reasons. In the Double Irish Chain, two featured fabrics move diagonally across the quilt; in the Triple Irish Chain, there are three featured fabrics criss-crossing the quilt. Usually, those designated fabrics march very carefully in their own diagonal rows, as shown. However, the designs are also very attractive when pieced from scraps.

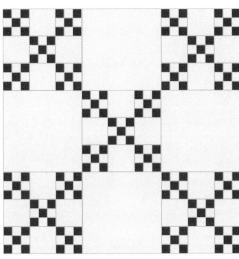

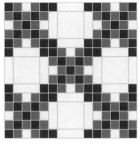

Double Irish Chain
161 Pieces

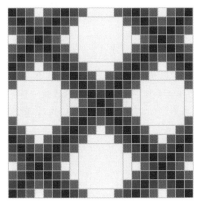

Single Irish Chain or Double Nine Patch
249 Pieces

Triple Irish Chain
313 Pieces

Bonus:

Irish Chain Quilts featuring Printed Panels

Fabric consumers often have no idea what to do with the many beautiful printed panels offered each season. With four printed panels, you have the perfect beginning for a Double or Triple Irish Chain wallhanging. Use the classic nine patch layout that has five Unit Blocks A and four Unit Blocks B. Unit Block A is pieced; select a printed panel for each Unit Block B position. The available printed panels will vary in size, and their size will

determine the strip width you cut. While the bamboo print framing the animals in the quilt shown is 10 inches across, I wanted the red and black print surrounding it to be visible, so my finished Unit Block B measures 14 inches square. However, complete the Unit Blocks A before cutting the panels, then measure your pieced blocks and use your O&O size for cutting the fabric panels.

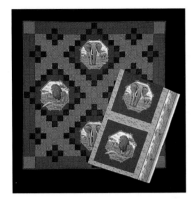

A finished size of 14 inches happens to be very convenient for the Triple Irish Chain. Unit Block A is seven squares across by seven squares down. To determine the size of the squares, divide the desired finished size of Unit Block B (your printed fabric panel) by the number of squares across Unit Block A. In this case, 14 inches divided by seven squares equals 2 inches finished size squares, or 2 1/2-inch cut strips. If you prefer to use the Double Irish Chain for Unit Blocks A, divide the desired finished size of Unit Block B by five. Fourteen divided by five, plus 1/2 inch for seam allowances, is not a convenient number. Double Irish Chain strips cut 3 1/4 inches wide, finishing at 2 3/4 inches wide, however, would make a 13 3/4-inch finished block. Although 13 3/4 inches is close enough to be a workable size to go with the 14-inch panel, I chose the Triple Irish Chain for this quilt.

Making the Double Irish Chain Quilt

Once you have determined the sizes of the squares, the rest is easy. If you have chosen a Double Irish Chain, the Unit Block A construction is just the same as for the previous quilts. Most likely, Unit Block B will have the single square appliquéd in the corners of the printed panel. Simply press

under 1/4-inch seam allowances on two adjacent sides of the square. Align the raw edges with the corner of the block and appliqué in place.

Making the Triple Irish Chain Quilt

If you have chosen the Triple Irish Chain, as pictured on the previous page and illustrated in **Diagram D**, there are more and smaller pieces. The obvious procedure to make Unit Block A, **Diagram A**, is to make four strip sets that have all seven fabrics, and cut across each set to make an entire row. You can, but I don't like to match that many seams when sewing rows together if it isn't necessary. Because all of the fabrics chosen are non-directional, I broke the block into four equal units and a center square. In this new sub-unit, there are only three strip sets with four fabrics each. Making 20 units is efficient and moves along quickly. Assemble the block by using a partial seam to add the center square to the first sub-unit. Add each section going clockwise and

complete the partial seam when the last sub-unit is added, **Diagram B**. Press and measure. Cut Unit Blocks B the same size.

Unit Block B is made basically the same as for the Double Irish Chain quilt, except that you need to appliqué a pieced sub-unit of three squares in each corner. Press under one seam allowance on two matching squares and join to a third square as shown, **Diagram C**. Press under two more seam allowances and appliqué the sub-unit in place on each corner of Unit Block B.

TIP
Make an Appliqué Irish Chain

If you did not realize you didn't have time to quilt until you had already started an appliqué project, you may have a few appliqué blocks lying around. If you have four appliqué blocks, substitute one for each Unit Block B position in the classic nine patch layout.

Unit Block A
Diagram A

Diagram C

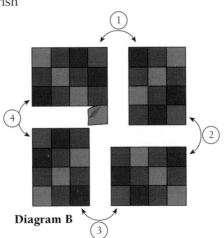

Diagram B

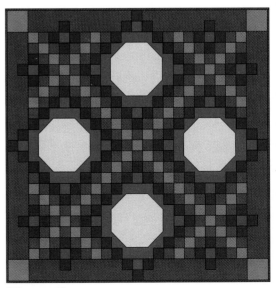

Diagram D

Radiant Squares

Snapshot

- Unit Block A: 84
- Unit Block B: 16
- Interior Arrangement: 84 Unit Blocks A accented by 16 Unit Blocks B, set 10 across by 10 down, **Diagram E**, page 148
- Strip Width: 1¹/₂" cut
- Borders: 1¹/₄" and 4¹/₂" cut
- French-fold binding: ¹/₂" finished

Unit Block A

Unit Block B

Wallhanging Size:
60³/₄" by 60³/₄"
154.3 cm by 154.3 cm

Block Size:
5" square
12.7 cm square

Materials Required:
1 yard of fabric #1 (light to medium color)

1 yard of fabric #2 (light to medium color)

¹/₂ yard of fabric #3 (light to medium color)

¹/₂ yard of fabric #4 (light to medium color)

¹/₂ yard of fabric #5 (light to medium color)

1 yard of fabric #6 (dark to very dark color)

1 yard of fabric #7 (dark to very dark color)

¹/₂ yard of fabric #8 (dark to very dark color)

¹/₂ yard of fabric #9 (dark to very dark color)

³/₈ yard of black fabric for border, cut crosswise and pieced

scraps of fuchsia fabric for border corner blocks

1¹/₈ yards of blue print fabric for border

3³/₄ yards of fabric for backing

3³/₄ yards of batting, or twin-size packaged batting

¹/₂ yard of fabric for French-fold binding

The Radiant Squares *wallhanging is a prime example of how to manipulate only nine different fabrics into a very dramatic quilt. Each of the one hundred 25-patch blocks contains all nine fabrics. Please refer to Introducing the 25 Patch, page 136, for basic instructions on making the unit block.*

Selecting the Fabric

For starters, avoid directional fabric designs. Much of the beauty of this quilt is dependent on rotating unit blocks. Directional fabrics may require the creation of different unit blocks for each quarter of the quilt.

At first glance, Unit Blocks A and B, **Diagram A**, may appear the same,

but a closer study will reveal that the fabrics in the 2nd and 5th positions, and 3rd and 4th positions, are reversed from Unit Block A to Unit Block B. In *Radiant Squares II*, page 149, the need to make two unit blocks was eliminated by selecting similarly-colored fabrics for the 2nd and 5th, and 3rd and 4th fabric pairs. Refer to the photograph on page 150.

To best develop the radiant design of the quilt, use light- to medium-colored fabrics for the first five positions, and dark- to very dark-colored fabrics for the 6th through 9th positions. Study both quilts in this book and analyze the fabric relationships as you make your selections.

Unit Block A

Unit Block B

Diagram A

rows of rearrangement

1	2	3	4	5	←Row 1→	1	5	4	3	2
6	1	2	3	4	←Row 2→	6	1	5	4	3
7	6	1	2	3	←Row 3→	7	6	1	5	4
8	7	6	1	2	←Row 4→	8	7	6	1	5
9	8	7	6	1	←Row 5→	9	8	7	6	1

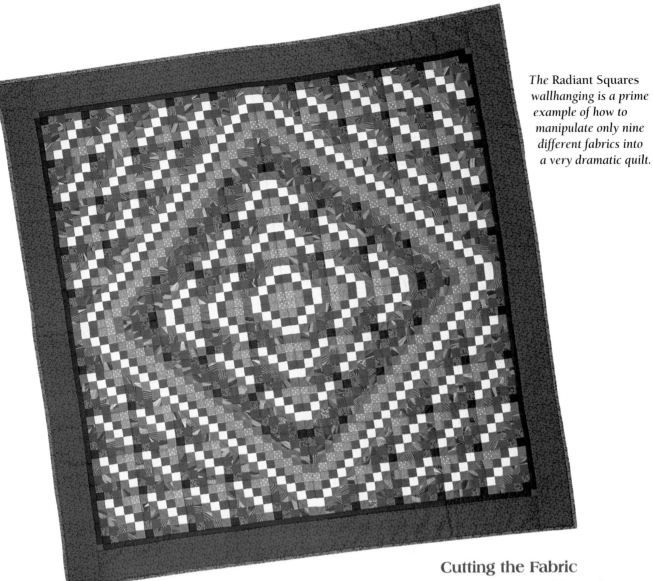

The Radiant Squares *wallhanging is a prime example of how to manipulate only nine different fabrics into a very dramatic quilt.*

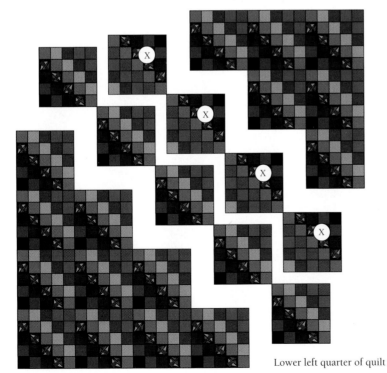

Lower left quarter of quilt

Diagram B

Cutting the Fabric

From each of nine different fabrics, cut designated number of lengthwise strips 1½ inches wide by 18 inches long per chart on page 148.

TIP

Make an actual fabric key for the unit blocks in this quilt. The block is very easy to make, but until you get the rhythm of the rows, it is also easy to make a mistake. A visual guide is good prevention.

Making Unit Block A

1. Referring to **Diagram C** and your unit block fabric key, sew the strips together into sets. Eight strip sets are needed for each row in Unit Block A.

Directional pressing is crucial to creating a flat quilt top with this many

147

small pieces. Alternate the direction of seam allowances in the strip sets. For example, press strip sets 1, 3 & 5 to the left and 2 & 4 to the right.

2. Cut 11 segments, $1^1/2$ inches long, from each strip set. Assemble 84 Unit Blocks A, **Diagram A** (page 146). The MCM for the unit block is $5^1/2$ inches square.

The direction of the horizontal seam allowances for the rows in the blocks is easily changed by pressing a second time. However, if you can remember to press half of the blocks up and half down, the number of necessary changes should be insignificant.

Making Unit Block B

Assuming you need a Unit Block B, proceed with step 1. If you have determined that you do not need a separate Unit Block B, sew the remaining strips together to make 16 additional Unit Blocks A.

1. Referring to **Diagram D**, sew the remaining strips together into two sets for each row. Pay careful attention to fabric position: Unit Block B differs from Unit Block A in that fabric #2 switches places with fabric #5, and fabric #3 switches places with fabric #4.

2. Assemble 16 Unit Blocks B, **Diagram A**. The MCM for the unit block is $5^1/2$ inches square.

Finishing the Quilt

The unit blocks are arranged in ten rows of ten blocks each. Study the one-quarter quilt layout thoroughly, **Diagram B** (page 147). Lay out 21 Unit Blocks A with four Unit Blocks B for each quilt quarter, rotating blocks as necessary to create the radiant design. Pay careful attention to the placement of Unit Blocks B. Assemble one quarter of the quilt at a time, and then join the four quarters. The MCM for the quilt interior is $50^1/2$ inches by $50^1/2$ inches. The borders were cut $1^1/4$ inches and $4^1/2$ inches wide (with

corner blocks in first border); binding strips were cut $2^5/8$ inches wide. There are many finishing options. Please read Finishing Your Quilt, page 179, and make your choice before cutting.

This quilt (shown in **Diagram E**) was machine quilted in the ditch using invisible thread. Additional machine quilting was done diagonally across the center row of each block.

STRIP CUTTING CHART

For quilt using Unit Blocks A and B, cut:

fabrics	#1	#2	#3	#4	#5	#6	#7	#8	#9
Unit Blocks A	40	32	24	16	8	32	24	6	8
Unit Blocks B	10	2	4	6	8	8	6	4	2
For quilt using only Unit Blocks A:									
Unit Blocks A	50	40	30	20	10	40	30	20	10

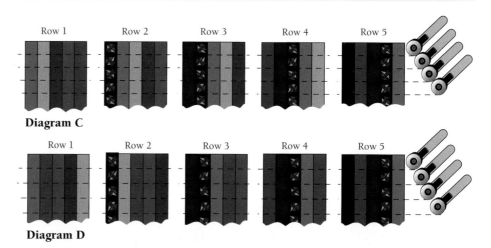

Row 1   Row 2   Row 3   Row 4   Row 5

Diagram C

Row 1   Row 2   Row 3   Row 4   Row 5

Diagram D

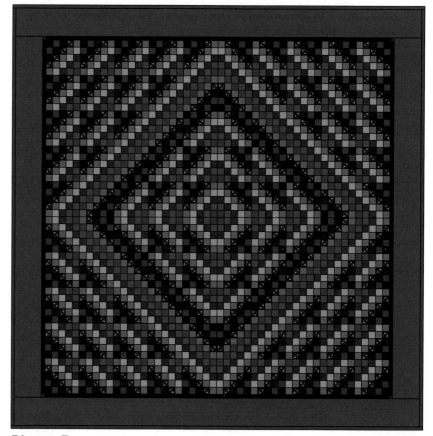

Diagram E

Radiant Squares II

Double Quilt Size:

81¹/2" by 96¹/2"
207 cm by 245.1 cm
*as shown in color picture, page 150,
and illustration in* **Diagram D**,
page 151.

Block Size:

7¹/2" square
19.1 cm square

Materials Required:

1¹/4 yards of fabric #1 (light to
medium color)

1¹/4 yards of fabric #2 (light to
medium color)

1¹/4 yards of fabric #3 (light to
medium color)

⁵/8 yard of fabric #4 (light to
medium color)

⁵/8 yard of fabric #5 (light to
medium color)

1¹/4 yards of fabric #6 (dark to
very dark color)

1¹/4 yards of fabric #7 (dark to
very dark color)

⁵/8 yard of fabric #8 (dark to very
dark color)

⁵/8 yard of fabric #9 (dark to very
dark color)

2 yards of fabric for first and third
borders

¹/2 yard each of three contrasting
fabrics for second border

5¹/2 yards of fabric for backing*

5¹/2 yards of batting, or queen-size
packaged batting

⁵/8 yard of fabric for French-fold
binding

* See On the Flip Side, page 151: You
may prefer to buy extra of each of
the front fabrics and do a pieced
back.

*If you have not read the instructions for
and/or made the previous quilt,* Radiant
Squares, *please read that section (pages
146 through 148) before selecting fabric
for this quilt. Refer to Introducing the
25 Patch, page 136, for unit block construction information, if necessary.*

Selecting the Fabric

Like *Radiant Squares*, you will need
nine fabrics to make *Radiant Squares
II*. Fabrics for the 2nd and 5th positions, and for the 3rd and 4th positions in the unit block should be
similar in color, but of a different
intensity, **Diagram A**. Planning your
fabric choices in this manner simplifies the construction and layout of
the quilt, eliminating the need for
the two separate unit blocks used
in *Radiant Squares*.

Making the Unit Block

1. From each of nine different fabrics,
follow the chart below to cut lengthwise strips 2 inches wide by 21 inches
long.

2. Referring to **Diagram A**, join
the strips to make eight strip sets for
each row.

3. Cut ten 2-inch segments from each
strip set. Assemble 80 unit blocks,
Diagram B. The MCM for the unit
block is 8 inches square.

STRIP CUTTING CHART

fabrics	#1	#2	#3	#4	#5	#6	#7	#8	#9
Unit Block	cut 40	cut 32	cut 24	cut 16	cut 8	cut 32	cut 24	cut 16	cut 8

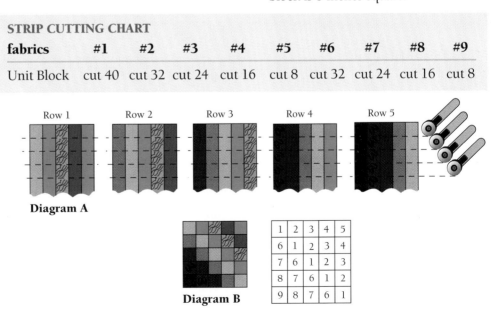

Row 1   Row 2   Row 3   Row 4   Row 5

Diagram A

Diagram B

1	2	3	4	5
6	1	2	3	4
7	6	1	2	3
8	7	6	1	2
9	8	7	6	1

Radiant Squares II *is similar to the* Radiant Squares *wallhanging (page 146) since it also uses nine different fabrics, but it has only one unit block.*

Finishing the Quilt

The unit blocks are arranged in sections four blocks across by five blocks down. Study the section layout, **Diagram C**. The three blocks that need to be rotated to create the radiant design are marked. Assemble using the Putting Pairs Together method, page 24. The MCM for the quilt interior is 60$^{1/2}$ inches by 75$^{1/2}$ inches.

Looking at the quilt, you might count five borders, but the second, third and fourth strips were cut 1$^{1/2}$ inches wide, sewn together and treated as one piece, making the second border 3$^{1/2}$ inches wide. The first border was cut 1$^{3/4}$ inches wide and the third border was cut 6$^{1/2}$ inches wide; corner blocks were added to the first and second borders (see page 182). The binding strips were cut 2$^{5/8}$ inches wide.

This quilt, **Diagram D**, was machine quilted in the ditch using invisible thread. Additional machine quilting was done diagonally across the center row of each block.

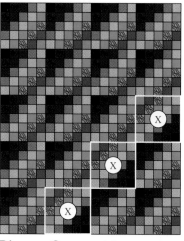

Diagram C   Upper left quarter of quilt

Diagram D

On the Flip Side

Like many of the quilts in this book, the back is pieced from the same fabric selection used for the quilt front. Depending on the availability of fabrics, some pieces are full 14-inch squares and some are triangles or even smaller scraps made into squares. Even though we know it isn't necessary for borders to match, it is easier for most of us to relax about them on the back of a quilt.

Tic Tac Toe

Snapshot

- Unit Block A: 13
- Unit Block B: 12
- Interior Arrangement: alternating blocks set 5 across by 5 down, **Diagram D**, page 153
- Strip Widths: 1" and 2" cut
- Borders: 2", 1" (pieced) and 4" cut
- French-fold binding: 1/2" finished

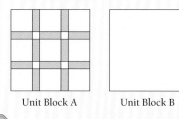

Unit Block A   Unit Block B

Crib Quilt Size:
39 1/2" by 39 1/2"
100.3 cm by 100.3 cm

Block Size:
5 1/2" square
14 cm square

Materials Required:

1 3/8 yards of novelty fabric (light), including first and third borders

10" wide by 20" long scrap of each of five different pastel fabrics, including second border

1 1/4 yards of fabric for backing
packaged crib-size batting

5/8 yard of white fabric for French-fold binding

Please refer to Introducing the 25 Patch, page 136, for further guidance on strip sets and unit block construction.

Give yourself an "A" if you immediately recognized this as a 25 patch.

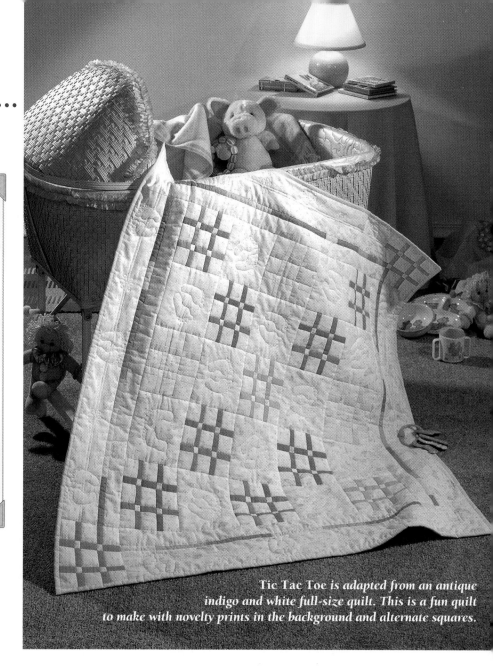

Tic Tac Toe is adapted from an antique indigo and white full-size quilt. This is a fun quilt to make with novelty prints in the background and alternate squares.

Most people don't. Even though Unit Block A is obviously five rows of five pieces, the pieces are different proportions from those of the *Double Irish Chain* and *Radiant Squares* quilts. This unit block includes rectangles and two sizes of squares, and that can be confusing at first.

Selecting the Fabric

Tic Tac Toe is adapted from an antique indigo and white full-size quilt. The simplicity of the small indigo strips set against the white background is striking, but the empty white square demands lots of quilting. People who *still* don't have time to quilt will find

Tic Tac Toe is fun to make with novelty prints in the background and alternate squares. There is enough unpieced area to let the chosen fabric make a statement. In this quilt, a delicate baby footprint fabric, combined with assorted coordinating pastels, makes a perfect newborn baby quilt.

Making Unit Block A

Two different strip sets are required to make each Unit Block A, **Diagram A**. In the photographed quilt, five different pastel fabrics are used in the 13 pieced blocks. It is easiest to cut strips long enough to make three blocks from each fabric. The two extra blocks provide flexibility in creating a random arrangement of finished blocks, or, as in the quilt pictured, use them as corner blocks on the border.

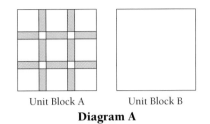

Unit Block A   Unit Block B

Diagram A

1. Refer to the cutting chart to cut lengthwise strips for 15 Unit Blocks A.

2. Sew the strips into sets for the rows, **Diagram B**. Press seams toward the darker fabric.

STRIP CUTTING CHART

	Rows 1, 3 and 5	Rows 2 and 4
novelty print	(15) 2" x 19"	(10) 1" x 7"
each of 5 pastel fabrics	(2) 1" x 19"	(3) 2" x 7"

3. From each color, cut across the strip sets for Rows 1, 3 and 5 to make nine segments, 2 inches long. Cut six 1-inch segments from the contrasting strip set for Rows 2 and 4.

4. Join the rows, **Diagram C**, to complete 15 Unit Blocks A. Continue to press the seam allowances toward the dark fabric. The MCM for the unit block is 6 inches square.

Adding Unit Block B

If your Unit Blocks A are not 6 inches square, use your O&O size in the following steps.

1. Cut three lengthwise strips of the novelty print, 6 inches wide by 27 inches long.

2. Chain piece ten Unit Blocks A to these strips, and press open.

3. Using the Unit Blocks A and a ruler as guides, cut across the strips in 6-inch increments to make ten pairs of Unit Blocks A and B. Also cut two 6-inch single Unit Blocks B from the strips.

Finishing the Quilt

Following the quilt illustration, **Diagram D**, join the blocks into five rows of five blocks each. Assemble the quilt interior. The MCM for the assembled quilt interior is 28 inches square.

The borders were cut 2 inches, 1 inch and 4 inches wide; binding strips were cut $2^{5/8}$ inches wide. The use of the corner blocks and random short pieces in the second border, illustrated in **Diagram D**, is purely optional. There are many finishing options. Please read Finishing Your Quilt, page 179, and make your choice before cutting.

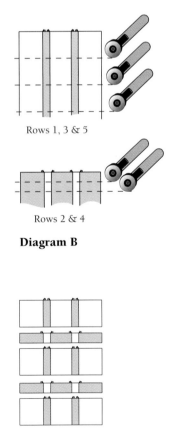

Rows 1, 3 & 5

Rows 2 & 4

Diagram B

Diagram C

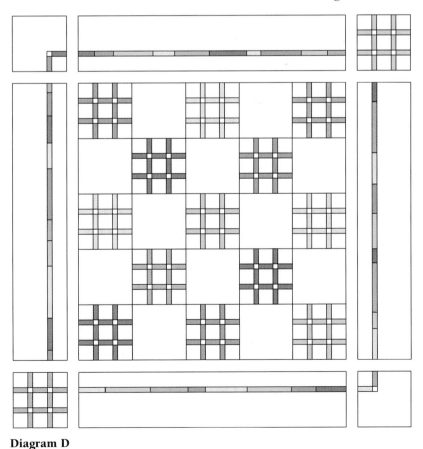

Diagram D

This use of corner blocks on a square quilt means that strips for the three borders are cut and pieced into four identical units, **Diagram D**. Refer to page 182 for information on adding borders with corner blocks. Two of the corner blocks are the extra Unit Blocks A. Two are 6-inch squares with the four small pieces of the corner unit pieced and then appliquéd. If using this option, piece two small corner sections and appliqué in place.

The continuous line baby foot quilting design, below, completes the theme. Mark the quilt top before layering. This quilt, **Diagram E**, was machine quilted in the ditch, and free-motion quilted using the footprint pattern and invisible thread.

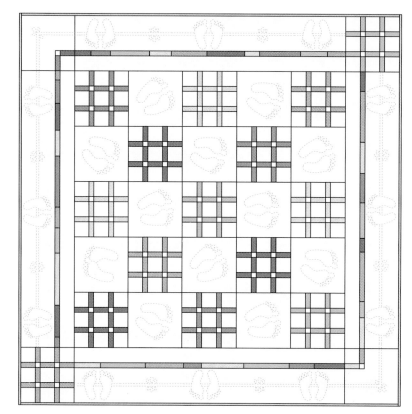

Diagram E

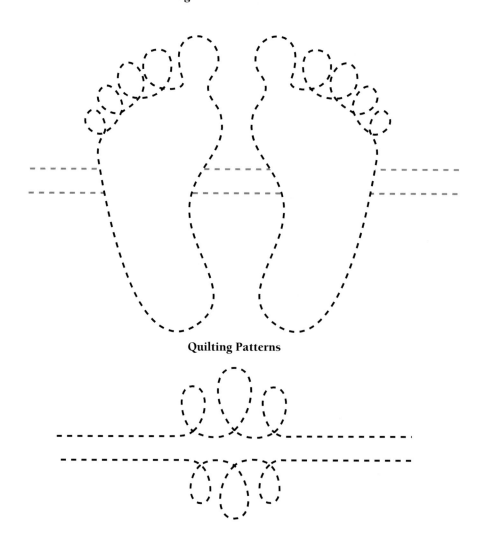

Quilting Patterns

Summing it Up

Burgoyne Surrounded Basic Quilt

Snapshot

- Master Units: 12
- Interior Arrangement: master units set 3 across by 4 down, with sashing, **Diagram H**, page 160
- First Strip Width: 1³/4"cut
- Borders: 4¹/4" (pieced), 4³/4" and (optional) 1³/4" cut
- French-fold binding: ¹/2" finished

Master Unit

Queen/Double Quilt Size:
83¹/4" by 105³/4" (including optional third border)
211.5 cm by 268.6 cm

Unit Size:
18³/4" square
47.6 cm square

Materials Required:
6⁷/8 yards of camel fabric (background), including pieced and second borders*
2¹/4 yards of red fabric (long diagonal lines), including pieced border and optional third border, cut crosswise
2 yards of navy fabric (circles), including French-fold binding

6¹/4 yards of fabric for backing
6¹/4 yards of batting, or queen-size packaged batting

* Look closely at the quilt photograph and you will see two camel print

The **Burgoyne Surrounded Basic Quilt** *is a very traditional quilt design and a great quilt to make to summarize the strip techniques used in this book.*

background fabrics. Using two fabrics was the solution when I didn't have enough of one fabric. Typically, only one light fabric is used.

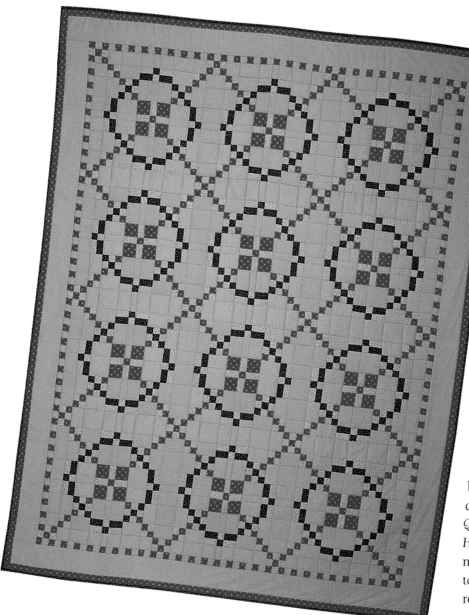

every antique Burgoyne Surrounded quilt I have ever seen used a layout of four master units across by five master units down, a total of 2,259 pieces, with the smallest square finishing to 1 inch, **Diagram B**.

This version, **Diagram C**, reduces the number of pieces by nearly one third, to 1,593. See Bonus: *Burgoyne Christmas* on page 161 for an even greater reduction of pieces. Add just 1/4 inch to the traditional size of the smallest square in the grid, use only 12 master units in a three by four arrangement and add 9 1/4 inches of borders to make the queen/double quilt shown. Even when using *Quilting for People Who* Still *Don't Have Time to Quilt* time-saver techniques, the easiest way to save time is to design attractive quilts that don't require as many pieces.

Selecting the Fabric

While surviving antique Burgoyne Surrounded quilts are more frequently found made with only two fabrics, red and white or blue and white, I prefer the three-color combination. Antique three-color quilts are often seen in red, white and blue, depicting the "Red Coats surrounded by blue-uniformed Colonists." As you consider other color combinations, it is most important to think dark, medium and light. Just like the Double Irish Chain quilts on pages 137 to 143, if you choose three fabrics that look good together, they can almost always be arranged in several very acceptable ways, **Diagram D**. Refer to *Burgoyne in 3/4*

If you have not made any quilts with four-patch or nine-patch units, please read Introducing the Basic Four Patch, page 62, and Introducing the Basic Nine Patch, page 98.

Burgoyne Surrounded is a very traditional quilt design, and a great quilt to make to summarize strip techniques as presented so far. The interesting name refers to the surrounding of English General John Burgoyne and his Red Coat army by Colonial troops in the United States War of Independence.

The quilt looks very complicated; the fun part is breaking it down to its very

simple components. The master unit for this quilt can be drawn on a grid, **Diagram A**. That means the size of the master unit, and thus the quilt, can be easily changed by changing the size of the smallest square. Nearly

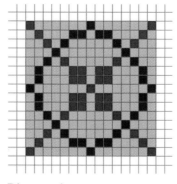

Diagram A

156

Time on page 162, and the *Floral Burgoyne* Bonus on page 164, to see how changing the positions of light, medium and dark fabrics can completely change the look of the quilt.

This quilt (refer to the photograph on page 156) employs a couple of tricks that allow the use of slightly larger pieces without giving the quilt a klunky look. By replacing the typical white background fabric with the camel-color, textured print background fabrics, the background space seems broken up and smaller. That also reduces the contrast between the background and the other colors. The

use of relatively low-contrast fabrics means the 1¼-inch finished squares will appear smaller than the same size squares would against a solid white fabric. Larger pieces of solid colors also demand lots of quilting, whereas printed textures almost reject heavy quilting.

The strip techniques used for making this quilt are written for non-directional fabrics only. For the most efficient construction, some of the sub-units are rotated in the master unit. This can be very distracting if directional fabrics are used. For guidance with the changes that are

required if you choose to use directional fabrics, refer to *Fenced-In Chickens*, page 108.

Finding and Dividing the Master Unit

It is easy to find the 12 master units in this quilt; they are set apart by sashing strips. The most important thing in a complex block like this is to break the master unit into easily-made smaller sections. The *Burgoyne Surrounded* master unit is composed of three different unit blocks, **Diagram E** (page 158). Each unit block is composed of sub-units or rows, **Diagram F** (page 158).

Diagram B

1 ▧ = 1"
Quilt = approximately 75" x 93"
Total number of pieces = 2259
Master unit is outlined in upper left hand corner

Diagram C

Each ▢ = 1¼"
Quilt = approximately 83" x 105"
Total number of pieces = 1593
Master unit is outlined in upper left corner

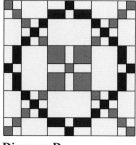

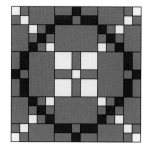

Diagram D

All strips are cut on the lengthwise grain. Narrow strips are cut the width assigned in the grid plus seam allowances, or in this case, 1³/4 inches wide.

Making Unit Block A

TIP

When fabric requirements include border fabric with fabric used elsewhere in the quilt, be sure to cut and reserve a strip of fabric along the lengthwise grain for the borders, before making any other cuts in your fabric. Refer to the cutting chart on page 160 to determine the strip width to be reserved for borders.

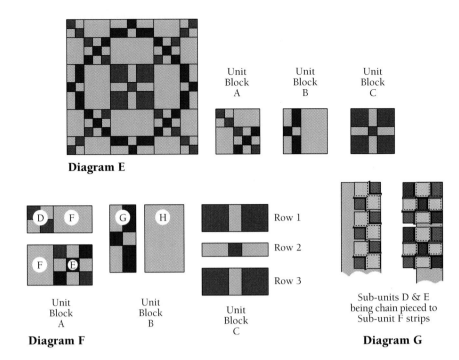

Diagram E

Unit Block A

Unit Block B

Unit Block C

Diagram F

Unit Block A

Unit Block B

Unit Block C

Row 1

Row 2

Row 3

Sub-units D & E being chain pieced to Sub-unit F strips

Diagram G

Because the light, medium and dark fabrics can be used in any position in this quilt design, the cutting charts refer to the fabrics primarily by their position, rather than by their value. In the photographed quilt, the navy (dark) fabric creates the circular designs, the red (medium) fabric creates long diagonal lines, and the camel (light) fabric is used as the background, **Diagram C** on page 157.

1. Follow the strip cutting chart below to cut strips for Unit Block A.

TIP

Keep in mind that reading directions for strip techniques may take longer than following them. Once learned, however, the techniques can be transferred to many quilts and repeatedly save time.

2. Sub-unit D is a four patch. Sew one of each color strip into sets, and press the seam allowance toward the darker fabric. Cut across the strip sets in 1³/4-inch increments. Assemble 48 four patches; the MCM is 3 inches square, **Diagram F**.

3. Sub-unit E is a nine patch. Sew the strips into the appropriate three-strip

sets for each row. There are enough strips to make four sets for each row. Press seam allowances toward the darker fabrics. Cut across the strip sets in 1³/4-inch increments. Make 48 nine patches; the MCM is 4¹/4 inches square, **Diagram F**.

4. The unpieced Sub-units F, used in opposite corners of the Unit Block A, are as wide as the four patch and as long as the nine patch, **Diagram F**. You could cut 96 pieces that size, and sew the ends of half of them to the four patches, and the sides of the remaining ones to the nine patches. However, I recommend these strip piecing techniques.

Follow the strip cutting chart below to cut the additional strips. The narrow size should equal the four patch

MCM or your O&O measurement; the wide size should equal the nine patch MCM or your O&O measurement. Sub-unit D is sewn to the wide F strips and Sub-unit E is sewn to the narrow ones, **Diagram G**.

TIP

Plan your sewing so that a pieced section is sewn to an unpieced section whenever possible. The unpieced section will usually have a newly-cut straight edge, so that making perfect ¹/4-inch seam allowances will be easier.

Using the pieced sub-units as guides, cut across the strips to create 48 each of sub-unit pairs D/F and E/F, **Diagram F**.

UNIT BLOCK A STRIP CUTTING CHART

	background (light)	diagonal lines (medium)	circles (dark)
Sub-unit D	(8) 1³/4" x 22"	(8) 1³/4" x 22"	-----
Sub-unit E	(16) 1³/4" x 22"	(8) 1³/4" x 22"	(12) 1³/4" x 22"
Sub-unit F*	(8) 3" x 27"	-----	-----
	(6) 4¹/4" x 27"	-----	-----

* Do not cut strips for Sub-unit F until Sub-units D and E have been completed and measured.

158

5. Join pairs of sub-units to create 48 Unit Blocks A, **Diagram E**. The MCM for the unit block is 6³/4 inches square. The seam allowances will create "automatic pinning" on the seam, just as they do when assembling four patches.

Making Unit Block B

Follow the Unit Block B Strip Cutting Chart below to cut strips for Unit Block B.

MAKING SUB-UNIT G

1. Join pairs of background and circle fabrics to make strip sets for Sub-unit G. Press seam allowances toward the darker fabric.

2. Look at **Diagram A**, and see if you can tell what the incremental cuts for the next step should be. Technically, the strips could be cut to any length, as long as the large squares in Unit Block C were cut the same size. For this quilt, however, the first incremental cut is the length of two grids plus seam allowances. Since the finished grid size is 1¹/4 inches, that means 2¹/2 inches plus ¹/2 inch, or a 3-inch cut to create the rectangles. The second cut for Sub-unit G should create squares the size of the grid, so for this quilt cut 1¹/4 inches plus ¹/2 inch, or 1³/4 inches.

Cut across 12 of the strip sets in 3-inch increments to make 96 pairs of rectangles. Cut across the remaining strip sets in 1³/4-inch increments to make 48 pairs of squares.

3. Join two pairs of rectangles with a pair of squares to complete 48 Sub-units G, **Diagram F**. The MCM for the sub-unit is a two-by-five grid plus seam allowances: 3 inches by 6³/4 inches, **Diagram A** (page 156).

ADDING SUB-UNIT H

1. Chain piece the Sub-units G to the strips for Sub-unit H. Press seam allowances toward the un-pieced strips.

2. Using the pieced sub-units as a guide, cut across the strips to complete 48 Unit Blocks B, **Diagram E**. The MCM for the unit block is 6³/4 inches square.

Making Unit Block C

Unit Block C is nothing more than a nine patch with three different sizes of pieces. Follow the Unit Block C Strip Cutting Chart below to cut strips for Unit Block C. The wide strip size should equal the four patch MCM or O&O measurement.

1. To create strip sets for Rows 1 and 3, piece a 3-inch wide strip of the "diagonal lines" fabric on each side of

the narrow background strips. Add a wide background strip to each side of the narrow diagonal lines strip to create a strip set for Row 2, **Diagram F**. Press seam allowances toward the darker fabric.

2. Cut across the strip sets for Rows 1 and 3 in 3-inch increments to create 24 rows. Cut across the set for Row 2 in 1³/4-inch increments to create 12 rows.

3. Join the rows to complete 12 Unit Blocks C, **Diagram E**. The MCM for the unit block is 6³/4 inches square.

Assembling the Master Unit

Join the unit blocks to make 12 master units, **Diagram E**. The MCM for the master unit is 19¹/4 inches square.

Making and Adding the Sashing

The master units are joined together by sashing strips, **Diagram H** (page 160). The exterior sashing strips are cut narrower, and pieced with checkerboard sections to create the first border. Nine patches within the sashing and pieced first border continue the diagonal lines across the quilt.

1. Follow the strip cutting chart on page 160 to cut the fabric. If the nine patch fabrics are not 36 inches long, cut twice as many strips 18 inches long.

2. To make the nine patches, begin by sewing the strips into the appropriate three-strip sets. Press seam allowances toward the darker fabric. Cut across the strip sets in 1³/4-inch increments. Assemble 20 nine-patch sub-units. The MCM for the nine patch is 4¹/4 inches square. Six of these sub-units are used in the interior sashing strips; the remaining 14 are used in the pieced first border.

3. Chain piece a nine patch to one end of six sashing strips.

UNIT BLOCK B STRIP CUTTING CHART

	background (light)	circles (dark)
Sub-unit G	(15) 1³/4" x 27"	(15) 1³/4" x 27"
Sub-unit H*	(12) 4¹/4" x 28"	-----

Strip width for Sub-unit H should equal the nine patch MCM or O&O measurement.

UNIT BLOCK C STRIP CUTTING CHART

	background (light)	diagonal lines (medium)
Rows 1 and 3	(4) 1³/4" x 22"	(8) 3" x 22"
Row 2	(2) 3" x 22"	(1) 1³/4" x 22"

4. Chain piece 11 of the master units to the remaining sashing strips.

5. Join the nine patch and sashing segments to six of the master units with sashing, as in **Diagram H**.

6. Join the 15 strips cut for the checkerboard sections in alternating fashion to make one strip set. The MCM for this strip set is 19¼ inches wide, the same size as the master unit. Cut across the strip set in 1¾-inch increments to make 14 pieced checkerboard-style segments, **Diagram I**.

7. Join the checkerboard segments to the sides of the 14 unpieced segments.

Finishing the Quilt

Following **Diagram H**, continue joining sub-units and master units until you have four horizontal sections, and one narrow border section at the top. Then join the horizontal sections together. The MCM for the assembled quilt is now 71¾ inches by 94¼ inches. The second border was cut 4¾ inches wide. The third border, cut 1¾ inches wide, is optional. The quilt is an ample queen/double size without it, and in other colors, it may not be needed. Binding strips were cut 2⅝ inches wide. This quilt was machine quilted in the ditch using invisible thread.

NINE PATCH, SASHING AND PIECED BORDER STRIP CUTTING CHART

	background (light)	diagonal lines (medium)
Nine Patches (20)	(4) 1¾" x 36"	(5) 1¾" x 36"
Sashing Strips*	(17) 4¼" x 19¼"	-----
1st Border (pieced)	(14) 3" x 19¼"	-----
Checkerboard Sections	(8) 1¾" x 27"	(7) 1¾" x 27"

Strip length should equal the Master Unit MCM or O&O measurement.

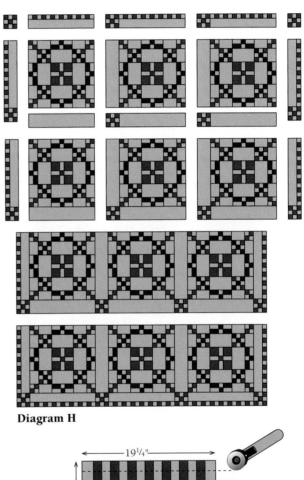

Diagram H

19¼"

27"

Diagram I

160

Burgoyne Christmas

Queen/Double Quilt Size:
83¼" by 105¾"
211.5 cm by 268.6 cm

Fabric Requirements:
5¾ yards of background (ecru) fabric
1½ yards of circles (red) fabric, including first border
3¾ yards of long diagonal lines (green) fabric, including second border and French-fold binding
6¼ yards of fabric for backing
6¼ yards of batting, or queen-size packaged batting

This Christmas quilt is almost identical to the *Burgoyne Surrounded Basic Quilt* on page 155. One exception is that the darker fabric (green) is used to create the diagonal lines and the medium fabric (red) is used to create the circles. In addition, this quilt does not use the checkerboard sections in the exterior sashing strips, eliminating 210 pieces. The sashing is followed by two borders: 1¼ inches and 4 inches

finished. Observing the changes, refer to the cutting charts and directions for the *Burgoyne Surrounded Basic Quilt* to make this Christmas version.

The quilting was done with invisible thread in rows every 1¼ inches to match the smallest square.

A Bigger Burgoyne

A simple way to get a king-size, approximately 106 inches square, Burgoyne Surrounded is to follow the instructions for making the Basic Quilt, but make 16 master units instead of 12. Just increase all yardage requirements and the number of strips required by approximately one-third.

A quicker way to get a king-size Burgoyne is to make larger master units. One student very successfully used a fairly large low-contrast print as the background and picked two colors from it for the circle and long diagonal lines fabrics. Her smallest square was 1½ inches finished. Each

master unit was 22½ inches square, so with 4½-inch sashing and a 10-inch border all around, nine master units would be adequate for a king-size quilt.

Burgoyne in 3/4 Time

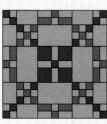

Master Unit

Wallhanging Size:

43³/4" by 43³/4"
111.1 cm by 111.1 cm

Unit Size:

11¹/4" square
28.6 cm square

Materials Required:

1⁷/8 yards of background fabric
³/4 yard of circles fabric
³/4 yard of long diagonal lines fabric
1³/8 yards of 60" fabric for backing
1³/8 yards of batting
³/4 yard of medium dark fabric for sashing and French-fold binding

This Burgoyne in 3/4 Time *wallhanging positions the dark fabric in the diagonal lines and the medium fabric in the surrounding circles. Please read* Burgoyne Surrounded Basic Quilt, *on page 155, for general information and complete instructions, if necessary.*

The master unit is composed of three different unit blocks, **Diagram A**; the smallest square in the grid is ³/4 inch finished. Even though using a small grid like this means more work, there are times when it is worth it.

Compare this to the *Floral Burgoyne Bonus*, page 164. The quilts are close to the same size, but the *Burgoyne in 3/4 Time* quilt has nine master units of almost 100 pieces each, while the *Floral Burgoyne* has only four master units.

Selecting the Fabric

Select non-directional dark, medium and light plum fabrics, or, if plum is not your color of choice, this look can be created in any monochromatic color scheme. A fourth fabric, medium dark, was selected for the sashing strips on the outside of the quilt to create the border. All strips are cut on the lengthwise grain.

Making Unit Block A

Refer to **Diagram B** when assembling the unit block.

1. Follow the Unit Block A Strip Cutting Chart below to cut the fabric.

2. Assemble 36 four patches (Sub-unit D); the MCM is 2 inches square.

3. Assemble 36 nine patches (Sub-unit E); the MCM is 2³/4 inches square.

4. Follow the chart to cut strips for Sub-unit F. The narrow size should equal the four patch MCM or O&O measurement; the wide size should equal the nine patch MCM or O&O measurement.

Chain piece nine patches to the narrow strips. Chain piece four patches to the wide strips. Press seam allowances toward the strips.

5. Using the pieced sub-units as guides, cut across the strips to create 36 of each pair of sub-units.

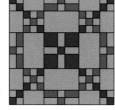

Diagram A

Unit Block A   Unit Block B   Unit Block C

Diagram B

Unit Block A   Unit Block B   Unit Block C

Row 1
Row 2
Row 3

UNIT BLOCK A STRIP CUTTING CHART			
	background	**circles**	**diagonal lines**
Sub-unit D	(4) 1¹/4" x 24"	-----	(4) 1¹/4" x 24"
Sub-unit E	(8) 1¹/4" x 24"	(6) 1¹/4" x 24"	(4) 1¹/4" x 24"
Sub-unit F*	(4) 2" x 27"	-----	-----
	(3) 2³/4" x 27"	-----	-----

Do not cut strips for Sub-unit F until Sub-units D and E have been completed and measured.

5. Using Sub-unit G as a guide, cut across the strips to complete 36 Unit Blocks B, **Diagram A**. The MCM for the unit block is 4¹/4 inches square.

Making Unit Block C

Unit Block C is nothing more than a nine patch with three different sizes of pieces.

1. Follow the Unit Block C Strip Cutting Chart below to cut fabric for Unit Block C. The wide strip size should equal the MCM or O&O measurement for the four patch.

2. Join the strips into sets for the rows, **Diagram B**. Press seam allowances toward the darker fabric.

3. Cut across the strip sets for Rows 1 and 3 in 2-inch increments to create 18 rows. Cut across the set for Row 2 in 1¹/4-inch increments to create nine rows.

4. Join the rows to complete the nine Unit Blocks C, **Diagram A**. The MCM for the unit block is 4¹/4 inches square.

Assembling the Master Unit

Join the unit blocks to make nine master units, **Diagram A**. The MCM for the master unit is 11³/4 inches square.

Making and Adding the Sashing

The master units are joined together by sashing strips, **Diagram C**. The use of a different fabric for the outside sashing strips creates the look of a pieced border. Nine patches within the sashing continue the diagonal lines across the quilt.

Burgoyne in ³/4 Time positions the dark fabric in the diagonal lines and the medium fabric in the surrounding circles for a different look.

6. Join pairs of sub-units to create 36 Unit Blocks A, **Diagram A**. The MCM for the unit block is 4¹/4 inches square.

Making Unit Block B

1. Follow the Unit Block B Strip Cutting Chart below to cut strips for Unit Block B.

2. For Sub-unit G, join pairs of background and circles fabrics to make strip sets. Cut across six of the strip sets in 2-inch increments (or your four patch O&O measurement) to make 72 pairs of rectangles. Cut across the remaining strip sets in 1¹/4-inch increments (or the grid width plus seam allowances) to make 36 pairs of squares.

3. Complete 36 Sub-units G, **Diagram B**; the MCM is a two by five grid plus seam allowances: 2 inches by 4¹/4 inches.

4. Chain piece Sub-units G to the strips for Sub-unit H. Press seam allowances toward the strips.

UNIT BLOCK B STRIP CUTTING CHART		
	background	**circles**
Sub-unit G	(8) 1¹/4" x 25"	(8) 1¹/4" x 25"
Sub-unit H*	(6) 2³/4" x 27"	-----

* Strip width for Sub-unit H should equal the nine patch MCM or O&O measurement.

UNIT BLOCK C STRIP CUTTING CHART		
	background	**diagonal lines**
Rows 1 and 3	(2) 1¹/4" x 20"	(4) 2" x 20"
Row 2	(2) 2" x 12"	(1) 1¹/4" x 12"

1. Follow the chart below to cut the fabric.

2. Assemble 16 nine patches; the MCM is 2³/₄ inches square.

Finishing the Quilt

Following **Diagram D**, complete the assembly of master units, nine patches and sashing into three horizontal sections. Join the sections together. The MCM for the assembled quilt interior with sashing is 43¹/₄ inches square.

Cut binding strips 2⁵/₈ inches wide and finish as desired. This quilt was machine quilted in the ditch using invisible thread.

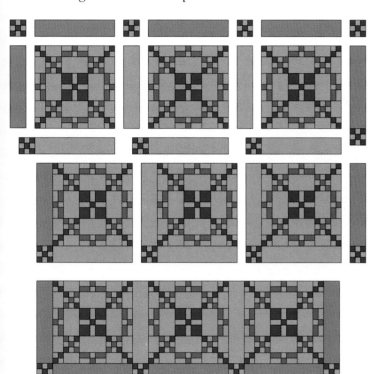

Diagram C

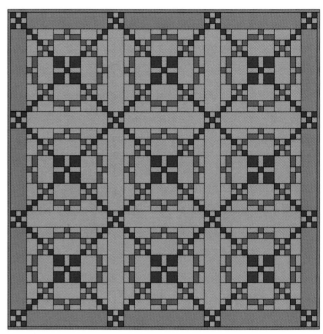

Diagram D

Bonus:
Floral Burgoyne

Wallhanging Size:
49³/₄" square
126.4 cm square

Fabric Requirements:
¹/₂ yard of long diagonal lines (rose) fabric
¹/₂ yard of circles (turquoise) fabric
1⁷/₈ yards of background (dark floral) fabric

¹/₂ yard of dark (navy blue) fabric for outside sashing, cut crosswise
¹/₂ yard of medium (lavender) fabric for French-fold binding
3 yards of fabric for backing
3 yards of batting

Combine the 1¼-inch finished size grid from the *Burgoyne Surrounded Basic Quilt* on page 157, **Diagram C**, and the use of a second fabric for the sashing strips to create the pieced border look, from *Burgoyne in 3/4 Time* on page 162. Then select a dark floral print for the background fabric. The finished result shown here is very striking and brings a more contemporary look to an old favorite quilt. This wallhanging, though not as delicate as *Burgoyne in 3/4 Time*, was much less work. The floral background fabric allowed a grid size ½ inch larger than the plum did, without looking klunky.

Even though this wallhanging has only four master units instead of nine, the final product is 6 inches larger.

Because the cut size of the smallest strip is 1¾ inches wide, as in the Basic Quilt, it will be easiest to refer to that quilt, page 155, for instructions.

Bonus:
Burgoyne Revisited

Miniature Size:
19³/₈" by 23⁷/₈"
49.2 cm by 60.6 cm

Fabric Requirements:
½ yard of long diagonal lines and circles (red) fabric, including French-fold binding
1 yard of background (ecru) fabric, including border
⅝ yard of fabric for backing
24" by 28" of Thermore® batting

Lisa Wesmiller Benson loves making miniature scrap quilts, but kept thinking she wanted to make a two-color quilt. Burgoyne Surrounded came to her mind as a quilt design that looks great in two colors. She was right! Lisa's beautiful quilt caught my eye in a display of winners from a national miniature quilt contest. It had received first place for quilts made with strip techniques and also the ribbon for the most pieces: 1,313!

The grid size for this miniature version of Burgoyne Surrounded is ¼ inch. The smallest strip is cut ¾ inch wide; strips were sewn together using ¼-inch seam allowances, which were trimmed to ⅛ inch after sewing. This quilt is the epitome of: the smaller the piece, the happier you'll be that you know how to use strip techniques.

Similar to the *Burgoyne Surrounded Basic Quilt* on page 155, the exterior sashing strips are cut narrower than those for the interior, but no checkerboard sections are added. Six-patch sub-units, and four patches in the four corners, are used in the exterior sashing to continue the diagonal lines across the quilt. The quilt is finished with a 2½-inch border and a ⁵/₁₆-inch French-fold binding.

The quilt was layered with Thermore™. Two colors of thread were used for hand quilting. Concentric circles were quilted with ecru thread in each master unit. The red diagonal lines of the quilt were continued with red quilting in the border. Halfway between the rows of red quilting, Lisa added another row of ecru quilting, a very nice subtle touch.

Refer to the *Burgoyne Surrounded Basic Quilt*, page 155, for further instructions.

As you can see, this miniature quilt has pieces smaller than the diameter of a thimble, but strip techniques made it easy to piece.

Not Such Hard Times Scrap Quilt

If you love scrap quilts and strip techniques, you'll really love Not Such Hard Times Scrap Quilt, *the final quilt of the Summing it Up Section.*

Sometimes people who are making scrap quilts overlook the ease of incorporating strip techniques. The method for making this scrappy quilt block should remind you to try strip techniques.

Snapshot

- Unit Block A: 30
- Unit Block B: 20
- Interior Arrangement: alternating blocks set in 10 diagonal rows with setting and corner triangles, **Diagram G**, page 170
- Strip Width: 2¹/₄" cut
- French-fold binding: ¹/₂" finished

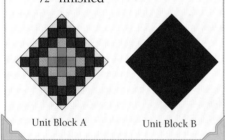

Unit Block A   Unit Block B

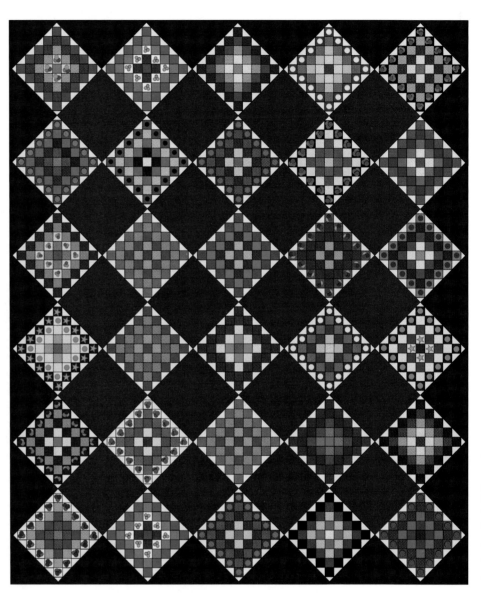

Not Such Hard Times Scrap Quilt Layout

Queen Quilt Size:
87³/₄" by 105"
222.9 cm by 266.7 cm

Block Size:
12¹/₄" square
31.1 cm square

Materials Required:
1¹/₂ yards total of three assorted fabrics for position #1 (ecru-on-ecru)
2¹/₈ yards total of assorted fabrics for position #2 (large print)*

1⁵/₈ yards total of assorted fabrics for position #3*
1¹/₈ yards total of assorted fabrics for position #4*
⁷/₈ yard total of assorted fabrics for position #5*
³/₄ yard total of assorted fabrics for position #6*
2¹/₂ yards of background fabric for alternate blocks

2 yards of contrasting fabric for setting and corner triangles
7⁷/₈ yards of backing fabric and finishing strips
5⁷/₈ yards of batting
³/₄ yard of fabric for French-fold binding

* Use assorted fat quarters and fabric scraps to equal fabric requirements.

Not Such Hard Times Scrap Quilt *was inspired by the Tennessee Hard Times quilt shown on the next page. This quilt interprets the design in a more orderly fashion, but each block uses a different combination of fabrics.*

You can see Tennessee Hard Times *is a product of an era whose theme was,* "Use it up, or do without."

This quilt was inspired by an antique quilt I call *Tennessee Hard Times* quilt. Look at the photo and you can see it is a product of an era whose motto was, "Use it up, or do without." Some of the unit blocks use random fabric and color placement; others are much more consistent and organized. This *Not Such Hard Times Scrap Quilt* interprets the design in a more orderly fashion. The fabric used in each position is consistent in each Unit Block A, **Diagram A**, but each block uses a different combination of fabrics.

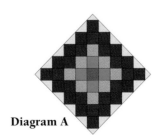

Diagram A

Selecting the Fabric

Each Unit Block A has six different non-directional fabrics. While every fabric in every block doesn't have to be different, fabric collectors like me love the opportunity to select just the right 150 fabrics for this quilt. The most time-consuming part of the quilt is picking the fabric. If you really want to be popular, cut a second set of strips while the fabric is out. One day you will find just the person for whom they are a perfect gift.

The fabric used in position #1 (the unit block setting and corner triangles) is always an ecru on ecru. Fabric position #2 is what could be called the theme print for the block. In this quilt it is always a relatively large print. The fabrics in the other positions coordinate with the theme fabric, but without a specific order of color value. Study the blocks to

see the many different combinations. Some blocks shade light to dark, some alternate, some have high contrast, and some have almost none.

Unit Block B, an unpieced alternating block, is a dark red print fabric. The fabric for the alternate blocks was selected first, then the theme fabrics (position #2). Fabrics were not considered for theme if they looked ugly with the alternate fabric. Some that clashed slightly were chosen. The surest way to make a boring quilt is to pick only fabrics that are very pretty together.

You may prefer to emulate the primitive look of the antique quilt. If so, you might want to make a few blocks with fabrics positioned consistently, as directed for the quilt, then mix up your pre-pieced scraps to make random blocks. Mismatched fabrics in the solid blocks, and not every block with the same accent color would continue the primitive idea.

Cutting Fabric for Unit Block A

Traditional quilt books instruct you to cut 61 separate pieces for each block and assemble them individually. But why would you do that, when Sew-Before-You-Cut methods allow you to make the blocks more accurately, and in a fraction of the time?

1. Refer to **Diagram C** on page 169 and the Strip Cutting Chart on page 168, cut strips for each Unit Block A. If possible, cut all strips on the lengthwise grain. If necessary, use the Optional Shorter Strip cutting instructions shown in the chart on page 169. Remember these instructions are for a scrap quilt. If you were making 25 or 30 blocks alike, you would make strip sets for each row as usual.

2. Because the squares in each unit block are set diagonally, small corner triangles are needed for each block. For each block, cut two 2½-inch squares from fabric #1. Cut each square in half diagonally to yield four triangles.

STRIP CUTTING CHART
For Full-Length Strips

fabric #	strip size
#1 bias strip	2½" x 32"
#2	2¼" x 36½"
#3	2¼" x 27"
#4	2¼" x 18½"
#5	2¼" x 9½"

OR

For Optional Shorter Strips (A)

fabric #	strip size
#1 bias strip	2½" x 18½"
#2	2¼" x 18½"
#3	2¼" x 18½"
#4	2¼" x 18½"
#5	2¼" x 9½"

(B)

fabric #	strip size
#1 bias strip	2½" x 18½"
#2	2¼" x 18½"
#3	2¼" x 9½"
#6	center square 2¼"

A NEW SECRET: BIAS STRIP REPLACES SETTING TRIANGLES

If you've read this book from the beginning, you remember Introducing Diagonal Set Quilts, page 40, and have successfully and repeatedly used The Secret of the Setting Triangles, page 43.

Since Unit Block A is like a small quilt set on point, and each block has 20 setting triangles, there are 600 tiny setting triangles in this quilt. Even using quick cutting methods, that's a lot of triangles; there must be an easier way! There is, and it's a wonderful new secret, especially useful for small setting triangles like these. Use the instructions that follow to replace the setting triangles with a bias strip. When the block is complete, there will be excess fabric on the outer edge of the block. Cut it off to make a square block, and you will have created perfect setting triangles with straight grain on the outer edge.

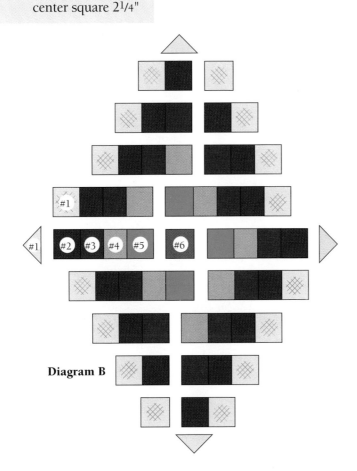

Diagram B

In case it sounds like I am making a big deal out of the idea of cutting bias strips, I am. True confession: the unit blocks were almost complete when it hit me to replace the setting triangles with bias strips. Personal experience makes me rave about this simple improvement. This block is both easier to make and more accurate with this method.

HOW TO CUT BIAS

In order to allow for seam allowances after trimming the unit blocks, the bias strips of fabric are cut ¼ inch wider than the other strips. For each Unit Block A, cut a total of 32 inches of bias strips of fabric #1, 2½ inches wide. Allow extra for pieced units. Avoid piecing if possible.

Cut bias from ½-yard pieces of at least three different ecru print fabrics. The easiest way is to first square off one end of the fabric. Align a 45-degree angle or ruler with one straight edge of the fabric. Then cut strips following the 45-degree angle.

Assembling Unit Block A

All the fabrics in each numbered position are consistent within each Unit Block A, but each block uses a different combination of fabrics.

1. Join the fabric strips #1, #2, #3, #4 and #5 into strip sets as shown, **Diagram C**. Press all seam allowances in the same direction.

2. Cut across the strip sets in 2¼-inch increments to make the sets of squares shown in **Diagram D**. Remove the square of fabric #1 from two of the five-square sets. They are the two single squares in **Diagram B**.

3. Lay out each Unit Block A as shown in **Diagram B**. Join the sets of squares and single squares into rows. Join the rows and add corner triangles to complete 30 unit blocks, **Diagram E**.

4. In the same manner as for trimming excess fabric from a diagonal set quilt, page 131, use an acrylic ruler and rotary cutter to trim the unit blocks. Line up the ruler on the block so that the 1/4-inch mark consistently passes through the block at the point where you want a seam, **Diagram F**. When the excess is cut away, a 1/4-inch seam allowance will be left.

The MCM for the unit block is 12 3/4 inches square.

Adding the Unit Block B

(If your Unit Blocks A are not the MCM, substitute your O&O measurement in the steps in this section.)

1. Cut ten strips of background fabric, 12 3/4 inches wide by 27 inches long.

2. Chain piece 20 Unit Blocks A to the strips of background fabric. Press seam allowances toward the background fabric.

3. Using the Unit Blocks A and a ruler as guides, cut across the strips in 12 3/4-inch increments, creating 20 pairs of Unit Blocks A and B .

Finishing the Quilt

1. To make the large setting triangles, cut five 19 1/2-inch squares from the selected fabric. Cut all squares on both diagonals to yield 20 setting triangles; 18 are required.

2. For the corner triangles, cut two 12 1/4-inch squares. Cut both

squares once diagonally to yield four corner triangles.

3. Lay out the unit blocks in ten diagonal rows. Join the blocks in each row, and add setting and corner triangles, **Diagram G**.

4. Continue assembling the quilt as desired, and square up the quilt interior.

The MCM for the assembled quilt interior is 86 3/4 inches by 104 inches from block to block. The photographed quilt has an additional 1/4 inch of float on each side; allow for a floating set on your quilt as desired. Bind as desired; the binding strips for this quilt were cut 2 5/8 inches wide.

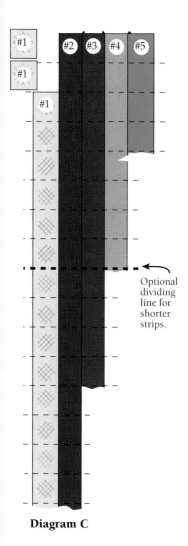

Diagram C

2 | #2 #3 #4 #5

2 | #1 #2 #3 #4 #5

4 | #1 #2 #3 #4

4 | #1 #2 #3

4 | #1 #2

Plus:

1 | #6   Fabric #1 is a bias strip

4 | #1   Cut 2 squares 2 1/2"

Diagram D

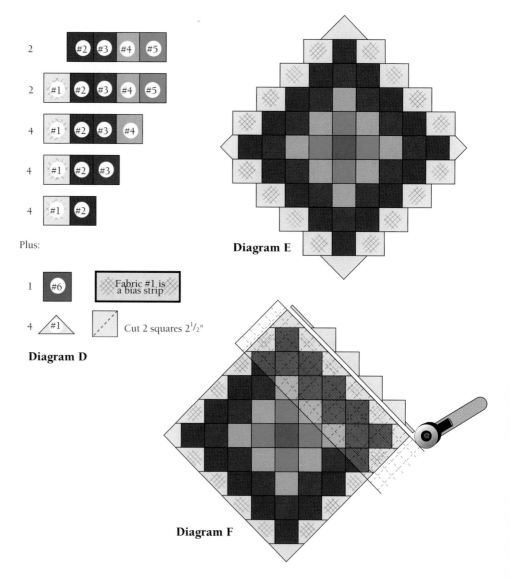

Diagram E

Optional dividing line for shorter strips.

Diagram F

170

Diagram G

Bonus:
Not-So-Hard-to-Make Other Sizes

Other sizes of the *Not Such Hard Times Scrap Quilt* are easy to make by planning your quilt using the sizes of strips and blocks shown in the chart at right.

Don't forget to cut the bias strips 1/4 inch wider for all strip sizes.

STRIP CUTTING CHART

Cut Strip Size	1½"	1¾"	2"	2½"
Finished Square Size	1"	1¼"	1½"	2"
Finished Unit Block	7"	8¾"	10½"	14⅛"
Unit Block Diagonal (approx.)	9¾"	12¼"	14¾"	20"

Tips on Fabric Selection, Tools and More

Fabric Selection

IN A NUTSHELL
There are a few things I feel duty-bound to say about fabric selection and fabric preparation. The nutshell synopsis is: I like to use 100% cotton fabrics that have been tested for shrinkage and fading. I cut my strips on the lengthwise grain. I like to think of my fabric selections as spirited, pretty, surprising or even off-the-wall (if that is the statement I want to make), but not dull or boring, which is different from comfortable or safe.

Is It True What They Say about 100% Cotton?

If cotton was King in "the old days," polyester was Queen from the late 1950s through the early 1970s. When I met an elderly Georgia mountain lady and quilter in 1970, I admit I originally considered her demand for 100% cotton an unsophisticated old wives' tale. Armed with my home economics degree and a lifetime of sewing experience, I felt very knowledgeable about fibers. At that time, 100% cotton was barely available. It was not recognized as a suitable fiber for women's clothing. I couldn't even remember sewing on 100% cotton. As a quilter, however, I developed a new appreciation for 100% cotton. Here are some of the reasons:

1. Cotton helps prevent distortion. In the process of sewing many small pieces together, suddenly—for some unknown reason—the carefully-cut shapes aren't matching. The seam allowance is perfect. What can it be? Nine times out of ten, you've chosen incompatible fabrics. Usually, the culprit fabric is a blend. Sometimes, it's just a different finish or weight, but using incompatible fabrics frequently results in distortion. This means the finished work isn't true, there is puffiness in places, and seams that are supposed to match, don't. This doesn't always happen, just often. (Once, when I was trying to make a visual aid showing a distorted block using incompatible fabrics, they simply wouldn't distort!)

2. Cotton holds a press or crease. When turning under the edge of a fabric for hand appliqué, a blend pops right back to its original position and is very difficult to press flat. The edges of a cotton appliqué "roll" more easily and permanently.

3. Cotton seems to reduce the risk of batting "bearding" or fiber migration. If the batting you use has a tendency to have little fibers coming through the fabric, the problem is much more prevalent with blends than with 100% cotton.

4. Cotton has better "give and take." This may be a different way of saying it distorts less, but I don't think so. There is a difference between a fabric's helping you through problems as opposed to just not causing them. In this case, I'm saying that using 100% cotton often helps you through problems because a good steam pressing can remove a puckered area and make a puffy piece flat.

5. Cotton is more comfortable.

6. Cotton is easier to hand quilt. Most hand quilters agree that 100% cotton is easier to "needle" than a blend. The larger the item you're quilting, the more important this is. Several hours a day of quilting on a quilt with fabrics that are blends becomes very noticeable in sensitive finger joints.

All of this is not to say you must use 100% cotton. It's just to say you should understand the possible problems if you don't. Generally, the more similar the fabrics are in weight and feel, the less the problem. A fabulous assortment of prints and solids are available today in 100% cotton. If you are a beginner, it will be easier if you start by limiting yourself to 100% cotton.

If you do mix fibers and you get rippled seams, there are a couple of tricks to try. Iron spray sizing onto the blend; the crisper finish seems to help control the fabric. Tear-away® stabilizer (a non-woven material usually sold where interfacings are sold), placed beneath the fabrics being sewn, may help control the stitching and prevent distortion.

More about Fabric Selection

Here are a few fabric selection tips:

1. It is easy to be boring. Most beginners tend to be very "matchy-uppy." Unsure of putting several different fabrics together, they will examine fabrics with a magnifying glass to make sure the blues match. Often the result is that when you step back a few feet from the finished item, the fabrics just blend together and all your work looks like a factory-printed patchwork.

2. Being happy with your quilt is most important. Because so many people express a desire to learn more about combining fabrics and color, most of the projects give pointers to help you stretch your fabric imagination. Additionally, wonderful color photographs and fabric selection information are given for almost every quilt. Use the pictures as a guide, but don't hesitate to change the colors, border sizes and arrangements. Your fabrics will look different from those photographed. Remember, the real key is that you are happy, because it is your quilt.

3. The fabrics set the mood of the quilt. Fabric does much more to set the mood of the quilt than the quilt pattern chosen. Look at the photographs of the *No-Name Four Patch Duo* quilts, pages 64 and 65. The strong contrast red and cream quilt looks masculine, country or contemporary, depending on the setting. The low-contrast peach and seafoam quilt is soft, feminine and romantic, even though the pattern is rigid.

4. The appearance of texture in fabrics should not be overlooked or underrated. In general, printed solids (defined as monochromatic or low-contrast small prints) just add texture. I almost always use them instead of solids. From a distance, the quilt has a softer, more muted look. Close up, a texture print does not demand fancy quilting. In fact, if you are planning lots of fancy hand quilting, I would recommend avoiding texture prints as they don't do justice to the quilting. Conversely, solids demand to be quilted, and can look very empty without lots of hand quilting.

5. Larger prints are not a no-no! When you cut a large print into smaller pieces, the images are often completely lost; only the colors and some random shapes remain. So if the colors are just perfect in a large jungle print with 10-inch elephants, you can probably make a *Double Irish Chain* without a trace of a trunk!

6. Random designs maximize the efficiency of strip techniques. Look carefully at your fabric choice. Directional fabrics can sneak in almost unnoticed. If in doubt, lay a small piece of fabric on top of and at right angles to the larger piece of fabric. If you would object to having some pieces going both ways in a quilt, it is directional. A fabric can be directional in either one way or two ways. Stripes are an example of a two-way directional fabric. Vertical stripes are meant to run up and down: sideways is obviously the wrong direction, but for many stripes, upside down has the same appearance as right side up. An animal print with all of the animals oriented in the same direction, however, is a one-way directional: there is only one way to place the fabric so the print looks like it was intended to look.

Conversely, fabrics with random patterns maximize the ease of strip techniques, require no special planning and will look fine when viewed from different angles. Refer to *Victorian Posy*, page 104, and *Fenced-in Chickens*, page 108.

7. Stripes and other directional designs need special consideration. The strong directional effect of stripes demands that special attention be given to the cutting and placement of striped pieces in patchwork. When done well, the illusions of motion and action created with stripes can be breathtaking. Real-life motifs such as trees, people or buildings, whose tops all point in the same direction, and other single-direction designs are very time-consuming to plan into a quilt. Nearly all one-way designs should be avoided in quilts designed on point.

8. Consider room color. If you are making a quilt for a particular room, that color scheme will influence your thoughts, but should not rule them. I encourage quilters to feel free about the fabrics they use and let their choices be right for the quilt, not the room. Funny thing is, usually what's good for the quilt is good for the room.

9. Stand back and look. Before you buy or cut fabrics selected for a quilt, stand back and look. We all tend to select fabrics at arm's length. But we tend to look at the finished quilt from "across the room." The fabrics can look very different then.

10. Be prepared to change your mind. Even the most experienced quilter can be surprised at the way selected fabrics look when they are cut and sewn together.

173

How Much Fabric Should I Buy?

In some ways, saying I buy as much as I can afford is a joke. In reality, once you start making lots of quilts, you will have a real appreciation for working from a stockpile of fabric. As quiltmakers, our fabric supply is our palette. If we don't have a fabric in a certain color, we can't use that color. The quilts in this book all include fabric requirements to make as shown. While I am flattered when others want to make a quilt just like mine, I encourage you to look at the quilt and make it your own way. One of my philosophies about quiltmaking is, "Why use only five fabrics if I can use 30?" You may laugh at this statement when you look at the quilts, but I believe I have used admirable restraint in choosing the number of fabrics used in most of the quilts.

If you get very serious about quiltmaking, you will probably start collecting fabric. Perhaps you are thinking about quilting because you have already collected a considerable quantity of fabric. Being an experienced speculative fabric buyer myself, let me pass on my standard purchasing amounts. Use these standards or create your own, but you will discover that having established standard purchasing lengths prevents embarrassing indecisiveness at the cutting table. If you have ever heard yourself saying, "I'd like ½ yard, please....No, make it ⅞....No, ⅝ should do....Oh, cut a yard and a half....No, just a yard. Yes, I'm sure," you know what I mean.

The least amount I ever ask store personnel to cut is 27 inches (¾ yard, or approximately 70 cm). That's not an arbitrary amount. I like to use many different fabrics in most of my large quilts and I also make quite a few small quilts. Using fabric in those ways, ¾ yard is almost always enough. Since almost everything I do starts with a strip, and because I cut my strips on the lengthwise grain whenever possible, 27 inches has also turned into my standard strip length. (Refer to Strip Piecing and Grainline, page 13.) Of course, if you plan to make full-size quilts with only two or three fabrics, you need to buy more.

If I'm crazy about a fabric and/or think I might want to use it as a border on a large quilt, I buy 3½ yards. That is the most I would need to cut a king-size border with mitered corners on the lengthwise grain. I can still cut small patchwork pieces down one side and leave a long wide piece of fabric along the other selvage for borders, **Diagram A**. Even though I rarely make a final choice of border fabrics until I have completed the quilt interior, that doesn't prohibit me from buying some border fabrics speculatively.

Fat quarters (18 inches by 22 inches), available in many stores, are a nice way to purchase a small quantity of a wide variety of prints and still be able to cut a meaningful strip on the lengthwise grain (18 inches). When you buy standard ¼-yard pieces, the lengthwise grain will only cut a 9-inch strip! Sometimes assortments or specialty fabrics are also available in the more usable fat-eighth and fat-sixteenth pieces, **Diagram B**.

How Much Fabric Do I Need?

Now, if the question is rephrased, "How much fabric do I need?" the answer is a little different. Just as there is no single fabric yardage requirement to make a dress, there is not one answer for how much fabric it takes to make a quilt. Here are some rules of thumb. The backing

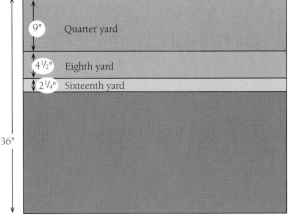

Diagram A

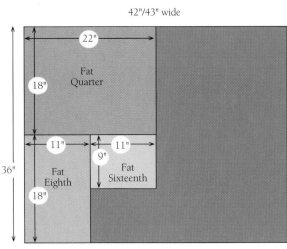

Diagram B

alone for a queen/double requires 6½ yards. So, if you add fabric for seams and some latitude in cutting, I say you need a total of 10 yards for the surface of a not-too-complicated queen/double quilt. Following the same line of thought, you need a total of 12½ yards for a king and 6½ yards for a twin.

The quilts shown have conservatively estimated yardage requirements based on a usable fabric width of 42/43 inches. You may want to increase the amounts slightly. Almost everyone agrees having extra is better than agonizing over running out. More and more I find I use my extra yardage for pieced backs for quilts or to make pillow cases—I put them on top of the quilt propped against the bed, then I don't have to fight the pillow tuck battle.

Two important things about fabric purchases are:

1. Learn not to panic or quit if you run out of fabric for a particular plan. Look at it as an opportunity to be creative in quiltmaking and problem solving.

2. Relax about having "just the right amount." With so many variables, expecting to come out even is not realistic.

What Size Is a Quilt?

IN A NUTSHELL
Sizes are given for all of the quilts in this book. This information will be most helpful as you start to create personal variations.

How much fabric you need to buy is really a function of what size quilt you are making. Finished sizes, as well as yardage requirements, are provided for the photographed quilts in this book. Of course, you always have the option

MY PERSONAL QUILT SIZE GUIDELINES

When measuring the bed isn't an option, I use these quilt size guidelines. Except for the crib size, they were developed by adding 9 inches for a pillow tuck at one narrow end and a 13-inch drop to the other three sides of the most common standard mattress sizes in the United States.

Crib - small: 30 inches x 45 inches; large: 40 inches x 60 inches; or small: 76.2 cm x 114.3 cm; large: 101.6 cm x 152.4 cm

Twin - 65 inches x 97 inches; or 165.1 cm x 246.4 cm

Double - 80 inches x 97 inches; or 203.2 cm x 246.4 cm

Queen - 86 inches x 102 inches; or 218.4 cm x 259.1 cm

Queen/Double - 84 inches x 100 inches; or 213.4 cm x 254 cm

King - 104 inches x 102 inches; or 264.2 cm x 259.1 cm

If you have a different-sized mattress, make your own similar diagram to get a feeling for the percentage and positioning of the design that shows on the surface of a bed.

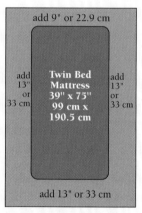

65" x 97"
165.1 cm x 246.4 cm

80" x 97"
203.2 cm x 246.4 cm

86" x 102"
218.4 cm x 259.1 cm

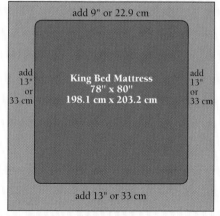

104" x 102"
264.2 cm x 259.1 cm

175

to make the quilt larger or smaller, depending upon your needs. When you make quilts for fun, that is, just because you want to, they can be any size.

Size is only crucial when you are making a quilt for a specific bed. Even then, personal choices enter into size decisions. Do you want it to hang to the floor or just skim a dust ruffle? Do you like a deep pillow tuck with huge pillows or will your quilt go under pillows? The best way to know what size you want is to put a large bed sheet on the chosen bed so that it hangs down and tucks and covers as you like. Then measure the sheet from edge to edge. Add 2 inches to 4 inches in both directions for the amount that the quilting takes up the size. That is your optimum size. Be aware that as you get into planning quilts for specific sizes, compromises often have to be made. A 12-inch unit block, for example, doesn't always fit the perfect number of times in both directions, leaving an equal amount for borders all around.

Then There Are Other Sizes

> **IN A NUTSHELL**
> *"Mini" and "miniature" are descriptive words I like to use for quilts smaller than 24 inches in either dimension. "Mini" just means distinctly smaller, as in mini skirt; while "miniature" really denotes a copy made to a smaller scale.*

"Wallhanging" is the term generally used in this book to describe a quilt not made for a bed. Many of those quilts could also be used as throws or decorative table covers just as easily; the choice is yours. They can be any size. If they are smaller than 24 inches in either dimension, they are generally discussed in other terms.

The words "doll," "miniature," "mini," "little" and "tiny" are all adjectives used to describe quilts that are small. Each is a perfectly fine word, but may evoke completely different images to different people.

There is no final authority on this topic, so I can only share the guidelines used in this book. Looking in the dictionary for help, I found that a miniature is a copy that reproduces something in a much smaller scale, while a mini is something distinctly smaller than other things of its type. In spite of sounding similar, they are the words I have chosen to use. "Tiny" is defined as extremely small. That sounded even smaller than miniature to me. "Little" is as indefinite as "small" and "doll quilts," by definition, must have been made specifically for dolls.

For me, two words that are completely unacceptable terms are "placemat" and "hot pad." Usually, they are only used by someone who has already exposed a lack of knowledge by calling a quilt an afghan or blanket. Regardless of how easy the techniques are, I'm not ready to put a 400-piece miniature 12 by 18-inch quilt on the table for someone to stain with spaghetti sauce!

Why Make Mini or Miniature Quilts?

If you have ever seriously priced antique mini and miniature quilts, you can easily see the financial value of making one instead. These quilts are more portable for hand quilting, and are a wonderful way to use scraps, test a color concept or audition different sets or a border treatment. If you have dolls and bears, they need quilts.

No matter what you call them or why you make them, the reason all of this is discussed at such length here is simple. The smaller the piece in the

quilt, the happier you will be that you are using strip techniques. They are easier, quicker and more accurate! In addition, when quilts are designed on a grid, as all of the quilts in this book are, you can make any quilt any size! There are mini and miniature quilts sprinkled throughout the book to remind you of that benefit.

Fabric Preparation

To Tear or To Cut?

> **IN A NUTSHELL**
> *I prefer to cut.*

Most fabric stores do one or the other and I accept their choice. My understanding is that before easy-care finishes were available, we tore. Then the next step was pulling on opposite ends to "straighten." With easy-care finishes, when you tear, there is often distortion in the fabric of as much as an inch in both directions. After you tear fabrics with an easy-care finish, you can wash them and pull them and press them and convince yourself that you've straightened the goods. The next time you wash the fabric, however, it will go right back to the distorted position.

So, as a matter of preference, I cut fabric and accept the fact that "what you see is what you get." (Please note that, in my opinion, tearing is not even an option regarding the strips to be sewn; they are cut!)

To Prewash or Not To Prewash?

There are many reasons why I don't automatically wash all fabrics. The colors and the finish are more appealing to me before they are washed. I like the feel of the fabric better before it's washed. The crispness of unwashed fabric makes it easier to work with when using the machine techniques promoted in this book. To the contrary, people who only hand

TIPS FOR MAKING MINI AND MINIATURE QUILTS

With strip quilt techniques, we can make great mini quilts—only faster, more accurately and more easily. Basically, it's the same thing—just smaller! Miniature quilts, however, may require special handling.

- *Remember, it's the size of the strip that determines the size of the quilt.*

- *Choose small prints and solids for the best scale.*

- *I like to use 1/4-inch seams and trim to 1/8 inch after sewing and pressing. The 1/4-inch seam allowance is more accurate than 1/8 inch, and trimming reduces bulk so the piece will lie flatter and be easier to quilt. Trimming after pressing ensures that the block will not be distorted. Use your rotary cutter and ruler to trim.*

- *Remember to think ahead and press logically so your little blocks will go together easily.*

- *Baste for quilting the same way you do a big quilt.*

- *Quilting stitches should be as even as possible because they are much more noticeable on small quilts than on large quilts. Do not over-quilt. Over-quilting can flatten a small piece, overwhelm the design and prevent the quilt from draping well. Machine quilting in the ditch is a good way to add loft and "hide" stitches. You can hand or machine quilt your miniature or secure the quilt interior with machine quilting and hand quilt the border. Or, tie your little quilt.*

- *If you like making miniatures and have a favorite finished-piece size, like 1/2 inch or 1/4 inch, cut lots of 1-inch or 3/4-inch strips and store them in a roomy box for easy access. Seeing all those values together will inspire you.*

- *To batt or not to batt: Antique mini and miniature quilts are filled with everything from cotton batting to cotton blanket material and even nothing at all. Experiment with different fillers to discover what you like best. You can use thin batting designed for use in garments, or peel regular batting apart and use one layer. If the quilt will be displayed on a small bed, try using batting just in the area that will be on top of the bed so the sides will drape down rather than stick out. Flannel or blanket material can be used in quilts that will be tied or machine quilted.*

- *Bind the same way you do a big quilt.*

- *Turn to the index, under "Mini/miniature quilts," to find more little quilts.*

quilt have told me they think pre-washed fabric needles more easily. Finally, I have acquired an amount of fabric that would have taken a considerable amount of time to wash.

An interesting thing to me, as an antique quilt collector, is my observation that there are two things people find especially charming about antique quilts. One is the quilt or top that "has never been washed." The other is the quilt that has almost a puckered look because it shrank evenly and considerably when washed. Prewashing fabrics was not an historic thing to do. I pick my traditions carefully and if "they" didn't prewash fabrics, I don't need to either. My choice is to test my fabrics for bleeding and shrinking before using, but not to automatically prewash.

HOW TO TEST

Cut 2-inch by 12-inch strips of each fabric you intend to use. Hold each strip under very hot water. If the color is going to run, you'll see it right there. Most bleeding is excess dye—that is, the dye is "spent" and will not permanently color another fabric, only the water—but you still need to deal with the fabric. Laundering to remove the excess dye is the safest. Then test again.

When no color runs, I squeeze out the excess water and iron the strips dry. It is heat on the wet fiber that really causes shrinkage. If any fabric shrinks beyond the 2% to 3% allowed by industry standards, I prewash that fabric or select another fabric. Shrinkage of 2% to 3% translates to a loss of 3/4 inch to 1 inch in a yard or 1/4 inch to 1/3 inch in 12 inches. If one fabric shrinks considerably more than the others, it is a greater problem than if they all shrink the same little amount.

HOW TO PREWASH

Sort by similar colors and put fabrics in your washing machine. Use the dial to bypass all steps except the last rinse and spin-dry cycles. Use cold water and no detergent (as it also facilitates color fading); hot water is not necessary, and may promote color fading. (Although it is heat on wet fibers that causes most shrinkage, the dryer will be adequate for the job.)

> **IN A NUTSHELL**
> *It's so easy to say prewash all your fabrics and just be done with it, but I don't do it or say it. In a nutshell, I pretest all fabrics as I select them for a particular project.*

Then dry the fabrics in your dryer, but don't overdry. Press each piece with a steam iron. If any fabric is unusually limp, spray it with sizing (not starch) when you press.

SUN TESTING

Everyone is allowed to work on at least one "masterpiece" quilt. I would sun test fabrics for that and for a wall-hanging. One fabric that fades unusually quickly will change the effect of the work. Sometimes Mother Nature is smarter, but it won't be what you had planned. Just put samples of the desired fabrics in your sunniest window. Compare to the original fabric after three days of strong sun. If there are some changes, but they're not major, I would leave the fabrics another week to see if there is further deterioration. If there are major changes, I would select another fabric.

Space and Tools

What About Your Work Space or Studio?

I highly recommend that you make quilts in a studio. You may physically be working on a folding table in the kitchen, but if you are mentally in "the studio," your results are definitely better.

A DESIGN WALL

A design wall is a wonderful tool that can easily be set up in part of your studio. It can be as elaborate or as simple as your space and budget allow. The ultimate would be an entire wall of your studio covered with felt or bulletin board material, so you can position fabrics and stand back to study the effect. The simplest is a piece of batting temporarily taped to a wall or wrapped around a large bulletin board or piece of foam core from the art supply store.

When selecting fabrics for the projects in this book, study the photographs to get a feeling for the number and use of the prints. The yardage figures and directions refer to the fabric colors in the photographed quilts for clarity, not because you are expected to duplicate the fabrics. I encourage you to experiment with your own fabric and color combinations. To help you decide on fabrics and positions, rough cut shapes, and position them on your design wall. Stand back and look. Change and reposition the fabrics until you are satisfied or make a sample block from your selected fabrics. Standing back to view the fabrics from a distance can make a tremendous difference in your selections.

The Sewing Machine

IN A NUTSHELL
You really do need a sewing machine to take full advantage of the techniques offered in this book. Don't panic, you don't need a fancy machine. It must stitch forward. The tension must be properly adjusted.

If you haven't used your machine in a while, dust it off, clean out the lint, oil it, put in a new needle (size 14/90) and adjust the tension. If the tension is too tight, you can get seams that are puckered; if the tension is too loose, fabrics may actually pull apart so that stitches show through on the right side of the seam. Consult your owner's manual for help.

Hand piecing can be very enjoyable for people who like handwork. It is almost a necessity for some very intricate piecing. It can be adapted to these techniques so that it, too, can move along faster; but if you want the real benefits of the *Quilting for People Who Still Don't Have Time to Quilt* techniques, piece by machine. Then, we'll learn how to machine quilt.

Threads

Use good quality 100% cotton or cotton-wrapped polyester for the machine piecing. Don't be tempted by cheap thread. You will use lots of thread, but cheap thread is false economy. In most cases, matching colors is not important, so you can sometimes find large spools or cones of natural that will save money without compromising quality.

When it comes to machine quilting, I often use a very fine nylon transparent thread on the top of my machine with regular sewing machine thread in the bobbin.

In previous years, the name "quilting thread" was reserved for a heavier, usually waxed thread that came in limited colors and was designed for hand quilting. That kind of thread should be reserved for hand quilting and not used in a sewing machine. Now, however, there are some brands of thread called "quilting thread" that are unwaxed, and come in a multitude of colors. They are designed for both hand and machine quilting.

Other Tools

Set up a steam iron and ironing board next to your sewing machine.

Most other tools are probably already in your sewing supplies: good small scissors, a seam ripper, thimbles, hand sewing needles, etc. You will probably soon want to add some specialized quilting tools like removable fabric marking pens and pencils, smaller acrylic rulers and squares.

Keep a small ruler or hem gauge handy for double-checking strip width and seam allowances; it's especially helpful for ensuring accuracy when using strip techniques.

Finishing Your Quilt

From One Person Who Still Doesn't Have Time to Quilt to Another

While the term "quilt" is loosely used to encompass all of the steps of planning and making a quilt, to quilt, the verb, is actually the process of permanently holding together the three layers that commonly make a quilt. Only those finishing methods used on quilts in this book will be discussed, which means that this section, like the rest of the book, stresses streamlined techniques.

Confirming Accurate Size and "Squaring Up"

IN A NUTSHELL
Measure across the quilt in several places and along the sides to confirm equal measurements. Correct any irregularities ("square up") before adding borders.

Most of the quilt directions refer you to this chapter as you prepare to add borders, after the quilt interior is complete. Before doing anything with borders, it is important to measure your quilt interior section carefully and accurately. Measure the length of the quilt from point to point, **Diagram A**. If the opposite sides match, great! Because you should have checked each unit block against the MCM or O&O measurement before assembling the quilt interior, the quilt sides will most

likely match each other. However, if they don't, square up your quilt interior by making any needed adjustments now. If you don't correct an error now, it just gets exaggerated with each border.

If you are adding borders traditionally, you may be able to adjust by easing the longer side of the quilt to the first border. Always ease the longer side to make it the same length as the shorter side; don't stretch the short side. If the quilt seems to ripple when you try to ease one side, it may be necessary to alter some of the quilt seams to correct the length. The goal is for opposite sides to be the same length.

There are two times when quilting is usually done before adding the borders: when adding Modified Quilt-As-You-Sew borders, page 181, and when tying the quilt, page 187. If you choose to use one of these techniques, turn to the appropriate page now.

Diagram A

Before Cutting Borders

IN A NUTSHELL
Choose the border(s) most attractive for your quilt. Cut borders the exact length needed on the lengthwise grain when possible. If you must piece borders, use a diagonal seam.

Fabric and Color Decisions

If you thought all your dilemmas were resolved once the blocks were made, think again! Even though measurements are included for the borders on each quilt shown, the first step in adding borders to your quilt is deciding if the measurements in the book are appropriate for the quilt you are making. It is important that you feel free to design your own borders. The fabrics and set of each group of blocks strongly affect a quilt's look. The number and width of borders (and binding) that complement strong country colors may not flatter a pastel print version. Borders should be designed to both achieve a certain finished quilt size, and make the quilt as attractive as possible.

Borders and Grainline

If there is one thing I'm adamant about, it is cutting strips on the lengthwise grain whenever possible. There is less fraying, there is less puckering in seams, and there is much added stability for pressing. (Review Learning About Grainline and Using Grainline Characteristics, pages 12 and 13.) Therefore, yardage requirements in this book are based on cutting borders and binding on the lengthwise grain, unless otherwise indicated. Please refer to the discussion about reserving lengths of fabric for borders, page 174.

Economics may require piecing the border and binding strips, especially if the fabric is not used elsewhere in the quilt. When this is the case, I use minimal piecing, avoiding more than two seams in each strip. The following examples illustrate my train of thought.

CUTTING BORDERS ON THE LENGTHWISE GRAIN WITHOUT BREAKING THE BANK

Let's say I'm ready to put a narrow 2-inch border on a 64-inch by 80-inch quilt interior. Cutting an 80-inch border on the lengthwise grain with no piecing would require $2\frac{1}{4}$ yards of fabric, **Diagram B**, and there would be lots of leftover fabric. If I am willing to make one seam in each border (and why not, since you certainly have to piece a strip cut on the crosswise grain), only $1\frac{1}{4}$ yards of fabric would

be required, but there would still be significant leftovers, **Diagram C**.

Cutting border strips crosswise and piecing them once would eliminate almost all the leftover fabric, and require only $\frac{5}{8}$ yard of fabric, **Diagram D**. Even though borders cut crosswise are not as stable, there is one reason I'm willing to do this. Most narrow borders, like this 2-inch example, are not the outside or final border. As long as the final border on a quilt is cut on the lengthwise grain, it will stabilize the quilt, and that is what counts the most.

So when yardage requirements in this book say something like, "$\frac{3}{8}$ yard of fabric for the border, cut crosswise and pieced," that is not a command, only an explanation that, to minimize the yardage needed, we calculated crosswise cuts. Please remember, if working from your stash, to cut border strips on the lengthwise grain whenever possible, and try to avoid placing more than two seams in a border.

The examples shown were for a very narrow border. As borders get wider, the fabric requirements increase and new ways of cutting borders on the lengthwise grain appear. The most common usable width of fabric is 42/43 inches wide. One and one-quarter yards is 45 inches. If your fabric requirement is less than $1\frac{1}{4}$ yards and you plan to cut borders crosswise, consider these two options:

1. Buy $1\frac{1}{4}$ yards of fabric instead, and cut border strips lengthwise. There will be no more seams than when they're cut crosswise.

2. Buy the fabric requirement listed, but cut lengthwise anyway; just piece more.

If You Must Piece the Borders or Binding

If you must piece the borders or binding, place the pieces at right angles and stitch diagonally as if you were piecing bias strips, **Diagram E**. Diagonal seams are less visible in a border, and eliminate bulk in folded bindings.

For each diagonal seam in a pieced border, allow extra length equal to twice the finished width of the border, plus $1\frac{3}{4}$ inches.

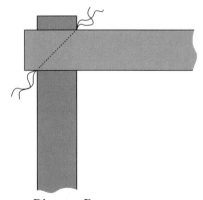

Diagram E

Diagram B

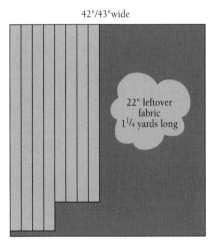

Diagram C

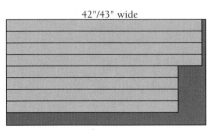

Diagram D

Decide on the Border Type

IN A NUTSHELL

In addition to deciding what styles of borders best suit your quilt, you have the opportunity to decide what technique of adding the borders best suits you.

Type of border can refer to both technique (traditional, Modified Quilt-As-You-Sew, etc.) and style (mitered, with corner blocks, etc.). The borders shown on the quilts in this book are all discussed in this section, but remember, it is not mandatory to use the style or technique shown.

Traditional Borders

Traditional borders are added to the quilt interior before it is layered with batting and backing; then the entire quilt top is treated as one unit.

CUTTING THE BORDER STRIPS

Some people add extra length to their borders, "just in case." But I say, cut your border strips the exact length they should be and make sure each border fits your quilt. If you cut any extra length and it gets unintentionally eased into the border, you are actually creating a ruffle. Granted, it has very little fullness, but it is fuller on the outside edge than on the seam edge and the border will never lie really flat.

1. Although cut lengths are given for the border strips for each photographed quilt, these are MCMs for the quilt as it was designed. No two quilts are alike. Please measure your quilt to determine the proper length to cut your strips (your O&O measurement), adding the necessary seam allowances if you are piecing your border, page 180.

Determine the desired finished width of the first border and add 1/2 inch for seam allowances.

2. Cut two side border strips the determined width and length.

ADDING THE FIRST BORDER

1. Mark and match the center points, quarter points and eighth points of both the quilt and the border strip, if necessary.

2. Add both side borders first. Lay the quilt top on a large, flat surface, right side up. Put one of the side border strips on top, right side down and with one long edge aligned with one long edge of the quilt. Pin in place. Stitch 1/4 inch from the raw edges.

3. Press the side borders open flat before sewing across the ends with the top and bottom border strips. Make sure the new corners are square and the opposite sides are equal lengths.

4. To determine the length of the top and bottom border strips, measure the new width of the quilt top. Cut two.

5. Add the top and bottom border strips in the same manner.

ADDING THE REMAINING BORDERS

Measure, cut and sew subsequent borders in the same way. Always attach the side border strips first, and complete one set of borders before starting the next.

The ends of each subsequent side border strip should line up with the ends of the previous top and bottom border strips. Subsequent top and bottom border strips should extend from end to end of the most recent side border strips.

Modified Quilt-As-You-Sew Borders

Many books I have written feature quilts made with Quilt-As-You-Sew blocks that are then finished with Quilt-As-You-Sew borders. After developing that technique (shown in ASN books #4111, #4120, #4126, #4146, #4160 and #4177), the natural evolution was Modified Quilt-As-You-Sew borders.

Instead of adding borders to the quilt and then layering and quilting traditionally, only the patchwork interior of the quilt is centered on the full-size backing and batting (refer to Layering the Quilt, page 184). After that section is quilted, Modified Quilt-As-You-Sew borders are added to the quilt. They are added just as they would be traditionally, except that you will sew through the batting and backing at the same time. The point is, you have to make a seam to add the border fabric to the quilt top, so why not quilt at the same time?

1. Measure and cut borders as for traditional borders. Mark and match the center points, quarter points and eighth points of both the quilt and the border strip, if necessary.

2. Add both side borders first. Stitch the border strip to the quilt edge through all thicknesses, sewing and quilting at the same time, **Diagram F**.

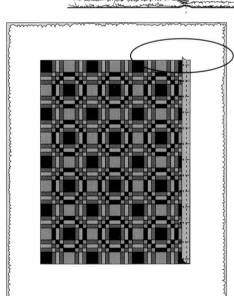

Diagram F

3. Open out the side border strips and pin or very lightly press them flat before adding the top and bottom border strips.

4. Add the top and bottom border strips in the same manner.

5. Repeat steps one through four for subsequent borders. Always attach the side border strips first, and complete one set of borders before starting the next.

Border Corners

There are only a few mitered corners in the whole book, and even they were really mock mitered. There are several reasons. Mitered corners take more time, more fabric, more skill and lots more luck than blunt corners. Even more to the point, when the same non-directional fabric is being used in the entire border, the resulting corners look the same whether they are blunt-seamed or mitered, **Diagram G**. In addition, I have a Theory....

THE MITERED CORNER QUOTA THEORY

I believe that we are all born with an unknown quota for the number of perfect mitered corners we can make in a lifetime. I would hate to be 85 years old and have a great floral striped border fabric that just had to be mitered and discover that I had used up my quota mitering something as undemanding as muslin. So I save my mitering for corners where it really counts.

There is a corollary to this theory that says, "Only three out of four mitered corners can be perfect on the same quilt on the first try!"

ADDING A MITERED BORDER

Borders that will be mitered have to be cut longer than blunt finish borders. When cutting blunt borders, the side borders are the exact length of the quilt, but the length of the top and bottom border strips is the total of the finished width of the quilt interior plus the width of two finished borders plus 1/2 inch. That same extra length must be added to all four border strips with mitered corners. Then they must be positioned perfectly and sewn to all sides of the quilt, stopping 1/4 inch from the end of the quilt interior. Press the seam allowances toward the quilt interior.

To stitch a traditional miter, fold the quilt at a 45-degree angle with the borders perfectly aligned on top of each other. Continue the fold line with the stitching, **Diagram H**.

For a mock miter, work from the top of the quilt with one border extended flat and the other folded and pressed to make the perfect 45-degree angle. Pin in place and carefully stitch by hand with a hidden stitch, **Diagram I**.

When corners are completed to satisfaction, trim away the excess fabric and proceed. It is okay to miter one border, perhaps a demanding stripe, and not the others.

ADDING A BORDER WITH CORNER BLOCKS

1. Cut two side border strips the desired border width plus two seam allowances, and the exact length of the quilt. Add as described in Adding the First Border, page 181.

2. Cut four contrasting squares the same size as the cut width of the border.

3. Cut the top and bottom border strips 1/2 inch longer than the width of the quilt before borders. Add one square to each end of the top and bottom border strips. Matching seams carefully, continue adding borders as described on page 181, see **Diagram J**, below.

Flaps Add a Special Touch

A flap is just that. In sewing terminology, it might be described as piping without the cord. A flap is used when

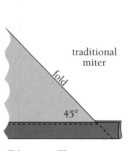

traditional miter

fold

45°

Diagram H

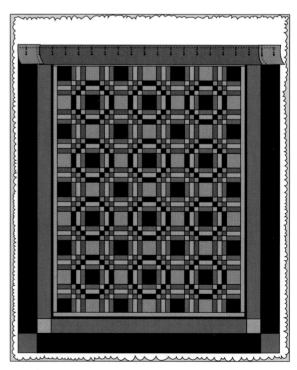

Diagram J

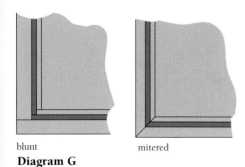

blunt   mitered
Diagram G

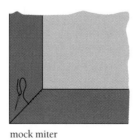

mock miter

Diagram I

182

you need a tiny bit of color as an accent or to delineate. Just as an extra mat with a tiny edge of color may be the perfect accent when framing a picture, a flap can be the perfect touch for a quilt. It can go between borders, or it can be added just before the binding.

While the flap looks like it is just tucked in between two layers of fabric when a seam is sewn, it isn't. It must be added separately, just like a border and in the same order as the borders, or the corners won't overlap correctly.

1. Cut a strip of fabric on the lengthwise grain, twice as wide as the desired finished width of the flap, plus 1/2 inch for seam allowances. The most common width of flap that I use is 1/4 inch, which means I cut a strip 1 inch wide.

2. Fold the strip in half lengthwise, wrong sides together, and press.

3. Align the raw edges of the flap with the raw edges of the last section of the quilt, and stitch, **Diagram K**. Add flaps to all sides. Then proceed with the next border or binding.

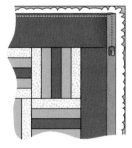

Diagram K

If you were stitching down both sides of a 1/4-inch border, any irregularities in the seam would be very visible. That does not happen with flaps. The little bit of dimension that a flap contributes is always very interesting. Although the flap does encroach 1/4 inch onto the underlying section, I have never found that to be objectionable.

What about Backing Fabric?

IN A NUTSHELL
Consider piecing your quilt back for a pretty way to use left-over fabric.

Traditional quilt backs are usually made from one fabric with minimal piecing. Although most people piece two fabric lengths for a full-size quilt with a lengthwise center seam, cross-wise seams are okay, **Diagram L**. A single 42/43-inch width of fabric will do for most crib and wall quilts.

Remember the possibility of pieced backs. They are fun and a great place to use any leftover fabric, especially if you are machine quilting and the bulk of extra seam allowances is not as much of a concern as it is to a hand quilter. Refer to On the Flip Side, page 25 (*Fence Rail Basic Quilt*), for an introduction to non-traditional quilt backs. More references to pieced quilt backs can be found by looking in this book's index, under the heading, "On the Flip Side."

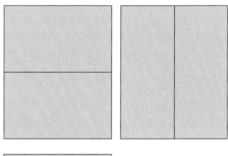

Diagram L

Selecting the Batting

IN A NUTSHELL
When making bed quilts with minimal machine quilting, my favorite batting is a medium-weight, bonded, soft polyester batting. For wall-hangings, try the new lightweight polyester battings. Some cotton battings are also very appropriate for wallhangings or for bed quilts with dense quilting.

What Kind?

My favorite batting for bed quilts with minimal machine quilting is a medium-weight, bonded polyester batting, sometimes called all-purpose. Batting that is very thin just won't puff enough; if it's too thick, it is difficult to handle. Look for batting that is bonded throughout, because surface-bonded batting can separate when washed. Find a bonded batting that is reasonably soft. Suitable varieties are Hobbs Poly-down®, Fairfield Light and many of the battings sold from a roll in fabric stores. Just make sure the roll battings aren't stiff. Machine quilting yields stiffer results than hand quilting, and a stiff batting makes for a quilt that is just too stiff. The new cotton battings like Hobbs Heirloom® are wonderful too, when doing lots of quilting on a bed quilt.

For wallhangings, I often use the new lightweight polyester battings, such as Thermore® by Hobbs, or one of the new cotton battings, such as Heirloom® Cotton by Hobbs. These battings give the flatter look I prefer in a wallhanging, especially because I frequently add more dense quilting, much of it free-motion, to the surface of a wallhanging.

Remember, batting choices are both personal and influenced by regional availability.

Preparing the Batting

As a rule of thumb when selecting packaged batting, choose the next size up from the size quilt you are making. The narrow width of typical roll battings (usually 48 inches) is not a problem for most crib quilts or wall-hangings. If you intend to use roll batting for a full-size quilt, you will need to shop for 80- to 84-inch wide roll batting or piece the batting. To piece, butt the lengths together, then join them with a diagonal basting stitch, **Diagram M**.

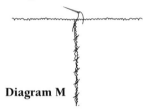

Diagram M

Remove packaged batting from its bag a day or two ahead of time so it can relax. A careful steam press eliminates humps and bumps. Put a lightweight fabric over either polyester or cotton batting to protect it from the hot iron.

Layering the Quilt

IN A NUTSHELL
This step is crucial; the way the quilt is layered will become permanent. The object of this endeavor is to center the quilt top on top of the batting, which is centered on the quilt backing. In addition, the goal is to do so without creating wrinkles or bubbles, and to secure the three layers together in a temporary fashion that can be removed when the quilting is complete.

If at all possible, do this step with a friend. It is so much easier with two people that you can layer one quilt for each of you in much less time than one person could layer two quilts.

Start with a freshly-pressed quilt top, quilting design marked if necessary, backing, and a prepared (flat) batting. I would love to layer on a waist-high flat surface as big as my quilt, no stooping or kneeling! My substitute is a long folding lunchroom table. Whatever surface you use, it should be smooth and impervious to pin pricks. I wanted a high table, but lacking that, I have a matching set of four cement blocks. The table is lifted up onto the blocks for layering quilts or when there is lots of cutting to do. It can be lowered again for everyday use.

1. Measure and mark the centers of both ends of the table with tape before you begin. Fold the backing in half lengthwise, then crosswise (into quarters), wrong side in. Mark the center of each edge at the fold lines. Do the same for the batting and quilt top, except fold the quilt top right side in.

2. Lay the folded backing fabric on the table, right side up, and unfold once. Align the lengthwise fold with the tape markings on the table, and pull the fabric smooth. Without shifting the fabric, open out the remaining fold. The backing should be wrong side up, and hanging evenly on all sides of the table.

3. Lay the folded batting on top of the backing so it covers one-quarter of the surface. Use a ruler to be certain the quarter-folded center corner matches the center of the backing. Unfold the batting.

4. Lay the folded quilt top on top of the batting, matching centers, and unfold it in the same way. The right side of the quilt top should be face up. Double-check all around the table to be sure the three layers are even and centered (use telephone books or other weights to hold things in place).

Pinning the Layers Together

IN A NUTSHELL
Securing the layers together with #1 safety pins is my choice—no basting!

At least 350 safety pins are required to pin-baste a queen/double bed quilt; a crib quilt takes at least 75. I prefer the rustproof, chrome-plated #1 pins. Straight pins are not an alternative because they catch on the quilt and scratch you badly as you are working. Hand basting takes longer and is more disruptive with one hand under the quilt. Some of my friends have adopted the new quilt tack tools with enthusiasm. Ask at your favorite shop for a demonstration if you are trying to decide whether to invest in safety pins or the tool.

Think about your quilting plan so you avoid pinning where you intend to stitch. Start in the center and work your way out, pinning approximately every 4 inches. I recommend using more pins than you think you will need, and using fewer when you are more experienced. Pin from the top of the quilt, and when the pin hits the table top, reverse direction; don't try to put your hand under the quilt to guide the pin. If you put your hand under it, the quilt is no longer flat.

When the first line of pins is secure, put one hand on the center of the table, reach under the quilt to the backing, and gently tug to make sure no wrinkles or folds have developed.

Each time you must re-position the quilt to pin a new section, check the back to make sure no wrinkles are developing. When you have finished pinning the entire quilt, turn it over and check the back to be sure it is as smooth as possible. Now you are ready to quilt.

Introduction to Machine Quilting

IN A NUTSHELL
I love both hand and machine quilting. I also love piecing. A stack of unquilted tops has very little appeal. The solution for me is more machine quilting.

I love hand quilting—both looking at it and doing it. Hand quilting aficionados, and quilters who have hand quilted anything, all have a great appreciation for the hours of work involved. The uninitiated, however, almost invariably look at a hand-quilted quilt, then look at you and say, "Did you do that by hand?" You beam, "Yes," and then simply cannot believe the next question: "Couldn't they invent a machine to do that?"

They have. It's a sewing machine. You can't, of course, use any machine to make a hand stitch. The sewing machine stitch doesn't look like a hand stitch either. But until you get within a few feet, or sometimes even inches, of a quilt, what you see is not the stitching, but the shadow created by the quilting indentation. Machine quilting actually gives a crisper indentation.

While I love hand quilting, I love making quilt tops more. I've learned that there is little personal satisfaction in a pile of unquilted quilt tops. I also love having people use my quilts. I can handle that with much more emotional ease when the quilts are machine quilted.

In the early years of the current quilt revival, machine quilting would hardly have been considered, but many people are more realistic today. Beginning to think about appropriate applications for machine quilting will change your life. Remember, everything is a trade-off. Piecing and quilting by hand, because it was once done that way and that is what you want to reproduce, is fine. Making quilts entirely by hand in order to make it a "real quilt" is not legitimate. Machine quilting is real. In fact, machine quilting may take more skill than hand quilting, but it is a different skill. It is also much faster. The quilter who can be comfortable with machine quilting will be more productive.

The straight design lines of the quilts in this book are perfect for straight line machine quilting. At the same time, free-motion quilting was used extensively. It is a wonderful way to add interest and texture to borders. While hand quilting can enhance any of the quilts, the overall graphic designs can stand alone without really missing the hand quilting. Refer to page 187 for more information on hand quilting.

Folding the Quilt

The trickiest part of machine quilting is fitting a big bulky quilt under the comparatively tiny arch of a sewing machine. The only way to handle this is to make the quilt smaller and more manageable. The lengthwise center seam will be the first place to quilt. Before sewing, I roll the right side of the layered quilt to within 4 inches to 5 inches of the center seam. Fold the left side in 9-inch to 10-inch folds to within the same distance from the seam, **Diagram N**. Then, roll up the quilt like a sleeping bag, starting at the end opposite where you want to start sewing, **Diagram O**. Now you are in control.

I hate to be the one to have to tell you, but you have to re-roll the quilt for nearly every seam. Sometimes, I can roll a quilt like a scroll without removing it from the machine. Machine quilting goes in fast, but it isn't fast to take out. You want to stay in control of the quilt. Getting sloppy with how you roll or don't roll your quilt is the easiest way to lose control. As you re-roll, check the quilt back for newly-sewn pleats. It's a personal decision, but I don't take out those little puckers most often found at seam crossings. It there's a tuck you could catch your toe in, you have to correct it. In between is a gray area.

Diagram O

Diagram N

Setting Up the Machine

Nearly everyone wonders if a fancy machine is needed for the quilting. I have successfully machine quilted with all kinds of machines from very simple to the most expensive. Check your machine's quilting I.Q. on scraps first. If you have any problem, or don't like the look of the stitch, the first thing to check is the pressure of the presser foot. Too much pressure can make an undesirable rippling effect. Nearly every machine has an even-feed attachment available that helps move all layers through the machine at the same rate. One brand of machine even has a built-in even feed, which, I must admit, is my favorite for machine quilting in-the-ditch.

For most in-the-ditch quilting, I like to use invisible nylon thread for the top thread only. In the bobbin use a cotton or cotton-wrapped polyester thread that matches the color of the backing fabric. Today's monofilament nylon thread is not at all like the 1960s version: thick nylon thread that resembled fishing line. The new thread is more like slightly coarse hair (ask for size 80 or size .004) and comes in two colors, smoky and clear. I use smoky for everything but the lightest fabrics. The clear seems to reflect light and show more than the smoky. If I will be stitching on or beside only one color of fabric, I prefer to use the 100% cotton thread on the top also.

It is usually necessary to loosen the tension for the nylon thread. It is very stretchy and if the tension is too tight, the thread stretches while being sewn and draws up and puckers when you stop sewing. I like a stitch length of 8 to 10 stitches per inch for quilting.

One of the things that has made machine quilting so much fun in recent years is the explosion of wonderful threads available. Shiny rayon, metallic and textured threads can all add interest to the surface design of the quilt.

Machine Quilting

In-the-Ditch Quilting

"In the ditch" refers to the space between two pieces of fabric that are sewn together. Granted, there isn't much space, so you create a little more space by pulling the fabric on each side slightly away from the seam just before it passes under the moving needle. That slight tension creates an extra-narrow channel for stitching. When your fingers release the tension, the fabric returns to its natural position and tends to hide the stitching "in the ditch."

1. Roll the quilt and place the exposed end of the lengthwise center seam under the sewing machine foot. Pull the quilt away from the seam with both hands to make a ditch. Position a friend or table behind the sewing machine to catch the quilt as you sew; if it is not supported, the weight of the sewn quilt will pull too much on the unsewn part of the quilt.

2. Re-roll the quilt and stitch the center horizontal seam. Stitch the remaining seams. I usually do two horizontal seams, one on each side of the center seam, then switch back to the vertical seams. Work outward from the center, re-rolling the quilt before each seam.

If you added your borders traditionally, quilt in the ditch between each border.

3. Clip the threads and remove the pins. If you are using traditional borders, the quilt top is finished and ready for binding. Otherwise, now is the time to add the Modified Quilt-As-You-Sew borders, page 181.

Straight Stitching on the Surface

You may wish to incorporate regular or straight machine quilting on the surface of the fabric, rather than in the ditch. The only differences are that you have to make a design or have a plan for the quilting, and the stitching is not hidden in a seam line. Follow a printed design in the fabric or mark a pattern, but minimize curves and eliminate as many turns as possible. Save them for free-motion quilting.

Free-Motion Quilting

Straight-line quilting on the machine is really quite simple once you understand how to control the quilt and make it manageable. But what if you want to quilt in circles? Traditional sewing, where the feed dogs pull the fabric through the machine, would require somehow rotating that whole quilt around and through the machine. No way!

So what happens if you disengage or lower the feed dogs? Well, basically, the needle goes up and down, but the machine doesn't move the fabric. That means you become the power moving the quilt under the needle, and you can move it any direction you want, even in circles. The good part is, you don't have to pivot the quilt around the needle!

That is why free-motion quilting is done with the feed dogs down. Most people like to replace the regular presser foot with the round embroidery or darning foot. When the presser foot is lowered, the darning foot doesn't actually touch the fabric, but it identifies where the needle will be stitching and is a safety buffer for your fingers. Even if you decide to stitch without a presser foot of any kind, the lever for the presser foot must be lowered, as that is the action controlling the tension on the upper thread.

"Free motion" means what it says. You can stitch in any direction you like. An effective, but very easy way to do free-motion quilting is with random movements that create a stippled effect. However, if you want to try fancy feather quilting on the machine, free motion is also the method you would use.

Keeping the fabric moving at a fairly calm, steady pace, and the needle moving fast seem to be the easiest ways to keep your stitch length regular. The hardest thing to believe is that the faster you sew, the easier it is to do. Practice on a small piece of layered fabric, but remember, your stitch length will not have the same consistency as it does when the feed dogs and needle are completely synchronized.

The place you are most likely to get puckers in machine quilting is where two stitching lines cross. A random motion that goes forward, curves back and cuts back again without actually crossing a previous stitching line will give you a nice quilted effect without puckers. Just a little practice and you'll be amazed at what you can do.

Tying the Quilt

IN A NUTSHELL
Tying the quilt layers together with yarn, or by using decorative machine stitching, is a quick and easy way to secure the layers of the quilt.

Tying may be used instead of, or in addition to, quilting. The *Fence Rail Basic Quilt*, page 20, is hand-tied between the quilt blocks with yarn. Any of several tying methods may be used.

1. Hand tie the quilt with yarn. Use a large-eyed, sharp-pointed needle with lengths of yarn as long as you can comfortably handle. Take a stitch in the center of each square or between the first pair of quilt blocks. Leave a loop between stitches as you continue making stitches across the quilt. Then clip the yarn between the stitches, **Diagram P**. Pull the yarn taut to be sure it is not loose on the underside of the quilt. Tie a square knot and trim the ends as desired. I like to leave the ends about 1/2 inch long.

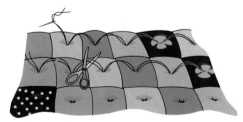

Diagram P

2. If you want to simulate a quilt hand-tied with ribbon, cut a 3-inch to 6-inch length of ribbon for each quilt block. Tie the ribbon into a bow, center it on the block and secure to the quilt with a narrow zigzag stitch across the bow.

3. Use a machine zigzag stitch, with both the stitch width and length set close to zero. Hold threads behind the needle, and stitch several times through all layers. This will secure the threads. Then adjust the stitch width to about 1/4 inch wide and stitch eight to ten times; adjust back to zero and stitch a few times more to secure the threads. Trim loose ends.

4. If you have decorative stitches available on your machine, experiment with a decorative stitch instead of zigzag. This is especially easy if you have the ability to instruct your machine to stitch one complete design and then stop. It is especially fun with some of the cute designs available.

Hand Quilting

Hand quilting is a very portable way to quilt. Some people find hand work very soothing; some consider it the only "authentic" way to quilt. That's obviously the case if you are trying to reproduce an antique hand-quilted quilt; but that is not the only way to make a "real" quilt.

It is true that, while pioneer women quickly converted to piecing by machine, they were more reluctant to quilt by machine. I believe they pieced by machine, a project traditionally done alone, in order to have more quilt tops in less time. Then they quilted by hand, in groups, in order to preserve their social time. Quilting around the frame gave everyone a chance to hear the news, to gossip, and to converse with other adult women. Lucky the quilter, today, who has a quilting group gathered around a large frame, because it is still fun and therapeutic.

Sometimes the combined use of machine and hand quilting is a logical response to different needs. Machine quilt in the ditch around large unit blocks and between borders, then hand quilt inside the unit blocks. That approach lets the machine do the long, tedious but necessary stitching, while the hand work is done where it will show to best advantage.

The Technique of Hand Quilting

Experiment with different methods until you find one you like. Don't forget to use a comfortable thimble. The quilting stitch is a small, consistent running stitch. There is a lot of discussion about the appropriate number of stitches per inch. The beginner should look for consistency first, and strive for smaller stitches later.

- In a full-size frame: There are so many different frames, and each seems to be used slightly differently, so just follow the directions for the one you own.

- In a hoop: Hand-held and floor-stand hoops are readily available.

- Without a hoop or frame: Some people prefer quilting without the tautness of the hoop or frame, especially if they are quilting by the block and then assembling the quilt.

THE NEEDLE AND THREAD

Most people prefer to use a fairly small "Betweens" needle. In fact, they are so commonly used for quilting that Betweens are now often packaged as Quilting Needles. I would suggest buying a package with assorted sizes and gradually working down to the smallest size.

In the past, most thread called "quilting thread" was intended for hand quilting only. Now there are some very nice threads labeled for either hand or machine quilting. The new quilting thread comes in a wide range of colors, but it is not as heavy as traditional hand-quilting thread.

Binding the Quilt

IN A NUTSHELL
My favorite binding is a separate French-fold binding, cut on the straight grain. The most common, but not the only, finished width is 1/2 inch. The corners are blunt, not mitered.

The French-fold binding is my favorite way to finish the edge of a quilt. It is cut four times as wide as the desired finished width plus 1/2 inch for two seam allowances, and 1/8 inch to 1/4 inch more to span the thickness of the quilt. The fatter the batting, the more you need to allow here.

What Width and Length?

My favorite finished width is whatever I think looks best on that quilt. Some quilts need a subtle narrow binding and others look best with a wide, high-contrast binding. The most common width, however, is about 1/2 inch finished, or 2 5/8 inches cut. With that width and an average full-size quilt, the equivalent of 5/8 yard of fabric is required for binding alone.

Measure the quilt to determine the length of the binding strips. Measure, cut, and sew the side binding strips first. My preference is to cut binding strips on the lengthwise grain of the fabric. Cutting on the bias is only necessary if the binding is going around curved edges or for decorative purposes. If you must piece the binding, do it diagonally as for piecing borders, page 180.

Sometimes a flat border will flare a little after quilting. Cut the binding on the crosswise grain and pull it taut while stitching. When it relaxes, the binding will calm the flare.

Preparing the Quilt for Binding

Before adding the binding, prepare the quilt. Unless I have quilted very close to the edge of the quilt, I stabilize it. Machine baste 1/4 inch from the raw edge of the quilt top on all sides of the quilt.

Adding the French-fold Binding

1. Fold the binding strip in half lengthwise with the wrong sides together and the raw edges even. Press. Binding strips are added in the same order as borders: sides first, then top and bottom strips.

2. Lay the binding on the quilt so that both raw edges of the binding match the raw edge of the quilt top, and machine stitch in place through all layers.

3. Now is the time to trim away excess backing and batting, but how much? To determine that, pull one section of binding flat, so it extends onto the excess batting. Because I like full-feeling bindings, I trim the backing and batting to be almost as wide as the extended binding. In other words, the extended binding will be about 3/16 inch wider than the trimmed backing and batting, **Diagram Q**. Assuming you wanted a 1/2-inch finished binding and you started with a 2 5/8-inch-wide binding strip and are measuring from the seam, not the edge of the binding, the batting and backing would be trimmed 7/8 inch from the seam line, or 5/8 inch from the edge of the quilt.

4. Roll the binding around the raw edge of the quilt to the back, and hand stitch in place using the row of machine stitching as a stabilizer and a guide, **Diagram R**.

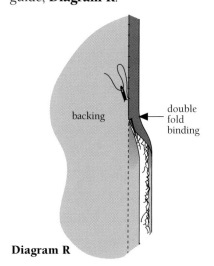

backing

double fold binding

Diagram R

The hand hemming stitch I use is hidden. The needle comes out of the quilt, takes a bite of the binding and re-enters the quilt exactly behind the stitch. The thread is carried in the quilt's layers, not on the outside.

5. To make blunt corners (I feel mitered corners aren't necessary on most bindings), complete the hand stitching on the sides of the quilt before beginning the end bindings. Trim batting out of the last 1/2 inch of binding before completing the hand stitching.

6. Measure the quilt ends for binding strips, and add 1/2 inch to each binding end. To eliminate raw edges, turn under the ends of the strips before folding the strips in half lengthwise. Continue in the same manner as above.

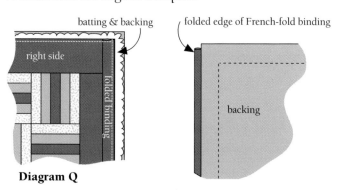

batting & backing

right side

folded binding

folded edge of French-fold binding

backing

Diagram Q

7. Complete the hand stitching for the ends of the quilt. At the corners, trim away enough batting and seam allowances to make the corners look and feel the same thickness as the rest of the binding. Carefully stitch ends shut.

MACHINE HEMMING

If you are hemming the binding by machine, attach the binding to the quilt back and bring to the front. Either top stitch with invisible thread or experiment with your machine hemming stitch, **Diagram S**.

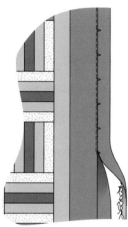

Diagram S

It's Not Done Until It's Signed

I always urge quiltmakers to sign their quilts, so that future quilt historians will know who made them and when. Quilts made by people who *still* don't have time to quilt are usually made to be used, not preserved, but that makes signing them even more important. Forget about the historians; sign and date the quilts you make for the people you know and love who are using them. Signing can be as simple or as elaborate as you like, and can go on the front or the back.

As more sewing machines are featuring built-in alphabets along with other decorative stitches, making a quilt label is a great way to make use of the feature.

A really simple way to sign a quilt is to use an indelible marking pen or laundry pen to write your name, date and any inscription on a piece of pre-washed muslin or other fabric, and hand stitch it to the back of the quilt.

Here is the label for the back of Basket Weave in Vivid Colors, *page 31.*

189

Index